MEN AND TENDENCIES

MEN AND TENDENCIES

by

dward

E. I. WATKIN

NEW YORK

SHEED & WARD

1937

To
MY DEAR DAUGHTER.
THERESA

PREFACE

SOME of the essays collected in this book are new, specially written for it, others reprinted. The following are completely new: H. G. Wells, The Frustration of Humanism; Galsworthy, In Darkness and the Shadow of Death; Havelock Ellis, To the Unknown God; Nation and State; Peace and War, and The Philosophy of Marxism. The following are reprints: A Philosophy of Moods; Science and Religion; The Best in this Kind are but Shadows; Dialectical Ideal Realism, all from the *Dublin Review*. They have however been revised and in some points modified to correspond with a development and clarification of the author's thought. The nuclei of Lord Russell, Religion without Reason, and Plotinus and Catholic Philosophy, Plato's Inheritance, were articles contributed to the *Dublin Review* and substantially reprinted here. They have however been expanded by a considerable amount of additional matter so that the essays as they now appear are by no means simply the articles originally published. The essay on Nationalism, Energeticism and the Totalitarian State is the combination of an article contributed to the *Colosseum* and an essay written for the Fribourg Congress of the Union Catholique d'études internationales. I desire to thank Messrs. Burns, Oates and Washbourne for kind permission to reprint articles from the *Dublin Review* and Mr. Bernard Wall for allowing me to reprint an article on Energeticism and the Totalitarian State. *St. Mary's, Sheringham.*

Feb. 15, 1937.

CONTENTS

MEN AND TENDENCIES

H. G. WELLS

THE FRUSTRATION OF HUMANISM

In his latest book, a book of despair and hope at loggerheads, the *Anatomy of Frustration*, H. G. Wells, through the mouth-piece of a Mr. Steele, discusses various aspects in which human desire and effort are frustrated. There is frustration by the subconscious, the frustration of socialism, of a world pax, of abundance, of youth, frustration through the conflict of cultural obsessions, frustration through self-indulgence, through the lack of a liberal morale, through sinfulness, through loneliness. But the supreme frustration passes unrecognised—the frustration of humanism. And by this I mean the inevitable frustration of any attempt to secure a permanent satisfaction apart from communion with God.

I would not deny that a vast amount of frustration arises from such causes as Wells enumerates and could be abolished by a more rational arrangement of human affairs. And therefore before coming to grips with the fundamental issue, that is with the fundamental frustration, a few remarks are demanded by these important, though not supreme issues. I whole-heartedly agree that world peace is impossible in a world of sovereign states. The national states must be subordinated to the supreme control of a world authority. And unfortunately it is more than doubtful whether a League of Nations or any similar federation of sovereign states will ever bring us to this point. It seems as though only the cosmic agony of another world war can break the idol of the sovereign national state, now more powerful than

ever before in the history of mankind. Wells, however, is
wrong in rejecting the positive value of national patriotism.
Divorced from the preposterous claim to sovereign independence, the differentation of national groups and the patriotic
attachment of their members would no more endanger world
peace than the Scottish nation and Scottish patriotism endanger the peace of the British Empire. On the contrary
not only is national grouping a natural instinct, like other
natural instincts to be controlled, not suppressed, it enriches
the total patrimony of mankind which an amorphous cosmopolitanism would impoverish. Here as elsewhere the right
answer to idolatry is not iconoclasm but the cult of images.
In his treatment of Socialism Wells is far more discriminating.
He will have none of the idolatrous orthodoxy which ascribes absolute truth to some particular Socialist scheme
and he opposes the Communist orthodoxy of Soviet Russia,
" this obdurate Eastern monster without eyes or ears." And
his description of its prophet is the reverse of flattering. " A
whole world which overrated Marx is now finding him out
—the essential snobbishness of his hatred of the bourgeoisie,
the pretentious crudity of his social psychology." Moreover
he sees that pure, that is absolute, socialism is a chimera.
" Men and women who can sit down to a serious discussion
of ' socialism versus individualism ' are fit only for institu-
tional treatment. Socialism is always a matter of degree."
That is to say the social ideal must be not the extinction but
the restriction and control of private property. It may be
that Wells restricts too closely the amount of private property
which would be tolerated in his ideal society. But it is as
much as the Jesuits permitted in their Paraguay reservations.
And his proposal to make the ownership of most classes of
goods dependent upon their proper use, though impossible
to carry out rigidly, for all ownership must involve some
power of abuse, points in the right direction.

Moreover, he states the ground on which Catholic sociology

has always maintained a right of private property against absolute Socialism. " Property . . . is the common guarantee against intolerable usurpation. Men without ownership and freedom and the pride (a Catholic would have termed it self-respect) that comes with these things are incurably careless with the goods of this world and spiritless in production." This is almost an echo of St. Thomas's defence of private property. " Every one is more careful to look after a thing that is his own private concern than after what is common to many, since everyone (where ownership is common) avoids labour and leaves to another to do the duty that belongs to a number of persons in common."[1]

In his views on education and literature Wells is haunted by his prejudice against the old as such, his notion that the new must always be better than the old. The classics have no permanent value, they will become mere museum pieces. He fails to perceive that inasmuch as they express with supreme perfection eternal truths they cannot grow old. He imagines he has discredited Shakespeare by the allegation that " no one can tell which of the plays and which parts of the plays ascribed to him were really written by that inimitable pen." But in fact controversy as to authorship arises not about the supreme plays or passages but precisely about plays and passages which fall below the highest Shakespearian standard. This dogmatic preference for novelty in every sphere is or perhaps was the illusion of an epoch dominated by the natural sciences in which the new does in fact replace the old, just as the contrary illusion of the Middle Ages that the best had been said and written was natural in an epoch dominated by theology and philosophy which do not progress

---

[1] (S.T. ii–ii, Quest LXVI, Art. i, trs. Fr. J. Rickaby, *Aquinas Ethicus*, vol. ii, p. 54.)

This truth must not, however, be pressed too far. There is always a minority of genuinely public-spirited people. Moreover it is more applicable to work not in itself of human interest, e.g. the mechanical production of goods, far less applicable to work interesting in itself and of a more intellectual and therefore distinctively human character, e.g., scientific research.

like the sciences by accumulating new facts. Wells of course has no use for a literary education such as that of our public schools. But although it is admittedly insufficient, an education in the humanities provides the best possible corrective of the crude utilitarianism which an exclusively scientific education is apt to foster.

" Art—the undying explorer. And with that emendation it seems to me most of the distinction between art and science disappears." It does indeed. For this definition does not define art at all. It misses its essence, the expression of significant form apprehended by aesthetic intution. It is a definition applicable not only to science as well as to art but to the curiosity of the cat or the local gossip. The excitement of the hunt common to animals as well as men is given precedence over the distinctively human apprehension and expression of truth, of ideal form.

Such a definition is inspired by the energeticism which prefers the action of search to repose in the enjoyment of what is found. Actually " the life of contemplation " is ranked with " reading detective stories, crossword puzzles and bridge " among " evasions of responsible life." This is the apotheosis of becoming as against being, the reverse of Platonism. Plato, it is true, also dreamed of an ideal society, though, as was natural in the fourth century B.C., it was conceived as a city state, not a commonwealth of mankind. But it was to be ruled by contemplatives and its noblest achievement was to be the production of contemplatives. Wells, it is true, recognises that the leaders of mankind must possess a wide vision. And this is a contemplation of truth. But this contemplation is subordinate to action, for whose sake it exists, and there does not appear to be any permanent truth to be seen. There is to be the town-planning of a cosmopolis. But there is no pattern of a city, eternal in the heavens, no order of the city of God to be reproduced on earth as far as our earthly limits permit.

Thus we are brought to the supreme frustration from which no world planning, however skilful, can deliver us, the frustration which, though never acknowledged, runs through the entire book. It is the frustration which I have termed the frustration of humanism.

For what in the last resort is to be the goal of all this planning? What is the value which Wells' ideal world order is to realise and whose attainment is to put an end to man's agelong frustration? Through his mouthpiece Steele, Wells proclaims that it must be something immortal. He sees clearly that it must be a satisfaction, a value which cannot be destroyed by death. And he also sees that it must consist in an identification with something beyond the interests and gratifications of the individual. It must in fact be an eternal life. He rejects, however, out of hand even the possibility of individual survival. For he can conceive it only as a survival of the empirical self, of the psychological surface. " Mrs. Bloggs . . . dressed rather differently perhaps but otherwise the same." He has no conception of a profound centre of the soul that does not change with the super- ficial psychological changes which follow each other from birth till death. Assuming the individual to be no more than this psycho-physical series he finds his immortality inconceivable, indeed self-contradictory. But he never seriously questions this assumption. To discover the abiding depth below the superficial series requires that profound contem- plation which he despises as lazy day-dreaming.

Having thus brushed personal immortality aside because it cannot be reconciled with his grossly inadequate psychology, Wells turns to the impersonal immortality which he regards as a sufficient substitute. There was a time when he set his face towards a transcendental religion. Though God the Invisible King was not truly transcendent, being built up by the successive generations of human spirits, he was at least a superhuman being whom man could serve and with whom he could enter into some sort of personal and religious relationship, a Wellsian version or perversion of Christ. But Wells has abandoned even this rudimentary and inconsistent transcendentalism. There is no Divinity beyond a purely immanent Life. And moreover this cosmic Life is practically identical with mankind. " He (Steele) believes that there is no truly rational objective, no sound and sure merger-immortality, enduring and practicable and satisfying, for any intelligent human being, except a thorough-going self-identification with the human will and intelligence considered as a synthesis of the will-drives and the mental drives of the entire species. He rarely writes it Humanity ; he writes it Life; but he admits that, outside the human range, consciousness of, much less participation in, anything of the sort is negligible." . . . " The only way of escape from ultimate frustration for every living intelligence . . . lies through this formula : ' I am life ' or what is practically the same thing, ' I am Man '."

When therefore a page or two later Wells speaks of " self-identification with the whole of life," it is plain that he should have written with the whole of humanity.

On the other hand this humanity is not after all the sum of human beings. " Man . . . means not the aggregation but the quintessence of human life." " This ' Man ' in whom all the best in every one of us participated is to be thought of neither as an individual being nor as the species considered collectively. He is a superindividuality (not a superindividual N.B.) arising out of the species. He is the sum of human knowledge and expresses the sustaining consciousness, the reasonable will of the race." Incidentally Wells glimpses here a profound depth in the human spirit " the best in every one of us " which he had ignored in his light-hearted denial of individual immortality. But what exactly does he mean ? Does he regard individual men as the passing waves upon an underlying ocean of human life, a cosmic humanity out of which they are born and into which they die ?

Turn a few more pages and you see that he does not hold even this minimum of transcendentalism. " He (Steele) is able to state his conception of our objective, the New Life, in terms at once extremely mental and extremely concrete. . . . He contemplates a world so unified, so understanding, so clarified and harmonised, that its advancing welfare and the vigour and happiness of its individuals reflect and complement each other." " We shall live in the All and the All will live in each of us." It is " the possible world community towards which life is thrusting now, the sort of All in which the individual is to live." This community however, is not an All, nor even a cosmic life. Nor is it the sum of human knowledge and will, " a synthesis of the will drives and the mental drives of *the entire species.*" It is simply a future human society organising the aggregate not of mankind from first to last but of the men and women who happen to be alive in it.

Nor is there anything in the least transcendental in a further statement " of the gist of all our religious, social and political desires : (1) Selfmerger in a world order, (2) participation in an unending research and adventure and (3) the attainment of a personal, shared and re-echoed happiness. . . ." Since the nature of this happiness is left undetermined it tells us nothing. And the endless adventure of a search which never finds is itself a frustration. No one would have set out to reach the Pole unless he had been convinced that it existed and could be reached by man, or would search for gold where he knew none could be found. As we have already seen this objective which is no objective, this search or " drive " valuable for its own sake though it can never win the goal, is an expression of the energeticism which exalts energy, life, above form, knowledge, and which is born of intellectual despair. In Wells, however, it contrasts strangely with an exaggerated rationalism which expects from man's unaided reason the achievement of an earthly paradise.

B

There remains the world order regarded as actually realizable. But why should even the best of purely human societies be invested with this quasi-religious halo? Why should it be identified with a quintessential human consciousness and will other than the sum of the minds and wills of its members? Why should it be identified with Life or even with Man? Life extends immeasurably beyond any conceivable human society. And Man includes the members of all the human societies which have ever existed and which Wells rightly finds so unsatisfactory. Evidently it is because Wells wants something far more than a rationally organised society, desirable though the latter may be. He wants a life unlimited even by death. " Almost all that ' living things ' desire either individually or in common, can be expressed as a freedom, as an escape from a limitation." But this desire for the unlimited, this chafing against all limits as frustrations is implicitly a desire for the only Being that is unlimited, for God. In a revealing aside Wells explicitly recognises the religious character of man's fundamental desire. " The crown of life is the religious crown, a proud realisation of one's own share of divinity." But what is this divinity in which we are to realise our share? As we have seen, when it comes to the concrete, it is nothing more than membership in an ideal human society. But we are not in fact members of such a society. Therefore we cannot realise a share in it. At most we can strive that our posterity may share in it. And this is a different thing and far less satisfactory. Nor could the most perfect social order conceivable give us the freedom from all limitations and therefore the perfect satisfaction for which we thirst. No amount of mystical personification can alter the fact that it could possess no consciousness or will other than the sum total of the consciousnesses and wills of its members. And these would be narrowly restricted by the limitations of individual earthly existence, and above all by death. " Proud realisation of one's own share of divinity." " Ye shall be as

gods." But the end is death. " Ye shall die." On the other
hand this urge to share in a Divine life to which Wells here
adds his testimony—so strange, so paradoxical in such a
feeble and short lived animal as man appears to be and indeed
is, so far as Wells's knowledge of him reaches—is not doomed
to frustration. For man can share by supernatural deification
in the infinite life of God. "I have said you are gods and
sons of the most High." But for Wells there is no Most
High, no being higher than a society, which despite his denial
is but an aggregate of individual men.

A rationally ordered society would no doubt put an end
to a host of frustrations—for example, frustration by poverty
and by war. And its command of scientific knowledge would
also remove a host of frustrations imposed by ill health or
psychological defects in the peripheral sphere, defects due to
faulty education, maladaptation to environment or nervous
derangements. But these successes could at most conceal
the profound dissatisfaction of the central spirit. For as
Wells himself realises, deep in the human soul is the desire
for an immortal and unlimited life. No society of mortal
men without supernatural and transcendental religion can
satisfy this desire. For God alone is infinite and an unlimited
life can be attained only by a supernatural participation in
His Infinity. And though the soul is naturally immortal,
only in relation to God has its immortality any significance.
As the Indians have perceived, an endlessness of natural living
must be endless dissatisfaction. Nor apart from transcendental religion have we any convincing proof that the soul
is immortal. Because here and now the soul can enter into
communion with the eternal God we know that it is not
like the body wholly subject to time, wholly perishable. But
there is no other proof. The attempt of spiritualism to
establish on empirical grounds the survival of the individual
and moreover on a plane of being as superficial as that of our
surface consciousness on earth has failed. It has demonstrated

only inexplicable capacities of the subconscious mind. In other words what Wells means by merger immortality is the ground on which we affirm the individual immortality which he rejects. But this merger is not strictly a merger. It is rather a submersion, a submersion in " the pacific Ocean of Godhead " which leaves what is submerged its distinct being.

Wells is like a man attempting to escape from a dark room. He glimpses a ray of light from outside. But he cannot find the door beneath which it enters and through which he might escape. He was groping his way towards the door when he wrote *God the Invisible King*. But his secularism with its proud confidence in human reason and its achievements was too strong. His persistent emphasis on pride as being a virtue instead of the supreme vice is significant. He retraced his steps. And now in this well-named *Anatomy of Frustration* he can but cast wistful glances in the direction of the light—the immortal and unlimited Life for which man is made. But he cannot move towards it. For he is sure there is nothing higher than man and his natural human life. His pride will not accept a divinity more than human. It demands a godhead in which he shares by natural right. And this human divinity in turn is conceived as an ideally organised human society, finite because a collection of finite individuals, mortal because a collection of mortals. And such as it is it is a Promised Land which mankind may never enter and which we certainly shall not enter. It would be impossible to draw a darker picture of man's immediate future than Wells has drawn in his *Shape of Things to Come*. And if we and our children are doomed to a hell on earth is it a sufficient comfort that a minority of survivors will produce grandchildren or great-grandchildren who shall receive the Wellsian promises ? Most of us would not think so. And Wells himself is not certain. For his latest mouthpiece, Steele, ends by taking an overdose of morphia. Whether this is deliberate suicide is left in doubt. In any case it proves that human pain cannot be sufficiently assuaged by the remote and dubious prospect of a future Utopia. If he is not to suffer frustration the individual must share in the unlimited Life which is not his own but God's Divinity. Steele's despairing moods and the manner of his death symbolise an invincible frustration in the heart of his creator. He struggles bravely against it and will no doubt continue to struggle against it until the end. But he cannot overcome it. For it is the essential, I might almost say, the absolute frustration of humanism, that is of humanity idolised as an absolute and sufficient value in the place of God. This humanist idol is the most powerful contemporary idol. Communism is one of its guises, National Socialism and Fascism are others. But it is also the idol of the humanist Utopians, of Russell and Shaw and Wells. And in the case of the two latter it is tending to produce the same evil fruit of intolerance which it has produced in practice when embodied in the totalitarian states. Shaw approves the painless extinction of men who resist his social panaceas. In the *Shape of Things to Come*, in the teeth of scruples surviving from the liberal milieu in which his thought was formed, Wells relates with approval the forcible suppression of all religions which acknowledge any Deity more than human. And although in his *Anatomy* he condemns " the doctrinaire intolerance " of Soviet Russia, he opens a door to intolerance. " It is legitimate to close a discussion and coerce, when decision is urgently necessary and opposition plainly malicious or mercenary." And he proceeds to white-wash the persecutions of past history, partly on the ground that their victims " were really malicious." They ought, I suppose, to have labelled Campion not the seditious but the malicious Jesuit.

In self-contradiction his liberal tolerance asserts itself. " Freedom of statement, freedom of discussion throughout the world is of as much importance to humanity as food or clothing." But what if the government chooses to regard a statement as malicious? And what freedom of statement is left to the representatives of religion by the founders of the new world order in the *Shape of Things to Come*? Wells is being pulled in opposite directions—towards toleration by his ingrained liberalism, towards intolerance by his religious cult of an efficient world society.

Clearly we must rank Wells among the apostles of the new energeticist humanism which is everywhere arising upon the ruins of liberalism to claim the place of God.

But we would not leave his latest manifesto with a negative criticism however justified. For not only does he bear witness to man's religious need ; he also voices a growing demand for a social order which shall be more than merely economic and political and shall embody a religious faith, a religious value. And the self-stultifying attempts to establish such societies on the basis of a religion which is the denial of religion because it rejects God—whether actually carried out, explicitly and logically by Communism, partially and implicitly by Fascism and National Socialism, or merely imagined, as by Wells—witness to the real possibility, indeed necessity, of the religious society which they caricature.

And there is precisely such a Society in existence, the mystical body of the Word Incarnate, the mystic and corporate Christ, the community of souls in supernatural union with God, in a word the Church. Its members are united by a common supernatural participation in the immortal and infinite Life of God, though it is a Life which is one with the Divine Wisdom, not a Life such as energeticism conceives it prior to Form, to the Word, and its parent. If this Supernatural Society could but take control of man's entire life a social world order would arise determined by Divine Reason and its eternal law and expressing it in every sphere. This order, however, must not be a domination of society by the clergy, the liturgical organ of the Church. Were such a domination possible it would involve, what it has always involved, the secularisation of the clergy. Nor must it be realised by an alliance between Church and State. For since the State is based upon force, alliance with it contaminates the Church with the alien principle of force, legitimate though the latter may be in its own sphere. It must be produced by the conscious realisation of their membership of the Church by the members of society as such and their determination to embody by a free collaboration whatever of Divine Truth and Life can be embodied on the secular plane, by social justice, for example, world peace or by art.

Not even such a society could finally satisfy man. For it would remain a society of sinful men subject to death. But it would be an expression on the earthly plane of the perfect society, the immortal society of immortals, the heavenly Jerusalem. And with that heavenly city the earthly city would be in organic communion, the Communion of Saints.

The epilogue to Shaw's *St. Joan* ends with her cry, " O God that madest this beautiful earth, when will it be ready to receive thy Saints ? " The hope of humanism that a society will be constructed on earth, whether the classless and stateless Society of Marxian eschatology or the similar society of Steele's (Wells's) New Beginning, which will be the abode of secularist self-sanctified saints is doomed to disappointment. Death and sin can never be destroyed by any social order however wise. But they witness to the profound longing of men for a society in which saints sanctified by God and participating in His supernatural life will mould the earthly city in the likeness of the heavenly, as man is made in the image and likeness of God. Though it could not be the home of saints, for we have on earth no abiding city, it would provide them with an environment immeasurably better than any yet achieved in which to prepare themselves and their fellows for their true and eternal home beyond the grave. The illusions of a crude millenarianism have led

Christians to forget the eschatological aspect of their religion. Though we cannot believe in a literal millennium in which Christ will visibly rule over a world free from suffering and sin we may and we should hope for a kingdom of God on earth in which the conditions of human life are fashioned by the Holy Spirit working through God's saints to a degree far beyond anything yet witnessed. Monasticism at its best and the Jesuit government of Paraguay are adumbrations of this ideal society. Of this kingdom the social experiments of Communism and Fascism are prophecies as well as parodies. In virtue of their fundamental humanism they are the kingdom of the beast whose number is 666. For it is the number which everywhere falls short of the symbolic number of perfection 777. It is thus the symbol of frustration. And these humanist societies, whatever they may otherwise achieve, are organised frustrations of man's desire for God's unlimited and immortal life. Great their performance may be, even so close an apparent approach to man's true satisfaction, as to present a deceptive semblance of it. Six approaches seven, and the best in a lower order foreshadows the higher order above it. But because this performance cannot exceed the merely human order it must be a mockery, not a fulfilment of man's true and profound destiny, six never becoming seven. The utmost achievement of a humanist society will be to provide the matter which the supernatural form of the religious society which must finally vanquish it will impose. "Only then will the life of a society, however well constructed be true life not frustrated activity."

But these attempts to reach man's goal by the wrong route point to the reality of that goal and the possibility of attaining it. Unless the city of God pre-exists in heaven it cannot descend to earth. Therefore those who deny that Divine city cannot build on earth the city of their dreams. The city of the man-god, of a self-deified human society must mock man's hope with the insufficience of human nature. But the

Divine city must descend to earth, as St. John saw it descend in his symbolic vision. Otherwise human history must lack its objective and therefore its significance; and the earthly society be abandoned by a false other-worldliness to disorder or servitude. Indeed modern humanism with its earthly Utopias is largely a reaction against this one-sided other-worldliness which has forgotten that God's kingdom must come on earth by the accomplishment of God's will on earth as it is in heaven. The perfect balance of the Lord's Prayer embraces the positive truth contained in the one-sided other-worldliness which looks for God's kingdom only in heaven and in the one-sided secularism which looks for no other kingdom than that of man on earth. And this balance has found another expression in the beautiful preface for the feast of Christ the King. It speaks of " a kingdom of truth and life; a kingdom of sanctification and grace; a kingdom of justice, love and peace." The mention of grace rather than glory shows that the kingdom is on earth not in heaven, though it comes from heaven and is fulfilled in heaven. This kingdom of God in man realises what is vainly hoped from kingdoms of man as God. It affords that Life which Wells expects from his human Utopia and which, as he sees, can alone satisfy man's desire and which in many guises man has persistently sought. But in opposition to modern energeticism it is primarily a kingdom of truth which produces the life, supernatural truth producing supernatural life, as everywhere throughout the hierarchy of creation form, the impress of wisdom, produces the energy-object. Wells demands justice if men are not to be frustrated. This Divine Kingdom is a kingdom of justice. It is a kingdom of love, a love not limited by the inevitable exclusiveness of sexual love. It is a kingdom of peace: a world pax. Here also the order is significant. In the past Christians have too often been content to make charity towards individual sufferers a substitute for social justice. And in reaction against this disorder Socialists have insisted upon social justice to the exclusion of love, a counter-excess whose terrible fruits have been the class war and Communist terrorism. Here justice and love are affirmed in their right order, the latter built upon the foundation of the former. And from both peace follows. As Wells points out, world pax will never be effected by the mere denunciation of war. It demands a strenuous positive effort to set up a just order. In God's Kingdom peace is the work of justice. And peace demands the provision of a substitute for the passion which war arouses. The passion of a charity as heroic and self-sacrificing as the devotion of the soldier can alone provide this substitute.

Moreover, when he speaks of a New Beginning as the preliminary step towards the construction of his humanist kingdom, Wells transposes onto the secular plane the condition laid down by Our Lord for entrance into the Kingdom of God. " Repent for the Kingdom of God is at hand." As the Greek term shows, this repentance—insufficiently rendered by the Douay, though not by the Westminster version, as penance—is a change of mind. Metanoeite, change your mind, your fundamental disposition. Only thus can you escape from the bondage of natural self-interest and become a member and disinterested servant of God's supernatural Kingdom. This change of disposition is the religious counterpart of the new beginning in which man's interest is converted from a petty self-interest to an identification (merger) with the kingdom of humanity.

Thus at every turn the Divine Kingdom here described meets and satisfies the contemporary demand for an ideal society which shall transform the conditions of human life and be an adequate goal of human effort and sacrifice. But it cannot achieve this task, cannot be embodied in an actual order of human society if it remains a pious ideal which no one expects to be realised. It is not enough to point a baffled and groping humanity to the sole remedy for their frustration. We must make a serious effort to bring it to them. Otherwise they will continue the hopeless search in a direction where there is no issue, only to experience in the end the inevitable frustration of humanism. This frustration with his hero's desperate efforts to escape it which is the burden of Wells' latest utterance should not merely console Catholics with the knowledge that they possess the true way of escape, and the true and sole satisfaction, the Life and the Kingdom of Life. It should urge them to the determination to do all they can by prayer and work to realise that Kingdom and embody its Life socially as well as individually and to bring their humanist brethren who seek life and its kingdom where they cannot be found, the life and kingdom of man, to this Divine Life and Kingdom, that we may all labour together in its service. We may be reminded by Wells of truths he does not himself know but for which he is seeking so earnestly. And that reminder should be a stimulus to realisation.

GALSWORTHY

IN DARKNESS AND THE SHADOW OF DEATH

By intention and temperament no man could be less of an energeticist than Galsworthy. A typical representative of the Liberal intelligentsia, his standpoint is that of an idealistic rationalist. A passionate hater of cruelty and the stupidity, individual and still more social, to which in the majority of cases it is due, he would persuade us to establish a more reasonable and humane order. A dull greed of money crystallized and even invested with an almost religious halo by the commercial middle class represented by his Forsytes, and in the class above it the worship of good form and the public school moral code must not be allowed to stifle the creative and living forces of art and love, or that intimate participation in the life and loveliness of nature which was such a dominant influence in himself. Social injustice, caste prejudice, brutalising and stultifying punishment, international incomprehension; such things destroy life and pervert the natural order of values.

This desire to replace an artificial and tyrannical order by a natural and liberating order arising from man's spontaneous experience of vital realities must command our sympathy. For it is a desire to base life, individual and social, on a genuine apprehension of values and their order. And this in the last analysis is an intuition of the forms which make these values what they are. That Wilfred Desert should sacrifice Dinny Cherwell's love and happiness to his sensitiveness to a social ostracism which she would so gladly have helped him to bear and overcome is indeed to sacrifice an evidently higher value to a lower, love to an exaggerated pride. As the writer displays the forms moral, biological and spiritual, we accept the unspoken verdict they pronounce.

Unfortunately, however, Galsworthy has no philosophy which integrates these forms in a comprehensive interpretation of the universe. He is unable to perceive the light they cast on reality as a whole. For he cannot rise above the sphere of nature and humanity. Why is nature so cruel as well as so lovely? Why are men so mean and so blind, yet so lovable, well-intentioned, noble, brave and self-sacrificing? Why is the blossoming of love so often frustrated, so often the source of agonising and barren pain? Galsworthy had no key to the enigma he felt so keenly. For the religious vision which alone could have shown him a supreme wisdom and love behind and beyond this baffling universe was dim and the metaphysical insight which would have established their absolute reality in the abstract was wanting. Had he belonged to an integral religion-culture, religious doctrine would have clarified and supplemented his religious vision, an adequate philosophy would have provided the lacking metaphysical insight. But for Galsworthy organised religion, particularly Christianity, meant nothing and the philosophy bound up with it less than nothing. The references to religion in his three final volumes display a pitiful ignorance of Christianity. It is simply a dying survival from the past with no place in the new order. He does not even pay it the Bolshevik tribute of hate. He would have been surprised at Mirsky's remark and, I dare say, scornful of it, that to the British intelligentsia no other alternative is open than Communism or Catholicism. To him Christianity in all its forms is but an empty formality to which the older generation clings from the force of social habit, not from conviction, and for which the younger generation has no use.

" What proportion of people in these days do you think really have religion, Uncle?"

" In Northern Countries? Very difficult to say. In this

country ten to fifteen per cent of the adults perhaps. In France and southern countries, where there is a peasantry, more, at least on the surface. . . ."

" Are you a Christian, Uncle Lawrence ? "

" No, my dear ; if anything a Confucian, and Confucius, as you know, was simply an ethical philosopher. Most of our caste in this country, if they only knew it, are Confucian rather than Christian. Belief in ancestors and tradition, respect for parents, honesty, kind treatment of animals and dependents, absence of self-obtrusion and Stoicism in face of pain and death. What more . . . does one want except the love of beauty."[1]

" Difference of religion is serious, Dinny, especially when it comes to children."

" Why, mother ? No child has any religion worth speaking of till it's grown up and then it can choose for itself. Besides, by the time my children . . . are grown up, the question will be academic."

" Dinny ! "

" It's nearly so even now, except in ultra-religious circles. Ordinary people's religion becomes more and more just ethical."[2]

There is no doubt a lamentable measure of truth in this estimate of contemporary religion. But Galsworthy clearly regards this irreligion as a natural and reasonable state of affairs. For him religion is but morality touched with a vague cosmic emotion of pantheistic colour. Nor can he really understand the religious believer. For him the faith of Catholic countries is the superficial varnish upon a peasant culture. The Catholic Mr. Dornford has no scruples about missing Mass to spend his Sunday morning with Dinny upon the river. " This," said Dinny, " is a nice exhibition of high purpose, I don't think. Something done isn't always what was attempted, is it ? No, but it's often

---

[1] *Flowering Wilderness*, Chapter vi.   [2] *Flowering Wilderness*, Chapter viii.

better."[1] We are not surprised that he is married in the Anglican church as a matter of course.

Moreover, Galsworthy is so convinced that there is nothing in religion, as the term is truly understood, that even his ecclesiastics do not possess it.

The Bishop, whose death introduces *Maid in Waiting*, is an agnostic departing to the unknown. And his slum parson, the Rev. Hilary Cherwell, in other respects a charming character, human, kindly, self-sacrificing and a man of mellow and tolerant wisdom, is devoid of genuine religious belief. A man so human and so wise obviously could not be a believer. Here are some of his private thoughts. " Was he or was he not based on revelation ? And if not on what was he based ? . . . He thought, I serve an idea, with a superstructure which does not bear examination. Still the good of mankind was worth working for. . . . One used forms in which one didn't believe and even exhorted others to believe in them. Life was a practical matter of compromise."[2]

It is not surprising that " of his many duties the deathbed was least to his taste." . . . And the best he can do for a dying child is to repeat the Walrus and the Carpenter before she passes into unconsciousness.[3] Though the picture is unfair to the multitudes of Anglican clergy with strong religious convictions, it is eloquent of Galsworthy's complete ignorance of the meaning of Christianity, and the arguments in favour of it. Indeed he has no suspicion that there is an intellectual case for it. Wishing to give us a specimen of an anti-religious poem by Wilfred Desert he can produce, as good poetry, the effusion :

> Into foul ditch each dogma leads
> Cursed be superstitious creeds
> In every driven mind the weeds!

[1] *Over the River*, Chapter xxxviii.   [2] *Flowering Wilderness*, Chapter xiv.
[3] *Ibid.*

There's but one liquor for the sane
Drink deep! Let scepticism reign
And its astringence clear the brain.[1]

That an artist of Galsworthy's delicate touch and sensitive
feeling can in all seriousness hold up to our admiration
this pitiful doggerel, and Desert is described as a poet of high
merit, as empty of sense as of melody, measures the depth
of ignorant prejudice with which he treats the religion which
has moulded the culture of Europe and claimed the allegiance
of a St. Thomas. It is painful to see a man of genius sink to
the level of the Hyde Park atheist. For Galsworthy is not
at bottom an atheist. Nor is his religion solely the emotional
morality with which he tries to content himself. Though
we cannot of course identify the sentiments even of his
favourite characters with his own, it is hardly possible not
to see in their confused gropings a reflection of their author's
search for an unknown God, his dissatisfaction with a
morality of human kindness set in a soulless universe.

" My old Governor is a dear old boy, but his services are
enough to kill all belief. Have you any left ? "

" In God do you mean ? " said Dinny. " Ye-es without
knowing anything about it. Don't you find it impossible
to think of God except in the open and alone ? "

" I have been emotionalised in Church."

" You want something beyond emotion, I think, you want
to grasp infinite invention going on in infinite stillness.
Perpetual motion and perpetual quiet at the same time."[2]

How close this description approaches the religious experience of God. An infinite energy which yet is an infinite
stillness—what is this but that unmoved energy which Aristotle perceived must be the nature of Absolute Being and
which is so experienced in religious contemplation ? But if
Galsworthy had not despised as outworn web-spinning the

---

[1] *Flowering Wilderness*, Chapter xix.   [2] *Maid in Waiting*, Chapter x.

philosophy handed down and developed by Catholic meta-physicians he would not have made the mistake of supposing that this infinite energy must be a perpetual motion. He would have understood that motion involves imperfection, the passage from one imperfection and incompleteness to another and that it is therefore incompatible with absolute rest. But though he is unable to state it correctly, he is evidently striving to express the intuition for which Aristotle found a more adequate formula. The train of thought is continued.

" Perpetual motion in perpetual quiet ? If that, indeed, were God, He was not of much immediate use to mortals, but why should He be ? . . . When Saxenden tailored the hare and it had cried had God heard and quivered ? . . . The million million blades of grass down there that made the texture of the deeper darkness, the million million stars that gave the light by which she saw that darkness, all all the result of perpetual motion in endless quiet, all part of God. And she herself and the smoke of her cigarette ; the jasmine under her nose whose colour was invisible and the movement of her brain deciding that it was not yellow ; that dog barking so far away that the sound was as a thread by which the woof of silence could be grasped, all all endowed with the purpose remote, endless, pervading, incomprehensible of God."[1]

Though we cannot assume that Dinny's meditations express her creator's thought, their harmony with Galsworthy's sentiment and attitude assures us that they represent the sort of religion which he found sympathetic. The vague pantheism never thought out is typical of so much modern religion. I am sure it is the creed of millions. " Part of God "—if all things are part of God how can He be so remote from the sufferings of men and animals ? Is there a perpetual quiet other than and beyond a universe in perpetual

[1] *Ibid.*

c

motion ? How can a God who is no more than the sum total of all things have a purpose ? And how is His purpose related to the conflicting purposes and desires throughout the world, for example to Lord Saxenden's purpose to kill the hare and the hare's conflicting desire to escape being shot ? The despised philosophy of the Catholic schools has thought out the problem of the relation between the universe and Absolute Being. Galsworthy seems content to enunciate incompatible notions and leave it at that. I cannot indeed prove that he was not aware of the confusion and contradiction had and had not his own answer, so that they are Dinny's and not his. But frankly I see no reason to think so. In any case there are millions of Dinnys for whom he is spokesman here.

And besides this problem with which philosophy can deal there is another here which I am convinced Galsworthy felt keenly. It is twofold. How can Absolute Being exercise a providence over individuals ? This indeed is plainly stated. How are personal relations possible between man and the Absolute and Infinite Being who in whatever fashion is the source of the universe ? This is implicit in the entire passage.

The former question falls indeed within the scope of metaphysics, which shows that the source of human personality must be more not less than personal. But only religion with its concrete experience of God can, I believe, assure us that God's infinite Transcendence does not make it impossible for us to enter into personal communion with Him. That is why the knowledge of God attainable by the metaphysical proofs of theism is too abstract to provide the basis of a living personal religion. But Galsworthy dismissing unheard alike the great positive philosophic tradition which establishes the validity of the arguments for the existence of God and the historical religion in which man attains the richest and fullest personal knowledge of God, perceives

only an insoluble enigma. Where he touches religion
closest he finds himself faced with facts and problems
to which these alone supply the key. But the key is flung
away without any attempt to discover whether it will fit the
locks of those doors which bar the way upon his search for
the ultimate secret. So the secret goes unsolved and the
last word would seem to be the melancholy agnosticism of
Desert's final poem : " Lie Still."

> The germ and I and sun we rise
> Fulfil our little lives and die ;
> And to all question God replies :
> Lie still! I cannot tell you why![1]

And this melancholy agnosticism is reinforced by Dinny's
despairing affirmation of a universal mortality.

" So one ran through life watching each venture coming
to shore and at the end lay still! Like birds who uttered their
songs, hunted for worms, preened their feathers, flew without
seeming cause, unless for joy; mated, built nests and fed
their young, and when all was over became little stuffed
bundles of feathers, and passed into corruption and dust."[2]

Those " superstitious creeds " so disdainfully rejected
would have returned a more satisfactory answer.

But what of energeticism ? Surely this rationalist scepticism
and ultimate resignation are no idolatry of life as the absolute ?
In reality they leave room for nothing else. Service sustained
by a noble if unintelligent class tradition, or by a personal
unselfishness lacking any vision of an ultimate goal, or
such restless energy as drives Desert into the wilds, above
all the flowering of sex in a love-life of mutual fulfilment ;
these things fill the lives and sustain the work of Galsworthy's
characters in these concluding volumes, when the wealth
earning drive of the Victorian Forsytes has spent its force.

[1] *Over the River*, Chapter xxv. [2] *Ibid.*

And they are forces social or biological which give men's lives what shape they possess but are not themselves determined by forms *rationally* seen and approved. Hence incoherence, insufficiency and disillusionment. Men are blindly pushed forward by forces they can neither estimate nor control. If there is nothing of the self-sufficient and triumphant energeticism which has found embodiment in the pseudo-religions of Communism and logical Fascism, here too energy is the ultimate and supreme reality—though it assumes many shapes which there is no attempt to co-ordinate. I am inclined to think that for Galsworthy the highest of these energies was the love of sex at its most perfect. Such at least is the impression left by his work. If this is true he approaches Lawrence on this point. But whereas Lawrence was under no illusions as to the biological character of sex, Galsworthy will accept it only when decked out with an illusion of romantic spirituality.[1] This romantic illusion is natural enough. Since man's spiritual soul informs his biological life, that life cannot be profoundly moved without affecting the spiritual level of his being, though these biological currents cannot reach the deepest depth where the centre of his spirit meets God. He is therefore easily persuaded to mistake biological passion for a spiritual love. And when as with Galsworthy, lack of religious belief leaves the spirit empty, he will unconsciously invest a biological force with a spiritual value and make an idol of romantic love. This however is to exalt a vital union as the supreme value—a species of energeticism.

If this view of sex-love seems too cynical I invite the critic to suppose that by the spell of a malevolent genie Wilfred Desert had been suddenly transformed into an aged man. Would Dinny still have loved him? That she would have been affectionate and sympathetic I believe. She might even have been prepared to marry him in a spirit of self-sacrificing

[1] Lawrence also ascribes a false spiritual value to sex—but to sex as biological.

love. But she could not have felt any sex-love for him. And the love of old couples has been built up by sex-love in the past, as a reef by corals once alive.

For lack of insight into the order of form which determines the order of energy, of the light which determines life, Galsworthy is an unconscious energeticist—and his lack of philosophy an unformulated philosophy of force.

Yet almost at the close of his life work, towards the conclusion of his last novel, the condemnation of energeticism is pronounced by one of his characters. " Shape IS life and when Life's gone, one cannot see why shape should remain even for the little time it does." Shape is life ; or rather it determines life. As an artist Galsworthy could give shape to his vision of life. But without metaphysics or clearly formulated religion he could not see the shape of life as a whole, the shape which determines the energies of the universe and co-ordinates them in an ordered structure. His view of the world, therefore, has a shapelessness which reflects the shapelessness of the inwardly disintegrated culture to which he belonged. It is a world in which men are the puppets of forces whose significance and place in the universal order are unknown. Their deficiencies are accepted with melancholy resignation as an ineluctable doom, their positive values isolated and idolised. The resignation and idolatry are accentuated in Galsworthy's attitude to sex—regarded as at once man's most relentless tyrant and inspiring divinity. For Galsworthy a rationalism ignorant of Reason has led inevitably to energeticism. And after all the energy life is but " sound and fury signifying nothing." Its end is death, "corruption" and "dust," nothing more. We catch the echo of the paganism from which the religion of Christ freed the western world. " Nos ubi decidimus quo pater Aeneas, quo dives Tullus et Ancus pulvis et umbra sumus." But Galsworthy's energeticism leaves not even a shade. There is but the " dust of formless corruption." Only when the world is known for the creation of an Infinite Intelligence and the human soul as an undying spirit made in His likeness is there place for a life which achieves abiding results and possesses an abiding significance. For only then can the universe be the product and incarnation of creative Form—the " shape which is life indeed."

ALDOUS HUXLEY

A PHILOSOPHY OF MOODS

As Mr. Aldous Huxley tells us himself, his article on "Pascal"[1] is not so much a study of its ostensible subject as an exposition of the writer's personal philosophy of life. It is therefore primarily Mr. Huxley's and not Pascal's views that I propose to examine here, but with him I shall take my start from Pascal.

Mr. Huxley agrees with Pascal in his philosophic scepticism, his preliminary pyrrhonism, disagrees with his Christianity. But is Pascal a typical representative of Christianity? Once Mr. Huxley admits that he was not—that his " was a special, a rather dreadful kind of Christianity." Elsewhere, however, he forgets this and treats as Christian what is the exaggeration and therefore the distortion of one among the many aspects of Christianity. This the Catholic mind has judged long since, condemning Pascal as at least a *Jansenisant*, and, with Mr. Huxley, pronouncing on the whole in favour of his Jesuit adversaries. Not a single orthodox theologian could Mr. Huxley find who would subscribe to Pascal's dictum about marriage that it is " *une espèce d'homicide et comme un déicide*." If Mr. Huxley desires to make his account with Christianity, he must choose another exponent than Pascal.

But no doubt it is Pascal's preliminary scepticism which has attracted Mr. Huxley. If he believed in the Christian revelation, he was at least too wise to believe in reason, at any rate when employed on ultimates. Mr. Huxley has, I think, misunderstood Pascal's " scepticism." It was not Pascal's intention to reject all rational certainty and base his Christianity on a pure act of faith without an intellectual

[1] Pascal. An Essay by Aldous Huxley. The Realist. Nos. 1, 2, 3.

foundation. His scepticism was directed only against discursive reasoning and in particular against the mathematical reasoning employed in the positive sciences. But above and beyond this geometrical reasoning man possesses what Pascal called the *esprit de finesse* or the *coeur* by which, prior to any revelation, he apprehends the profound truths of reality. In other words Pascal was not a fideist but an intuitionist. Truth, inaccessible to the discursive reason, is known by intuition. This intuitionism however is not scepticism. For it holds that man can attain truth by a natural function of his spirit.

In many respects indeed Pascal's epistemology was defective. He should not have contrasted intuition, the *esprit de finesse*, with discursive reasoning, the *esprit de géometrie*. For if we examine the nature of discursive reasoning, we shall find that in the last analysis it consists in the intuition of truth, of form, and the discrimination of intuitions. Mathematical reasoning differs from the profounder intuition which Pascal calls the *esprit de finesse* not because it also is not intuition, but because it is the intuition of clear abstract forms whereas the latter, Pascal's *esprit de finesse*, is a more obscure and more concrete intuition of form. And it was most misleading to attribute the obscure concrete intuition to the heart. Its intellectual character is indeed admitted by Pascal when he speaks of its " supple *thought* "— " *souplesse de pensée*." Because it is concerned with the great concrete realities of human life, it is coloured by an emotion foreign to the cold apprehensions of those abstract truths which are the subject of the mathematical sciences. But this does not make it an emotion. On the contrary it is the highest exercise of the intellect, the power which apprehends forms, whether the clearer and more abstract and comparatively superficial forms which are the object of the mathematical sciences, the abstract but more obscure forms apprehended by metaphysics, or the dim but more concrete and more profound forms which are the object of moral, aesthetic and above all religious intuition. And in his reaction against the mathematicism of the Cartesians, Pascal failed to realise that even the abstract forms apprehended by the mathematical sciences, by his *esprit de géometrie*, are not conventional symbols but the objective properties of real objects, even though they cannot exhaust the full concrete reality of those objects. M. Meyerson by his comprehensive studies of scientific reasoning has proved that it is essentially realist, concerned not with a manipulation of convenient symbols, substitutes for a reality wholly unknowable, but seeking, and with a large measure of success, to discover the nature of things as they objectively exist.

This undue scepticism however of mathematico-scientific reasoning and a certain confusion between the higher intuition of the intellect and the emotion with which it is normally invested does not affect Pascal's conviction that the human mind can and does attain truth by its natural power. The *esprit de finesse* is not faith, but knowledge.

Thus although his language gives a handle to the sceptic, Pascal was not a sceptic. Mr. Huxley, on the contrary, is a genuine and almost a complete sceptic. Almost—for grudgingly and illogically he admits that objective knowledge of the sensible world is attainable. True, what he gives with one hand he takes away with the other. Even in this order the denial of the most evident, the most ineluctable facts—*e.g.*, that Socrates is mortal, that two and two make four, is simply " outrageously bad taste universally condemned," and these facts no better than " rationalizations of psychological experiences more or less uniform for all men." This is a desperate attempt to keep the sceptical flag flying to the last, despite the overwhelming attack of common-sense. For Mr. Huxley is obliged to admit—an admission fatal to pure scepticism—that to deny the facts of sensible experience is to collide not merely with the consent of one's fellow men but with things. " The hero," he remarks, " of

Dostoievsky's *Notes from Underground* protests against the intolerable tyranny of two and two making four. He prefers that they shall make five, and insists that he has a right to his preference. And no doubt he has a right. But if an express train happens to be passing at a distance of two plus two yards, and he advances four yards and a half under the impression that he will still be eighteen inches on the hither side of destruction, this right of his will not save him from coming to a violent and bloody conclusion." In other words, his alleged right is meaningless. The universe, truth disallows it. Practically, then, Mr. Huxley admits that our senses and the intellect which through their data apprehends the forms of things give us knowledge of objective reality.

However, though not, save perhaps in words, a complete sceptic, he restricts the sphere of knowledge considerably. As we have seen, he disbelieves in historical truth. Here indeed, he is self-confuted. If historical truth be unattainable —or at best only a knowledge of external facts—how comes he to be discussing the opinions and sentiments, the interior life of Pascal, and, further, utilizing for that purpose not only Pascal's actual writings, but his sister's biography? Moreover, he illustrates his thesis by quoting, as historically authentic, sayings of Jesus recorded in Gospels which he argues elsewhere cannot give us a reliable account of His life. Mr. Huxley has certainly made generous use of " that non-existent thing, the Historical Truth." But we need not take this attack upon history too seriously. It is but a casual stick taken up to beat the apologist who appeals to history. The heart of his scepticism is not here. It is the denial that *philosophic* truth is attainable—that is to say, that we can have any certain knowledge of the ultimate nature of reality. To maintain any view of reality as a whole—its ground, its meaning, its end—is for Mr. Huxley a contemptible " rationalism," due largely to the weakness which demands fixed truth as the basis and goal of life—in fact, to habits implanted in the European mind two thousand years ago by Christianity.

So far as sense knowledge and the physical sciences based upon it are concerned, we grant that they do not, and cannot, give us a knowledge of ultimates. Science is confined to quantitative measurements amenable to mathematical treatment. Of the matter thus measured we know only that it exists outside ourselves. Even the spatial and temporal properties which in our normal experience are inseparable from it perhaps hold good only of material complexes, not of the ultimate units, the electrons and protons. The latter indeed may perhaps have no existence independent of these complexes, which may thus strictly be the ultimate energy-objects in the descending scale of being. So far Mr. Huxley is right, though he might perhaps remember that when those incurable "rationalists" Aristotle and St. Thomas taught that quantity was an *accident* of matter, and *materia prima* an unintelligible potentiality incapable of existing apart from form, they anticipated these humbling confessions of modern science. Moreover, as I have pointed out above, these measurements are forms, quantities of an objective reality, and therefore give us a genuine, if incomplete and abstract, knowledge of that reality. But is sensible knowledge scientifically organized our total knowledge of reality? Why this arbitrary limitation? Throughout his essay Mr. Huxley allows the reality of a host of experiences more or less transcendent of the sensible and measurable order—ecstasies (we use the word here in the widest and most untechnical sense) of every description, from the ecstasy of sex or drugs to the ecstasy of the mystic. Their existence is, he admits, as certain, although of course less common than the existence of sensible experiences. Why, then, am I to allow objective reference to the latter and deny it to the former Why is it reasonable to believe my senses and my intellect, as it apprehends in their data the outer forms of objects, but "rationalism" to regard more or less super-sensible experiences—or rather all experiences other than quantitative, and therefore the intellect as it apprehends forms which are not quantitative as affording knowledge of a reality other than the emotion of the experient? Because, Mr. Huxley replies, whereas the "psychological experiences" on which scientific theories are based "are more or less uniform for all men and for the same man at different times," the experiences on which a metaphysical world view is based "are diverse, irrational, and contradictory." No doubt the higher experiences are comparatively rare; mystics are few. But directly religious experiences of an inchoate semi-conscious type are extremely common—I think universal—and experiences of a lower order, which, nevertheless, transcend measurement and mechanism, are as much a part of normal human experience as the measurable and mechanical aspects of experience on which the mathematical sciences are based. That from their very nature these qualitative experiences cannot give us that distinct scientific knowledge of reality, which is by definition quantitative, does not in the least invalidate a reference equally objective. But they are diverse—why not? We should expect —and no one expects it more than Mr. Huxley—richness and diversity in the universe. They are contradictory? Mr. Huxley does not prove it, and on occasion, to the jeopardy of his entire thesis, admits that after all they may be, not contradictory, but complementary, and that "each" of the views of reality which rationalize such experiences—a fortiori, therefore, the experience itself—may "represent one aspect of the whole." Elsewhere[1] he tells us that "art deals with many more aspects of internal reality than science." This implies that art reveals a profounder level of truth than science, to which, as we have seen, he so grudgingly concedes an assured reference to objective truth. The fact is, and this I believe

[1] *Do What You Will*, p. 4. Essays by Aldous Huxley. (Chatto and Windus.)

is the reply to Mr. Huxley's semi-pyrrhonism (has the complete pyrrhonist ever existed?) there is not and cannot conceivably be a purely subjective experience—an experience which conveys *no* knowledge of external reality. A wholly subjective experience is a contradiction as meaningless as the complete lie or the wholly evil man or deed. If, *e.g.*, I dream that I am King of England, my dream is only possible because, outside dream and dreamer, England exists and kingship exists. The illusory or purely subjective element in my dream is simply a wrong relationship between the objective realities—monarchy, England, and myself. Every desire, moreover, contains an element of knowledge. I cannot desire the simply non-existent. " From the fact of change and decay," writes Mr. Huxley, " the logic of desire deduces the existence of something changeless. . . . It is desirable that there should be noumena " (by this Kantian phrase he understands permanent spiritual realities) ; " therefore noumena exist. . . . A similar conjuring trick produces the One out of the deplorably puzzling Many, draws the Good and the Beautiful out of the seething hotch-potch of diverse human tastes and sensibilities and interests, deduces Justice from our actual inequalities, and absolute Truth from the necessary and unescapable relativities of daily life. *It is by an exactly similar process that children invent imaginary playmates to amuse their solitudes, and transform a dull, uninteresting piece of wood into a horse, a ship, a railway train, what you will.*" The sentence I have italicized gives away Mr. Huxley's entire case. Unless playmates really existed in *rerum natura* children could not invent imaginary ones. If there were no real horses, ships, and railway trains there would be no toy horses, ships or trains. What child before the first half of the last century ever " transformed a piece of wood into a railway train " ? Only because playmates, horses, ships, and trains pre-exist and enter somehow into their experience can children desire them, and, to satisfy their desire, form mental or material

images of these things.[1] And it is because the " One," the
" Good," the " Beautiful," " Justice," and " absolute Truth "
actually pre-exist, and somehow are experienced by us, that
by a similar process we form, not indeed images of these
things, as like as children's toys to their originals—the gulf
is too wide for that—but true, if obscure, notions of them, as
transcending yet partially reflected in the imperfect unities,
goodness, beauties, justice and truth of our human experience.
Moreover, as a child's dissatisfaction with its loneliness presupposes the existence of human companionship, the essentially
social nature of man, our dissatisfaction with the relative and
changing presupposes the existence of the Absolute and
Unchanging. How could we object to the sight of " change
and decay in all around " unless we possessed some, however
dim, experience of the changeless and abiding ? The insect
does not chafe against its ephemerality, nor the cat lament
the passing of youth and love.

But, objects Mr. Huxley, the rationalizations of our transcendental experiences are various and conflicting. We deny
the assertion. They are by no means so various as is usually
supposed ; on the contrary, almost fatiguingly alike : and
contradictory, only in so far as they deny or distort, enlarge
or restrict unduly, either the experimental facts which they
profess to explain or the data or implications of other
experiences equally authentic.

First a necessary distinction.

Analyzing Pascal's " conversion " experience as recorded
in his " Memorial," Mr. Huxley insists on the distinction to
be made between the pure, we may say, the raw experience
—for example, " Feu. Pleurs de Joie "—and its intellectual
interpretation—for instance, " Dieu d'Abraham, Dieu d'Isaac,
Dieu de Jacob . . . Dieu de Jésus Christ." The distinction
is true and important but insufficient. We must further

---

[1] Imaginary objects are but compounds of real (e.g., the dragon—lizard, wings,
fire) and *do not represent another order of being.*

distinguish between the intellectual interpretation of the
experience based wholly on its own data, and the interpretation which consists in relating that experience to data derived
elsewhere. No doubt both interpretations blend and cannot
be completely separated. But roughly the distinction may
and should be made. Take, for example, the following lines
of the " Memorial " :

> " Dieu d'Abraham, Dieu d'Isaac, Dieu de Jacob
> Non des Philosophes et des Sçavans
> Dieu de Jésus Christ."

All this is interpretation, but the interpretation is not of a
piece. It moves on two levels.

There is first the direct, the internal, interpretation which
(terminology apart) makes use of no data external to the
experience. The " Being " *experienced* by Pascal, and simply
as experienced by him, is not an abstract conclusion, but a
living and active Being in personal relationship with the
soul, is therefore more not less than personal—which
is the true meaning of the much misunderstood expression
a personal God. This is the primary sense of the lines,
especially of the second. The interpretation is directly based
on the experience it interprets, and would be what it is and
equally true if Abraham, Isaac and Jacob, and even Jesus
Christ, had no existence.

These, on the contrary, belong to the secondary interpretation, which relates the experience to data external to itself.
Pascal's experience warranted the interpretation that he had
experienced the presence and operation of a personal God ;
it did not, and of its nature could not, warrant the further
statement that the God thus experienced had revealed Himself
to three Jewish patriarchs over three thousand years before,
or was in a unique sense the God of Jesus Christ. The truth
of this secondary indirect and partially external interpretation
cannot be established by the experience it interprets. It is

essentially a relationship between that experience and facts or beliefs wholly outside it.

Before, however, we complain of the diversity and contradiction which exist between the rationalizations of religious experiences (indeed of higher experiences of every kind), we must eliminate all those based on interpretation of this second class. Not, of course, that such interpretation, such relating, is necessarily false or illegitimate. But it is no part either of the experiences whose validity is in question, or of their direct rationalization. We cannot, therefore, object against the validity either of the experiences or of their direct rationalization, divergencies and contradictions due to this secondary and indirect interpretation, which, therefore, *from our present standpoint*, must be left out of account.

When this has been done, and we confine our attention to the religious experiences themselves and their direct intrinsic interpretations, we are struck not by the diversity but the similarity between them. To convince ourselves of this we have but to compare such a typical product of Christian mysticism as Ramon Lull's book of the Lover and the Beloved with the psalms of the Hindu mystics Kabir and Dadu. The experience of God which underlies these prose poems, as described and directly interpreted in them, is substantially identical. This is not to claim for all religions an equal level of value and truth. The direct religious experiences of the individual are not the whole of religion, and the interpretations of the second degree which relate them to a total world view vary enormously in truth and value from one religion to another. Nevertheless, the likeness which obtains between the experience of mystics of every age, country, and creed constitutes a massive witness to its objective validity and to the truth of, at least, its direct, its internal, interpretation. Mr. Huxley, however, denies this. "Mystical experiences," he tells us, "which in Europe are interpreted in terms of a personal God, are interpreted by the Buddhist in terms of an entirely godless order of things." This appeal to Buddhism, common with those who wish to discredit the powerful and world-wide witness of religious experience to God is, I am convinced, a travesty of the facts. I will concede, though it cannot be regarded as proved, that the teaching of Gautama was atheistic—that is to say, that for him the ultimate reality was a sheer nonentity. But his fundamental experience of the deficiency and vanity of all things mutable, therefore of human life in as much as it is occupied with and involved in these passing things and is itself passing away, implied a positive experience of an Absolute and Immutable Good—the background against which this emptiness of the contingent and the mutable was apprehended so powerfully, even if this positive apprehension was but implicit and not fully conscious. And if the Buddha's explicit doctrine was in fact negative, atheistic, the history of Buddhism is the history of the transformation *under the pressure of religious experience* of an original atheism into a practical theism. For Mahayana Buddhism, and even in large measure for the more primitive Hinayana school, the Absolute is not, save (since the original terminology survives), to some extent, in words, Nothingness, but a Being above, not below determination; thus practically, as the object of religious experience, though not theoretically for metaphysical interpretation, it is identical with the Brahman of Vedanta. How are we to differentiate such an Absolute from the super-determinate Deity—the super-God of Christian mysticism, as formulated in the classic treatises of the pseudo-Dionysius? The most that can be said is that in Buddhism, as in the Advaita Vedanta, the real existence of creatures is insufficiently safeguarded, and the *doctrine* of Deity is too often formulated in terms of an acosmic pantheism or theopanism for which God is in such wise the sole Reality that nothing exists that is not Himself or Itself. This error however is not in the primary interpretation of the religious experience, the affirmation of

D

Absolute Being, but originates in the secondary interpretation which relates other aspects of reality to it. Also, it is an error of denial—*i.e.*, it refuses to do justice to the distinct reality of the creature—not of affirmation, and an error not about the Being of God, but about the being of creatures. For the Christian mystic also his experience of God involves an experience of the comparative non-reality of everything else, including himself. If he is saved from the further step of denying any real being to creatures, it is due to a creed and a philosophy which supplement the immediate data of his experience as a mystic. And after all, we may doubt whether the acosmism of Buddhist or Vedantist is at bottom anything more than this appreciation of the comparative non-being of creatures, their *utter* dependence on God. Fr. Johanns, S.J., has shewn that the philosophy of Sankara, the founder and metaphysician of Advaita Vedantism, whose system is generally supposed to be sheer pantheism, is not really pantheist, but though incomplete, is, in so far as concerns the nature of the Absolute, entirely compatible with Christian theism. Nor do we think that a similar examination of great Buddhist teachers would lead to a very different conclusion. Of religious experience we may safely affirm that with one voice in every place and in every epoch it proclaims the Being, Presence and Operation of God.

Nor do lower forms of qualitative, more or less sense-transcending, experiences—the experiences, for example, of the artist or the lover—imply world-views incompatible with that of the theist. It is indeed impossible in the compass of an essay to prove a universal proposition of this kind; but neither does Mr. Huxley bring forward any fact which disproves it. " The life-worshipper," he writes, " is in a position to accept all the partial and apparently contradictory syntheses constructed by philosophers." " Partial," certainly; " apparently contradictory "—examination reduces the contradiction either to mere appearance or to that unwarranted exclusion and rejection of other aspects of experience which Mr. Huxley himself so rightly repudiates. "He [the life-worshipper] is at one moment a positivist and at another a mystic . . . now a pessimist and now, with a change of love, or liver, or even the weather, an exuberant believer that God's in His heaven, and all's right with the world. . . . *Each belief is a rationalization of a prevailing mood.*" Falser philosophy and falser psychology than those expressed in this quotation it would be difficult to find.

False philosophy in the first place. Positivism, in so far as it affirms the reality of the material and mechanical aspects of the universe, is not opposed to mysticism. On the contrary, it valuably supplements and corrects it—is a salutary check on such exclusive preoccupation with the direct experience of God (evidently not His Will for man on earth) as might lead the mystic to deny or unduly minimize the value and reality of creatures, especially bodily creatures, and our necessary occupation with them. Only when the positivist presumes on the strength of this in itself true and valuable experience of the reality and worth of the material and the mechanical, to deny the mystic's—indeed generally the religious man's—experience of God and the soul, does his positivism contradict mysticism. Human experience reveals God, the soul, bodies, machinery, and measurement, and if the true philosophy must accept all the data of human experience, it cannot, like Mr. Huxley, acquiesce in an alleged incompatibility between them. Christian philosophy, at any rate, if not always the individual Christian, has found room for all these facts.

In the second place there is false and extremely crude psychology.

Mr. Huxley actually confuses, in the teeth of everyday experience, mood and belief, emotional colouring and intellectual judgement. He shuffles off this confusion by making use of the ambiguous terms pessimism and optimism. These words denote two different things : moods and judgements. As moods, pessimism and optimism have little intellectual significance. They witness respectively to the obvious facts that there is much good, also much evil, in human experience ; and that is all. Whether we are at a particular moment more sensible of the good or the evil is indeed largely a matter of mood, dependent, as Mr. Huxley remarks, on love, liver, or weather. But they may also be judgements—optimism that the good exceeds the evil, pessimism the reverse. Here, indeed, a genuine conflict arises ; but it is an insult to a professedly reasonable being to suggest that his decision should depend on the accidents of his individual experience or bodily constitution. No doubt it often does ; but even Mr. Huxley will hardly maintain that whatever is ought to be. When the question is considered from a rational stand-point it is plain that there is much evidence to support both views, and that an ultimate decision must depend, not on an impossible calculus of the good and evil in human life, but upon a world-view based on other grounds. But the evidence excludes both the absolute optimism of Pippa's "All's right with the world," which, one need not say, Browning did not believe himself, and the absolute pessimism of Hardy's *Tess*—to which Mr. Huxley opposes it. But, we may be sure, neither Browning nor Hardy would have seriously maintained *as deliberate intellectual judgements* that the world is good after dinner, a success in love, or on a fine day ; that it is evil before dinner, after an unsuccessful love, or on a rainy day. For although even our moods give us *some* knowledge of reality, to found upon them considered judgements of the universe, " world-views," is the bankruptcy of reason. Mr. Huxley's philosophy of moods is the abdication of the intellect in favour of the most superficial emotion, the canonization of chaos.

Indeed, we doubt if such a " philosophy " could ever have been propounded except as a reaction against three excesses

—two theoretical and one practical. One theoretical excess is the attempt to construct a philosophy in terms of one aspect only of experience, suppressing or distorting by unnatural interpretation all evidence to the contrary. Such an excess is at the root both of idealism and of materialism. The other is the belief that a complete philosophy is attainable ; that not only all the views and aspects of experience ought to be taken into account (as Mr. Huxley and Catholic philosophy would agree) and cannot be really incompatible, for truth is self-evidently one (though Mr. Huxley questions this, it is the presupposition of every attempt to give a rational account of experience, and therefore of the special sciences), but that we can attain so complete an understanding of reality that we can see clearly how they are harmonized. This is indeed an excess of rationalism, of confidence in human reason and knowledge. Though we know enough to be certain that the jig-saw puzzle of experience does present one coherent design—too many pieces fit together for this to be reasonably questioned—we cannot and never shall be able to put together that pattern in its entirety. Only the knowledge of God sees the whole and every detail. Plato, haunted by a beatific vision of the Good, believed it attainable on earth, craved such knowledge of the universe as would enable us to assign a final cause why trees are green. It was an impossible idea, knowledge not for mortals. Moreover, in consequence of the element of irrationality due to the *comparative* non-reality of creatures and increasing as we descend the hierarchy of being, there may not be an explanation other than a purely mechanical one for every quality of material bodies. Nor even of the riddles presented by the fundamental aspects of experience do we possess a solution. Why is there suffering, and such suffering, in the creation of a good God ? In these dim regions of ultimate truth we can see only " through a mirror and in an enigma ": must be content with obscure intuitions of truth—

stammering formulations. But the fact that we cannot hope to possess the loaf of complete knowledge is no ground for saying with Mr. Huxley that there is no bread, or even less bread than there is.

The practical excess from which Mr. Huxley reacts, and which he finds not unfairly in Pascal, is the attempt to act as if only one type of experience possessed value for man. Mr. Huxley, on the contrary, argues that we should treat all types of experience as possessing equal value.[1] A more rational attitude than either extreme is that expressed by the Vulgate text " ordinavit in me caritatem "—" He set charity in order within me." Obviously experiences are not of equal value. The enjoyment of a good dinner is self-evidently less valuable than the enjoyment of poetry. But it does not follow that we should wholly sacrifice the art of cookery in favour of the art of poetry. For if the value of good cookery is inferior to that of poetry, the former is a distinctive value not to be omitted from the complete experience of mankind. (Not that there is the least danger of this!) Moreover, when occasion arises to cook or appreciate food, we should do it whole-heartedly. Neither the cook nor the diner will wisely divide their attention between the dishes and the study of Shelley. But to go farther than this and object to any and every sacrifice of a lower to a higher order of values, even to deny that such an order is possible—is to make life as irrational and chaotic in practice as the rejection of any certain world-view does theoretically. Mr. Huxley bids us worship life. But order is the very essence of life ; disorder, that is to say, disintegration and corruption, is death.

And though it is true that the experience of the race ought to find place for every type of experience, it does not follow that the experience of every individual must do the same.

---

[1] Yet in his essay entitled " Fashions of Love " (*Do What You Will*) Mr. Huxley condemns *purely* physical love-making as destructive of love itself and finally of pleasure. If, however, physical values were equal to spiritual, as his theory demands, this would not be the case.

We must specialize in practice as in study. Though, for example, all men should value art, not all need practise it. And similarly, though all should hold sexual relations in honour, not all need marry. It may, however, be urged, and this in fact is the peculiar excess in Pascal which annoys Mr. Huxley—that since God is the Absolute Good we *all* ought to sacrifice as far as possible every other activity to the direct practice of religion. If, indeed, we could see God as He is, we should practise and enjoy all other activities and experiences formally or eminently in Him, and should *need* nothing beyond. " Deus meus et omnia." Since, however, we can at best apprehend Him only in the darkness of an incomprehensible intuition, the secular aspects of experience contain and reveal values and aspects which, though eminently in God as He is, are not contained in His revelation to man on earth. Therefore, even in presence of the fullest possible knowledge of God, these secular experiences and activities have claims upon us, urgent in proportion to their rank in the scale of values. This, indeed, is the radical fallacy of St. Augustine's conclusion that it is enough to know God and the soul, and we are no better if we know other things besides. If we could know God as He is, this would be a truism. Since in fact we cannot do so, man (not necessarily Augustine) needs to know these other things which reflect uniquely aspects of His Being of which we should otherwise be ignorant, and thus indirectly increase our knowledge of Him.

But it does not follow that the Saint should devote much of his time and energy to these lower values. He is entirely justified in sacrificing, indeed it is his vocation to sacrifice, them, for the sake of a more continuous and deeper communion with God. If Mr. Huxley objects, he is objecting to all specialization, expecting the individual to realize powers and functions which can be realized only by the united work and experience of the community. We can legitimately complain only when, as we must admit is too frequently the case, the Saint expects all his fellows to specialize in holiness, and despises, depreciates, or even denounces the lower experiences and activities he is himself called upon to surrender. And holy men and women have no doubt in practice unduly starved the non-religious experiences and needs of human life, natural affections and emotions. Hence a nervous tension which too often mars the serenity and impairs the complete sanity of their lives, incidentally depriving them of much of that attractiveness they would otherwise possess. But even these excesses are not, as Mr. Huxley terms them, death-worship, or necessarily the product of a sickly weakness of the natural desires. St. Augustine's view of life—as he holds it up *as a law for others*—was, no doubt, too exclusive ; but in view of his history to ascribe it to a weakness of natural desire would be absurd. And to call it death-worship is caricature. The Saint, even a somewhat perverse saint like Pascal, seeks life, to say the least, as ardently as any of Mr. Huxley's life-worshippers. But he will be content with nothing less than the eternal and complete life of God, and that not simply or primarily as a promise of the hereafter, but as present and operative here and now. " With Thee is the well of life." " That they may have life and have it more abundantly." These are not the accents of death-worship. That holy men have dwelt too long and too delightedly on the death which inevitably awaits all life merely natural is no doubt true. Every excess—therefore also Mr. Huxley's—is the reaction against a counter-excess. But they did not therefore worship death. Nor is their ecstasy, as Mr. Huxley will have it, negative—the contemplation of death and its void. It is a possession by the plenitude of a Life transcending the partial determinations which limit while they characterize and diversify the life of nature and the normal life of man.

The true life-worshipper, while *duly* prizing every manifestation of life, will prize supremely the life of God, communicated to the soul, and will be glad that there are men called to partake it so fully, that they reject to a large degree, though of course never completely, those lower modes of life which the majority do, and should, live. And knowing, moreover, that everywhere life is the achievement of form and unity, the integration of multiplicity in a comprehensive whole, he will be convinced that although man's short vision may not see it, and the deficiency inevitable in a world so remote from the eternal and perfect life of God may involve an inevitable element of disorder and irrationality, as a whole the universe, which man so diversely experiences, manifests a harmony, increasing in perfection and fulness as created life—in its lower degrees we call it energy —approaches the life of God, but absent nowhere. And so convinced he will, not by himself alone, but working in his due place with his fellows, endeavour, theoretically to discover and understand the harmony and order in the world, practically to introduce it into his own life and the life of society, both thus made more alive.

Mr. Huxley himself perceives that unrestrained abandonment to any and every desire is death, though his refusal to accept a hierarchy of values leads him to apply this so perversely to the desire for God. This, however, is implicitly to admit that life itself demands a co-ordination and subordination of desires. And this in turn involves the scale of values and " fixed point of reference," theoretical and practical, against which he rebels. Life, no doubt, welcomes—nay, requires—every form of human experience and action, but only in its appropriate place and scope, which is by no means the same for all experiences or for all men. And the complete life can be only the life of the entire human race, with its saints, its artists, its scientists, also its dressmakers and its cooks. All must specialize—but not equally. The saint must specialize more than the artist, the artist more than the cook.[1]

---

[1] Not necessarily in the amount of time actually spent in the preparation or practice of his art, but in the reference to it of his experience as a whole.

For everywhere the higher manifestations of life must be preferred to the lower, and the lower exist to subserve, not directly even the highest—not even the mystic's *knowledge* of God is the *summum bonum*—but that which is revealed most adequately in man's highest activity, mystical experience, least in his lowest activities—though fully in none and partially in all—namely, God Himself, that is to say, Life itself, the Life that is the source of all life beside. This is the life-worship of the theist, balanced, sane and full, not the tight-rope walking between unco-ordinated excesses to which Mr. Huxley invites us, but a climb, at least equally thrilling with adventure and risk, to a summit where the entire being of man, individual and social, is alive with the Life of God and ecstatic with the Vision of His Beauty.

LORD RUSSELL

RELIGION WITHOUT REASON

" Educ de custodia animam meam ad confitendum nomini tuo " (" Bring my soul out of prison that I may praise thy name.") Whatever may have been the psalmist's thought when he wrote these words, they are pregnant with a meaning so wide that it is co-extensive with the entire field of religion. Human knowledge and human belief are in the last analysis formulations, interpretations of human experience. If there be a God and He has revealed Himself to man, it is within human experience that the revelation has been made. When, therefore, the Christian affirms his belief that there is a God and that He has made Himself known to man, he implicitly affirms his belief that God is an object of human experience. Why, then, are His existence and self-revelation (as Max Scheler points out,[1] since God is personal, all our knowledge of Him natural or supernatural must be His self-revelation) denied by so many men of goodwill and sound intellect? They are in prison—cut off by some spiritual or intellectual barrier from frank acceptance of that total human experience in which God is given.[2] It may be that, owing to some congenital defect analogous to aesthetic blindness or from lack of religious education, they have never themselves enjoyed religious experience, and for some reason or another—e.g., a philosophy, explicit or implicit, which denies or explains away religious values—will not accept the testimony borne by the religious experience of their fellows. Such men are in a windowless dungeon, close-shuttered from the light of

[1] *Probleme der Religion, Vom Ewigen im Menschen*, Bd. I.
[2] For the purpose of this essay the further question of a special historic revelation such as Catholic Christianity claims to be can be left out of account. For it arises only at a later stage than that with which the present controversy is concerned.

God. But there are others who do enjoy religious experience, yet will not accept its data as objectively valid. Their dungeon has windows, but the door is fast bolted. It is to the latter class that Lord Russell belongs. He is *anima naturaliter religiosa*. He does not accept even a minimum of religious belief. He accepts, praises, and himself possesses religious experience, yet will not allow that it bears witness to the nature of objective reality. What are the bolts, the bars which confine him in the prison of denial? Are they really so strong as he supposes? If a thinker of his eminence has tested them so often, and so often proclaimed them inextricable and unbreakable, is it not because they are so in fact?

A. REALITY OF RELIGIOUS EXPERIENCE ADMITTED

Over and over again Lord Russell gives emphatic testimony to the reality and value of religious experience. In his *Principles of Social Reconstruction* he divides human activities into three groups derived respectively from impulse or instinct, from mind and from spirit. To the life of the spirit belong " art, reverence, and worship," and " deeper than all these the sense of a mystery half-revealed, of a hidden wisdom and glory, of a transfiguring vision in which common things lose their solid importance and become a thin veil behind which the ultimate truth of the world is dimly seen." " Such feelings," he continues, " are the source of religion, and if they were to die out most of what is best would vanish out of life."[1] In an article contributed in 1912 to the *Hibbert Journal*,[2] he attempts to construct a religion without the dogmatic beliefs on which religion has hitherto rested. Here also the existence and the supreme worth of religious experience are emphasized. " Acts inspired by religion have some quality of infinity in them." " The quality of infinity makes religion the selfless, untrammelled life in the whole which

---

[1] *Principles of Social Reconstruction*, pp. 207-8.
[2] *Essence of Religion: Hibbert Journal*, October, 1912.

frees men from the prison house of eager wishes and little thoughts." " Worship " must at all costs be preserved. " It brings joy in the contemplation of what is worshipped. But joy alone does not constitute worship ; there must be also some reverence and a *sense of mystery not easy to define.*" In his latest utterance indeed *Religion and Science* (1935) this religious affirmation is significantly weaker. Long years of repression by a positivist mind have had their effect upon the religious soul thus thwarted and starved. Nevertheless, it has not been wholly silenced. In fainter tones, and in the background, it repeats its former witness. " The mystic emotion . . . may give something of very great value—the same kind of thing, though in a heightened form, that is given by contemplation. Breadth and calm and profundity may all have their source in this emotion in which, for the moment, all self-centred desire is dead, and the mind becomes a mirror for the vastness of the universe. . . . In the realm of emotions I do not deny the value of the experiences which have given rise to religion." The distinctive quality of religious experience and its irreplaceable value for human life are thus fully recognized by Lord Russell. He does not attempt to explain religious experience away as a perversion of sexual instinct, as infantilism, or some form of pathological hallucination. Yet, although religious experience is thus real, distinctive and valuable, he refuses to regard it as objectively valid.

B. THE OBJECTIVE VALIDITY OF RELIGIOUS EXPERIENCE DENIED

In his chapter on Mysticism in *Religion and Science* Lord Russell attempts to invalidate the witness of the mystics by pointing to its divergence. " Catholics," he writes, " but not Protestants may have visions in which the Virgin appears." This is in the main true. But it affects, not the essential experience of Absolute Divine Reality nor the interpretation immediately suggested by it, but merely secondary phenomena conceptual or imaginary which, as the great mystics have insisted, are not part of the essential mystical experience. He also appeals to the fact that drugs, for example, "opium, hashish and alcohol," may produce experiences of illumination not unlike those claimed by the mystics. For the most part these intoxications resemble, if anything mystical, those secondary phenomena in whose production the subconscious self admittedly plays a large part.

"We can make no distinction," writes Lord Russell, "between the man who eats little and sees heaven, and the man who drinks much and sees snakes." Any vision of heaven belonging to the same visual order as a vision of snakes would not be an apprehension of God, but, like the latter, the work of the subconscious imagination, at most stimulated by a contact with God itself formless. And in fact the great mystics have always admitted that physiological conditions play their part in producing visual phenomena. St. John of the Cross was well aware of it centuries before Lord Russell has pointed it out.

It is not, however, impossible that the action of a drug may release a genuine experience of God. For although the essence of such experiences is a union of the fundamental will with God, which can be produced only by Him, their secondary aspect, the conscious intuition of this union and thus of God's special presence and action, is not produced by the union alone. Since the union with God takes place in the centre of the soul, it is normally subconscious. And though as it becomes closer and more complete it tends to enter the field of consciousness, this largely depends upon the psychophysical complexion of the subject. A more opaque subject may be unconscious of a union with God which far exceeds that possessed by a more transparent subject in whom the threshold of consciousness is passed more easily. Although culpable intoxication by its offence against God's law must in proportion to its culpability diminish or destroy the supernatural union with God experienced by a mystic, inculpable intoxication, produced for example by an anaesthetic, might by bringing into consciousness the contents of the subconsciousness produce the conscious intuition of a union with God previously unconscious. In this sense the drug would produce a genuine and valid mystical experience. Moreover, the natural union with God possessed by every soul in virtue of its spiritual nature, but of which there is normally no distinct perception, might under the influence of a drug emerge from the penumbra of an obscure and unrecognisable contact into clear consciousness. In this case the drug would occasion a valid though merely natural religious experience. Mystical experience is not, therefore, invalidated by the experiences of drug addicts or patients under an anaesthetic.

Finally, Lord Russell persists in ascribing to the mystics a doctrine they do not hold, the absolute as opposed to the comparative unreality of time. Though time has no place in the Divine Eternity with which the mystic makes contact, and in this contact transcends the time series, it does not follow that there " is nothing in reality corresponding to the apparent distinction between earlier and later events." " To say we are born . . . and then die must be just as false as to say that we die . . . and finally are born." We have only to imagine a Christian mystic holding that it is as true that Christ died before He was born as that He was born before He died, to realise how preposterous is this attempt to foist upon the mystics a doctrine which they would have regarded as sheer lunacy. Surely Lord Russell must know that the mystics do not hold that time is unreal in its own order, though it has no part in the Divine Superreality. Why then does he attempt to discredit the testimony of the mystics by so grossly misrepresenting it? Evidently he is hard pressed by its unanimity and strength but cannot surrender his positivism. Hence these desperate shifts to evade evidence whose force is powerfully felt but which must on no account be accepted.

In his famous essay entitled the *Free Man's Worship*, Lord Russell asserts in the most emphatic terms that man, with his entire mental and spiritual life, is " but the outcome of accidental collocations of atoms," and that sooner or later material forces will extinguish both his individual and his racial life. In *What I Believe* (1925) he again expresses his disbelief in God and Immortality, " since they find no support in science." The *Essence of Religion*—the article mentioned above—sketches the sort of religion still in his opinion possible on the assumption that any spiritual interpretation of the universe—theist or pantheist—is untrue. And in *Religion and Science* he is equally uncompromising in his refusal to accept any religious truth. Science has disproved all the arguments for the existence of God and a soul whether mortal or immortal. The dualism is glaring. Religious experience is a part, and the most valuable part, of human experience. Yet it is not an experience of anything external to the subject, for the universe is fundamentally unspiritual. The world revealed by science is " alien and inhuman," the work of " blind Nature," man's entire life " the outcome of accidental collocations of atoms." The world is a " pit of hell," and the knowledge of the world " unyielding despair." " Man as a curious accident in a backwater " (that is to say as the product of blind and unintelligent forces) " is intelligible : his mixture of virtues and vices is such as might be expected to result from a fortuitous origin." Therefore, what is valuable—religious experience—is objectively unreal. What is objectively real—a mechanically determined world of non-spiritual forces—is not valuable.

It would be strange if this dualism were the last word. Heart and mind, the apprehensions underlying our emotions, and the unifying urge of thought reject it.

Lord Russell's dualism, the appreciation of religion as a

subjective experience, the denial of religion as an experience of objective fact, or, as he puts it himself, religion without dogma—itself the consequence of a wider dualism of value and of reality—is artificial (therefore *a priori* suspect), self-contradictory and metaphysically unfounded.

C. LORD RUSSELL'S DUALISM ARTIFICIAL

"It may be not belief, but feeling, that makes religion."[1] Mysticism "may be essentially a feeling of peace."[2] Such an interpretation of the religious experience of mankind has an artificial air and rings false to the simple directness of actual life. Religious men have not valued, and do not value their religion primarily for the feelings which it evokes, but as a means of contact with a Divine Reality outside themselves. Lord Russell's subjective explanation of religious experience in which, as we shall see, Havelock Ellis agrees with him, does not arise naturally from the experience it seeks to explain away but is a *tour de force*, a violence offered to the facts. We detect indeed the same violence and the same artificiality in many other opinions and *obiter dicta* of Lord Russell's. That the individual is non-existent, merely a cinematographic hallucination caused by a series of psychic atoms nearly alike and succeeding each other so rapidly that the interstices are not felt; that men become magistrates in order to indulge "the pleasures of vindictiveness and moral superiority";[3] that, at least in the belief of mankind hitherto, "a good man is one whose opinions and activities are pleasing to the holders of power," are instances of judgements so widely divorced from the sound common sense of mankind, and so contradictory of experience, that I am tempted to say of Lord Russell what Dr. Johnson said with less justice of the metaphysical poets, his "thoughts are often new, but seldom natural; they are not obvious, but neither are they just; and the reader, far

---

[1] *The Essence of Religion.*   [2] *Mysticism and Logic.*

[3] *Roads to Freedom*, 112.

E

from wondering that he missed them, wonders more frequently by what perverseness of industry they were ever found." Though *vox populi* be not *vox Dei*, nor the common judgement of men an infallible oracle, a proposition, and still more an entire philosophical position which runs counter to the general consent of humanity, must stand under a strong prejudice of falsity and should be accepted at no easier rate than demonstration. Such a position is most emphatically that of a religion without doctrine of any kind, a religion which reveals nothing of the nature of the universe, supremely valuable, but wholly unreal.

A further *a priori* consideration which creates at least a strong probability that Lord Russell's scepticism is false is suggested by his division of human activities into those of instinct, mind, and spirit. The supreme activities of instinct are sexual and parental love; the supreme activity of mind, the discovery of abstract truth, scientific, mathematical, metaphysical; the supreme activity of spirit, religion. That sexual and parental love imply an object external to the lover is undeniable; they bear witness to the objective existence of sexual union and procreation. That knowledge of objective truth is attainable, if denied theoretically by a handful of sceptics, is admitted by the overwhelming agreement of mankind including Lord Russell. Thus the activity of instinct and the activity of mind admittedly imply an object other than the experient himself; a contact with external reality, an apprehension of the nature of the universe. It is, therefore, only reasonable to suppose the same of the third and highest form of activity, the activity of spirit. The activity of spirit, no less than the activity of instinct or mind, must surely imply an object other than the experient, a special contact with external reality, a peculiar apprehension of the nature of the universe or its ground. And, further, since, as Lord Russell himself holds, the activity of spirit is higher and more valuable than the activities of instinct and mind, we should presume that its object is more valuable than theirs, its contact with a higher sphere of reality, and that its mode of apprehension perceives a truth nearer the ultimate. Spirit thus reveals not far less—as would be the case were its reference subjective —but far more of reality than instinct or mind. A position which denies to the highest form of experience an objective validity allowed to the two inferior forms runs counter to all reasonable probability, and is extremely unlikely to be true.

When, therefore, Lord Russell comes forward as the advocate of so extreme, so abstract, and so artificial a subjectivism, we are entitled to demand rigid proof that it is not only a possible, but the necessary explanation of all the relevant facts. That proof is not forthcoming. On the contrary, his dualism—religious value, non-religious reality —is (1) self-contradictory, (2) metaphysically unfounded.

D. LORD RUSSELL'S DUALISM, SELF-CONTRADICTORY

For Lord Russell—and in this he is unquestionably right —religion involves worship. He proceeds[1] to distinguish in worship two varieties: "selective worship," which demands that its object shall be good, and "impartial worship," which can be given to whatever exists regardless of its goodness or badness. He requires both. In default of a God, whether transcendent or merely immanent, selective worship is to be given to "the ideal good," [2] impartial to everything which exists, good and evil alike. Lord Russell never clearly explains what in his opinion the ideal good is. Is it my private ideal? In that case religious worship could not emancipate the worshipper from his own desires, as he expects it to do. Is it the ideal of the best men? That would involve a universal validity of ethical values which Lord Russell, as we shall see, is not prepared to concede. In any case, if the ideal good is not realized somewhere and somehow in the external universe—a conviction which involves

---

[1] *Essence of Religion.*   [2] *Essence of Religion, passim.*

some kind of religious dogma and which Lord Russell emphatically rejects—it must be a creation of the human imagination, a world, to use his own words, " of our imagining."[1] Man, therefore, is to render selective worship to a non-existent figment of his own making—" the work of his own hands." But an attitude of worship is impossible towards what the worshipper recognises as his own creation.[2] For worship, as Lord Russell truly says, comprises reverence, and the superior cannot reverence the inferior, the workman his own work. Moreover, worship is possible only if its object is believed to exist. But the ideal good, if it is only man's creation—as it must be if religion has no objective ground and reference—is non-existent. Even if human effort can in some degree realize, and ought to realize, the ideal good, that realized good is equally the work of man himself, therefore no object of his worship and reverence. Moreover, in a mechanical universe such as Lord Russell depicts in his *Free Man's Worship*, the ideal good *cannot* be fully or finally realized, must always remain to a large extent a nonentity, and must in the end perish completely. Selective worship, therefore, must be largely directed to a non-existent object.

The impartial worship is undoubtedly directed to a real object. But it violates the human soul by worshipping objects seen to be unworthy of worship, objects which reason must condemn. Lord Russell argues that, if the fundamental evils are due to the blind empire of matter and are the wholly necessary effects of forces which have no consciousness, indignation is absurd.[3] Indignation certainly is absurd, but condemnation and opposition must remain our response to such evils, and it is hard to see how we can worship—*i.e.*, " reverence " and " contemplate with joy "—that which we must condemn and to the utmost of our power resist. Can

---

[1] *Principles of Social Reconstruction.*
[2] The image worshipped by the pagan is believed to contain or represent a deity by no means of human manufacture.
[3] *Essence of Religion.*

we really contemplate with joy, still more reverence, such objects as a leper colony, the life of the convicts on Norfolk Island as depicted in the biography of Bishop Ullathorne, the condition of the slaves in the Roman ergastula or on American cotton plantations, Ivan the Terrible in his torture chamber, the atrocities of the Spanish Civil War, or the Messina earthquake? The bare suggestion is an outrage on the healthy intellect and heart. For intellect and heart must pronounce such things to be evil—Lord Russell himself judges them to be evil—and that which is evil is *ipso facto* no object of pleasurable contemplation or of reverence. Lord Russell, indeed, says elsewhere that we ought not to attempt to feel delight towards all sentient beings impartially. "There are many in whom we cannot feel delight because they are disgusting; if we were to do violence to our nature by trying to see beauties in them, we should merely blunt our susceptibilities to what we naturally find beautiful. Not to mention human beings, there are fleas and bugs and lice."[1] In an earlier passage he says we cannot be compelled to admire anything because it is a "law of nature." This is sound common sense. But what has become of impartial worship? In the *Essence of Religion* Lord Russell bade us adopt an attitude of reverence and joyous contemplation towards all things alike—including, therefore, the laws of nature. Now he tells us we need not, indeed ought not to admire every law of nature. The contradiction is patent. Perhaps he has changed his mind, and, though so far as I know, he has not retracted his former position, he no longer believes impartial worship possible. But if impartial worship is, as he maintains, an indispensable component of his undogmatic and purely subjective religion, that religion must disappear if impartial worship is impossible.

Lord Russell's non-dogmatic worship thus involves a selective worship of what is mainly non-existent and an

[1] *What I Believe*, p. 34.

impartial worship of evil and good alike, both self-contradictory. But this non-dogmatic worship is essential to his un-doctrinal religion. The latter, therefore, is self-contradictory.[1]

Not only is Lord Russell's undogmatic religion self-contradictory in its implications ; it is a formal self-contradiction. For, as stated by himself, it demonstrably involves certain judgements of fact, certain beliefs—in other words, dogmas. One of these is that the ideal good is good, is possessed of ethical value. For this dogma Lord Russell's subjective and pragmatic account of ethical values as statements of human desire leaves no room. Another dogma, the corner stone of his undogmatic religion is the reasonableness and value of worship, selective and impartial. Here are two dogmas. The contradiction becomes verbal when Lord Russell writes of " a faith wholly independent of beliefs as to the nature of the actual world." By definition a faith is a belief about something other than the act, or, if Lord Russell prefer the emotion,[2] of faith itself, refers therefore to a reality external to itself—that is to say, it makes some affirmation as to the nature of the world.

Here there emerges a further contradiction inherent in Lord Russell's position—his affirmation of a value which is

---

[1] Yet in the very passage in which this position is expounded Lord Russell charges Christianity with " a confusion of thought " in inviting action against evil, while believing that since " apparent evil is in accordance with the will of God, it cannot really be evil." Not Christianity but Lord Russell is chargeable with confused thinking. For the former does not teach, has never taught, that evil is in accordance with the will of God. It is permitted by Him for the sake of a greater good : an entirely different proposition. Does not its holiest prayer end with the petition *Libera nos a malo?* Is it not essentially a religion of redemption from evil—from real, not imaginary, evil ? But the point needs no labouring. We can only wonder that Lord Russell can pronounce so light-heartedly on the fundamental teaching of Christianity when any serious study of the Christian faith proves his accoun of it utterly mistaken. But Lord Russell is fond of flinging out at haphazard such wild misrepresentations of Christian belief. In his chapter on Mysticism (*Mysticism and Logic*) he ascribes to the mystics a series of propositions, including this very tenet of the unreality of evil which every Catholic mystic would repudiate. And in *What I Believe* (p. 51), he lays down that the accepted moral code regards " sexual intercourse as wicked unless accompanied by *desire* for offspring." What social or legal code of any Christian country, what Christian body has prohibited or denounced the marriage of the sterile or the aged ? However Lord Russell may disrelish Christian doctrines, he need not misrepresent them so wilfully.

[2] Faith, however, is not an emotion but an act of the intelligence.

purely subjective, or, from the epistemological standpoint, an emotion which does not imply a judgement. In his *Essence of Religion*, Lord Russell proclaims a union with the world which demands nothing of it, and implies, therefore, nothing as to its character, being wholly contained within the soul of the experient. "Religion," he writes, "seeks union with the universe by subordination of the demands of self, but this subordination is not complete if it depends upon a belief that the universe satisfies *some at least* of the demands of self. Hence, for the sake of religion itself *as well as because such a belief appears unfounded*, it is important to discover a form of union with the universe which is independent of all beliefs as to the nature of the universe." Incidentally he affirms that the universe does not satisfy "*some at least*" of the demands of self. Surely, on a moment's reflection, it is obvious that this is untrue. If the universe—that is to say, our external environment—did not satisfy *some at least* of our demands, we could not live in it at all. And in fact when he wishes to refute the argument that the adaptation to man of his environment is a proof of design he makes this very point. "It seems fairly evident that if creatures having likes and dislikes were to exist at all, they were pretty sure to like *some* things in their environment, since otherwise they would find life intolerable." (*Religion and Science.*) That the universe satisfies *some* human desires (demands of the self) which he denied as an "unfounded belief" is now, when it suits his controversial purpose, regarded as what indeed it is, a truism, "fairly evident." Whether it is an unfounded belief or "fairly evident" depends, it would seem, on the controversial exigencies of the moment. When it appears to favour theism it is the former. When Lord Russell thinks he can shew that it does not, it is the latter. This method of argument is of the heads I win, tails you lose description.

A more fundamental contradiction, however, lies in Lord

Russell's view that there can be a union with the universe whatever its nature may be. Can there be a union thus purely one-terminal, a union which involves nothing as to the nature of the other term? Surely union is impossible unless both terms are such that they can enter into union—that is to say, possess some measure of affinity. If the universe be *wholly* alien to the spiritual character and needs of man, it cannot be the object of that religious union which Lord Russell requires. Failure to perceive this underlies his contention in the same essay that mystical intuition involves no " perception of new objects," but " is simply a different way of regarding the same objects." To prescind from the question whether religious and *a fortiori* mystical experience does not present, however obscurely, an object wholly transcendent of ordinary experience, it is at least certain that if religious and mystical intuition differ in any way from ordinary experience—a difference which Lord Russell not only admits, but on which he lays great stress—their object cannot be simply identical with the object of ordinary experience, but must *at the least* present some new quality, some new value, therefore some new aspect of reality not apprehended by non-religious experience. The distinction between the two forms of experience must be more than a difference in the quality of emotional reaction. For an intuition is essentially a mode of cognition. And if the distinction were merely one of emotional quality, the *world* would not be *seen* by the religious intuition in a new *light*, as Lord Russell himself affirms that it is.

" The liberating intuition," Lord Russell tells us, " may be occasioned by ' the night-wind in the trees.' " What distinguishes this experience from a merely physical experience of the wind or on a slightly higher level from a sense of the refreshment it may bring? Surely not any sensible or abstract cognition of the physical constituents and character of the breeze and the foliage. They are experienced as sacramental of a spiritual quality, a value and a reality which on any view of its nature transcends the purely mechanical and physical events, which constitute the physical reality of the wind in the trees. Indeed, Lord Russell in a passage already quoted admits as much. For he calls the supreme vision of spirit, the religious experience or intuition, " a transfiguring vision in which behind the veil of ' common things ' the ultimate truth of the universe is dimly seen." Here he escapes the self-contradiction of his purely subjective position. But he also admits, though in its vaguest formulation, a religious truth. Elsewhere and more normally, as in the *Essence of Religion*, he is content to speak of a new vision which, notwithstanding, sees nothing new.

In its psychological expression this self-contradiction inherent in Lord Russell's position is the belief in emotions which imply no judgement. You can feel joy in the contemplation of an object (here the universe) without judging it of a nature to cause joy; reverence it without judging it worthy of reverence—that is to say, as at least higher in value than oneself; and love it without judging it lovable— that is to say, good. This is another of those artificial abstractions in which Lord Russell murders the truth of experience in dissecting it. Like every other emotion, joyful contemplation, reverence and love contain implicitly, at least, value-judgements about their object. Pure feeling is never found without cognition, and cognition is always a knowledge of objective reality. Not even the most rudimentary feeling—*e.g.*, a vague sense of happiness or well-being—is of purely subjective reference. It implies, even if due to some purely physical, possibly even pathological, cause—*e.g.*, the action of a drug —the judgement that there exists somewhere *in rerum natura* a ground of the happy feeling and experience, something which is pleasurable, and the further judgement that the universe must be such that it causes some pleasure to man, therefore that absolute pessimism is false. Emotional attitudes (*e.g.*, worship) devoid of judgements are artificial abstractions.

The internal contradiction of Lord Russell's position is further revealed by inconsistent and obscure admissions of an objective reality manifest or operative in religious experience.

To the finite life and self of ordinary experience Lord Russell opposes the infinite self or life, "the infinite part of our life," revealed in religious experience.[1] He also speaks of the infinite nature in one man and the infinite nature in another, of "a union of all the infinite natures of different men" and of "that one universal nature which embraces what is infinite in each of us." Only an objective metaphysic of a spiritualist nature can give any meaning to such phrases. Lord Russell here affirms as a datum of religious experience an infinite life or nature distinct from and even hostile to the natural finite life of the individual and of higher value than that life. Evidently this infinite life or nature is a distinct entity existent *in rerum natura*. For religious experience releases its subject from the bondage of his purely individual emotions and desires by bringing him into contact with a reality whose value at least exceeds that of his ordinary psychic life, and which, therefore, is either spiritual or more than spiritual, not material. This, however, is distinctly a dogma, a doctrine about the nature of the universe —the doctrine, namely, that in the universe there exists a reality of a value and a spirituality exceeding those of normal human life. The spiritual character and value of this universal nature is also implied when a few pages later it is termed the universal soul. It is no mirage created by the imagination of the individual subjects. For it is the one universal nature which embraces in actual fact what is (not what is merely imagined to be) infinite in each of us. Neither religion nor metaphysics, indeed, can leave the matter at this point. They must go on to enquire what is the relation between this universal infinite nature on the one hand, and individual men and the mechani-

[1] *Essence of Religion.*

cally determined phenomena of the universe on the other. But, at least, by its admission Lord Russell has contradicted his pure " undogmatic " subjectivism. Nor does he identify the universal nature with all that is ; it is a universal *soul*, and embraces not all things without distinction nor even the entire life of man, but only what is infinite in each of us— " the infinite part " of our life. A hierarchy of value and reality is implied. Further, if the infinite life in man is in conflict with his ordinary finite life, it must be *at least* equally real ; no mere image or abstraction, no ideal created by the imagination or thought of the normal self could fight—and even defeat—its creator. The contest must be between two realities alike existent in the real world. Nor can this infinite life which struggles—at times successfully—against the super-ficial life and self of normal experience be a mere epipheno-menon of that self, as it would be if it were its creation, " a world of its imagining " ; still less the mere epiphenomenon and product of a mechanical collocation of non-spiritual forces, such as is depicted in a *Free Man's Worship*. If the flesh lusteth against the spirit and the spirit against the flesh —and Lord Russell's conflict between the infinite and finite self is a statement of that experience in other terms —the spirit cannot be a product, epiphenomenon or aspect of the flesh.

Nor are these the only admissions inconsistent with a subjective interpretation of religious experience to which the stress of that experience has forced Lord Russell. " The sense of a mystery half-revealed."[1] " Worship involves a sense of mystery."[2] Lord Russell is right. There can be no doubt that a sense of mystery is an essential characteristic of religious experience. But there is no room for mystery in a mechani-cally determined universe. Of this Lord Russell is himself aware. " Physical Science," he writes,[3] " is approaching the stage when it will be complete and therefore uninteresting.

[1] *Principles of Social Reconstruction.*   [2] *Essence of Religion.*   [3] *What I Believe*, 11–12.

Given the laws governing the motions of electrons and protons, the rest is merely geography. . . . It is difficult to imagine anything less interesting. . . . It is like climbing a high mountain and finding nothing at the top except a restaurant where they sell ginger-beer, surrounded by fog, but equipped with wireless. Of this physical world, uninteresting in itself man is a part." He means, of course, only a part and nothing more. In this dreary mechanically determined universe, this ginger-beer house in a fog, what place is there for a transcendent mystery, "a mystery half-revealed, a hidden wisdom and glory"? For the entire context implies that in Lord Russell's view the fog is impenetrable and will never lift, at least for human vision. If, therefore, religion postulates mystery, and religious experience is an experience of mystery, and without mystery religion dies, either the universe, including man, is not in every respect mechanically determined or religious experience is sheer illusion and religion doomed to extinction. Lord Russell cannot have it both ways. He must either accept the deliverance of religious experience as valid testimony to the nature of the universe, or abandon mystery and with mystery religion. And even more directly inconsistent with his subjectivism are his admissions that in the highest experience of spirit " the ultimate truth," not of the experient's feelings, but " of the world," is " seen "; that " a truer image of the world . . . is attained by picturing *things* as entering into the stream of time *from an eternal world without*.[1] and that ' the unknown ' contains not mechanical sequences, but ' a shining splendour ' which it is the work of the human spirit to bring down and incarnate in creative thought."[2] In utterances like these—so powerful is the compulsion of the religious experience which Lord Russell is describing—the subjective standpoint is for the moment abandoned. And these plain statements of the objective reference and validity of religious experience cannot

---

[1] *Mysticism and Logic*, 21.   [2] *Principles of Social Reconstruction*, 168.

be retracted by such awkward qualifications as those which are inserted in the following passage : "Life to be fully human . . . must serve some end which seems *in some sense* outside human life. . . . Those who best promote life do not have life for their purpose. They aim at what *seems* like a bringing into human existence of something eternal, something *that appears to imagination* to live in a heaven remote from strife and failure and the devouring jaws of time. Contact with this eternal world—*even if it be only a world of our imagining*—brings a strength and a fundamental peace."[1] Here we watch the writer struggling desperately to escape the felt inconsistency between his admitted experience of an objective religious value outside himself and the purely subjective explanation demanded by his philosophy. In this passage the self-contradiction inherent in the non-dogmatic— *i.e.,* purely subjective—religion preached by Lord Russell obtrudes nakedly and forces itself on the attention.

There is a further contradiction which we may characterize as pragmatic. Lord Russell ascribes supreme value and the most potent efficacy to religious experience. "Mysticism reveals the possibility of a nobler, happier, freer life than any that can be otherwise achieved."[2] "If the feelings which constitute the supreme intuition of spirit—*i.e.,* religious experience—were to die, most of what is best would vanish out of life."[3] The life of the spirit "liberates those who have it from the prison house. . . . of mundane cares. . . . It brings the solution of doubts, the end of the feeling that all is vanity." In these passages he insists upon the ethical values produced by religious experience. And the entire essay on the Essence of Religion is a paean in praise of the value revealed and achieved by religion. If, however, religious experience has no objective reference, does not bring the experient into contact with an external reality, it cannot

---

[1] *Principles of Social Reconstruction,* 245.   [2] *Mysticism and Logic.*
[3] *Principles of Social Reconstruction.*

produce these effects. Illusion, unless it be merely the defective interpretation of a value objectively real, cannot effect moral good. Nonentity cannot work, nor can creation improve its creator, who must already possess the value he produces. Once more we need go no further than Lord Russell himself. "Subjectivism," he writes, "the habit of directing thought and desire to our states of mind rather than to something objective, inevitably makes life fragmentary and unprogressive."[1] But if the eternal world experienced by religion be only "of our own imagining," and religious experience purely subjective, religion directs "thoughts and desires to our states of mind rather than to something objective." It must, therefore, on Lord Russell's showing, make life fragmentary and unprogressive. How can it, then, be the source of most of what is best in life, or produce the moral and spiritual values which, as we have seen, Lord Russell ascribes to it? The antithesis between value and reality implicit in Lord Russell's view of religion, and affirmed explicitly in *What I Believe*,[2] is therefore false and self-contradictory.

In the chapter on mysticism in *Religion and Science* the same purely subjective explanation is restated. Significantly however nothing is said of a "transfiguring vision" which "behind the veil of common things" sees the ultimate reality of the universe. Presumably Lord Russell has realised the objective and indirectly the theistic implication of such a statement and will not repeat it. Nothing is any longer admitted beyond "an emotion in which all self-centred desire is dead and the mind becomes a mirror for the vastness of the universe." Incidentally this contradicts an earlier statement, of which more later, that even scientific knowledge is not a "Mental mirror of the universe but is merely a practical tool." The vastness of the universe however is not a new truth apprehended by mystical experience but a truth already known from the discoveries of astronomy, the object of

[1] *Principles of Social Reconstruction*, 290.　　[2] 22 *sqq.*

astronomical knowledge, rather than mystical intuition. There is nothing distinctively spiritual or mystical about it. It is purely material. The ginger-beer house in the fog offers nothing more satisfactory for being enlarged to the palatial dimensions of the Ritz. The materialist idolatry of physical size which finds a social expression in the Bolshevik devotion to large scale construction and planning has Lord Russell in its grip. He supposes[1] that the time occupied by the formation of the earth and the evolution of man is an argument against a Divine Creator and Providence. He evidently thinks that if God exists, the time which measures His work must measure the Operation which has produced it. And man cannot possess the importance ascribed to him by religion, because the earth is so infinitesimal in comparison with the universe. Physical extent, however, whether of time or space is irrelevant. It is no fit object for man's selfless adoration. The humblest intelligence is of its nature superior to an infinite universe of matter, to endless time or boundless space. But a religious attitude or emotion directed to an object on a lower plane of value than the worshipper is misdirected—idolatrous not truly religious. In his *Free Man's Worship*, Lord Russell had himself opposed man to an unintelligent and unmoral universe as a defiant Titan spiritually victorious over the material forces which must annihilate him. Now however man is to worship those forces because of their superior size. The reference to an ultimate reality transcending the empirical universe which is implicit in all religious experience and which Lord Russell has himself perceived is now denied. But along with it is denied the distinctive quality and value of mystical experience in spite of the attempt to justify them on a purely subjective basis.

By dropping his admissions that a reality which transcends the empirical universe is apprehended in religious experience Lord Russell has indeed removed a glaring and formal self-con-

[1] *Religion and Science.*

tradiction. But it is at the cost of evacuating religious experience of its specific character and reducing it to the mere worship by the human spirit of a material " vastness " inferior to itself.

E. LORD RUSSELL'S DUALISM METAPHYSICALLY UNFOUNDED

It has, I hope, been sufficiently proved that Lord Russell's religious subjectivism—a wholly undoctrinal religion, with its implicit dualism of value and reality is self-contradictory. It is a subjectivism which, as is evident from his own admissions, contradicts the deliverance of the religious experience it professes to interpret and whose artificiality produces a strain felt even by himself. Why, then, does he maintain it so persistently despite the audible clamour and energetic recalcitrance of his own deepest experience ? To suit the exigencies of his metaphysical position. This system is, however, radically false—founded upon an untenable restriction of human knowledge.

1. *Experience involves Objective Existence.*

A philosophy is an interpretation of experience. Its measure of truth is the measure of its capacity to accept and reconcile all forms of experience. If its explanation of one sphere or form of experience, or of the whole in terms of that sphere or form, involves the denial or misinterpretation of another sphere, level, or aspect of experience, it is therefore erroneous because inadequate to the total body of facts which it professes to explain. Without logical self-contradiction it is possible to deny the objective validity of every experience except the actual sensation of the moment. There is no logical refutation of the man who is willing to argue that only his own successive states of consciousness have real existence. But unless one is prepared to adopt some form of solipsism—and Lord Russell naturally is not—we must allow the self-evidence of experience. Within limits, therefore, he does accept it. That experience of sensible objects is evidence at least of external stimuli, sense data, therefore of an external reality he is prepared to allow—also, to some extent at least, that the laws of logical reasoning reflect relations obtaining in the outside world. But neither religious nor ethical nor aesthetic experience is allowed to bear the same evidence. " The object of selective worship," he writes, " need not exist."[1] It is true that the object of experience—though of sensible experience as much as of any other form—may be incorrectly interpreted or misplaced. Error and hallucination are only too possible. We may wrongly complete the form apprehended as when fear invests a white sheet with the properties of a ghost. We may insert the form apprehended into a false context as when the victim of delirium inserts the green rats of his hallucination into the context of his physical environment. Or we may fail to discriminate correctly a form apprehended, as when we confuse a distant peak with the clouds. But we always apprehend the form of an object actually existing in some context, in some order of reality be it physical or mental. There cannot be unmixed error, pure hallucination. The positive value or reality experienced must exist somewhere and somehow. I dream I have come into a fortune. Only a dream. Yet I could never have dreamt it, if wealth were not a fact of the external universe. Similarly, a man may imagine and worship false gods—Milcom, for instance, or Apollo. But they could not do so if the positive values of these gods did not exist, formally in creatures, eminently in the one true God.[2] The self-evidence of religious (as also of ethical and artistic) experience is the same as that of perception through the senses, though, since its object is so much more obscure owing to its transcendence of humanity and nature,

---

[1] *Essence of Religion.*

[2] Only Lord Russell's curious inability to perceive this point can explain his belief that the existence of the Christian God is on a par with the existence of the gods of Olympus, the question being the same in both cases (*What I Believe*, 13, 14). *Ex hypothesi* the Christian God is eminently all the positive value contained in the gods of Olympus. A god whose being was of the same category as theirs would not be the Christian God.

F

it cannot possess the same clearness. All forms of experience are experiences of realities which in the last resort are given self-evidently in the experiences of them. And a sensible man will accept the experience of his fellows—e.g., a colour-blind man the existence of colour as experienced by other men— even if he has not shared it himself. Lord Russell's philosophy explains away the evidence—the admittedly powerful evidence —of what, on his own showing, is the profoundest and most valuable form of human experience. It cannot, therefore, be an adequate interpretation of human experience.

2. *Value involves Reality*.

We have seen already that from the pragmatic standpoint Lord Russell's divorce between value and reality cannot stand. Only being works. It is equally false ontologically. An experience of value is an experience of something as good, as an object of desire and will. We cannot deem good, or desire what is not. For what does not exist cannot be known, and what cannot be known cannot be desired. " What we think good," writes Lord Russell,[1] " what we should like *has no bearing whatever* upon what is." If the world were other than it is, human desires would be other than they are. Therefore our desires afford at least some indication of what exists. Every perception of value is a perception of reality. We may locate the value wrongly—as we may place an object of sense perception in the wrong context—and we may also perceive it obscurely and misinterpret it in terms of conceptual reason. Nevertheless the value carries with it its existence somewhere, somehow in the universe. " Only in the mind." Not only in the mind of the individual experient, for he apprehends the value—and no one more than Lord Russell has stressed the fact—as essentially transcendent of the merely individual, as a universal.[2] Therefore it must exist somehow, somewhere as a universal.

[1] *What I Believe*, 22.   [2] See *Essence of Religion*.

"The philosophy of nature," as Lord Russell tells us, meaning by nature objective existence, "is one thing, the philosophy of value is *quite* another."[1] What is united in experience cannot be thus cleft asunder. Experience is a whole and all its aspects interconnected, however obscure the connection may be to our necessarily limited understanding. The dualism of value and existence is an instance of that dualism of experience and existence already criticized. It is an abstraction which cuts away the ground of religion at the cost of cutting away the ground of any complete and coherent account of experience. It is metaphysical bankruptcy.[2]

A divorce between value and reality is fatal not only to religious but to ethical value. It is not, therefore, surprising that Lord Russell denies that our moral valuations are anything more than the expression of our desires. The good means simply what men desire. "I do not think," he writes, "there is, strictly speaking, such a thing as ethical knowledge. . . . All moral rules must be tested by examining whether they intend to realize ends that we desire. I say ends that we desire, not ends that we *ought* to desire. What we ought to desire is merely what someone else wishes us to desire. . . . Outside human desires there is no moral standard." "The part of morality not included in prudence" (enlightened self-interest) "is analogous to the rules of a club. It is a method of enabling men to live together in a community in spite of the possibility that their desires may conflict."[3] "Our desires confer value."[4] "Human ethical notions . . . involve, when used in metaphysics, an attempt . . . to legislate for the universe on the basis of the present desires of men

[1] *What I Believe*, 22.
[2] It is this artificial division between value and reality which has made possible Lord Russell's belief that the physical size of the earth has a bearing upon man's place in the scale of being (*What I Believe*, 23). The intelligence that can discover the elements which compose Sirius is far more wonderful, more valuable and higher in the scale of being than Sirius itself.
[3] *What I Believe*, 39, 40, 45. [4] *Ibid.*

. . . Ethical metaphysics is fundamentally an attempt . . . to give legislative force to our own wishes."[1] "When an animal has arrived at the dignity of the metaphysician, it invents ethics as the embodiment of its belief in the justice of its own herd."[2] "Questions as to value lie wholly outside the domain of knowledge. . . . When we assert that this or that has ' value ' we are giving expression to our own emotions, not to a fact which would still be true if our personal feelings were different."[3] "Ethics is an attempt to give a universal and not merely a personal importance to certain of our desires."[4] "If two men differ about values there is not a disagreement as to any kind of truth but a difference of taste. If one man says ' oysters are good ' and another says ' I think they are bad ' we recognise that there is nothing to argue about. . . . All differences as to values are of this sort."[5] "Questions of values lie outside the realm of truth and falsehood."[6]

The violation of experience in the interest of a theory is extreme. Not only is it denied that moral values are a manifestation of the character of reality, their very existence as objective *values* is called in question. What is morally good is only that which enables as many human desires as possible to be fulfilled. If the majority of the human race desired to get drunk, or to commit some hideous form of sexual perversion —measures being previously taken that no one could offer violence to his neighbour—why not ? If deliberate hypocrisy —*e.g.*, a pretence to hold tenets not really believed—promoted best the happiness of the individual and did not interfere with the happiness of others, why not ? The perception that moral values are valuable in and for themselves, with the consequent perception of moral obligation ; the sense of moral obligation expressed by the " ought " which Lord Russell dismisses so cavalierly, is rejected as not even sub-

---

[1] *Mysticism and Logic*, 107–108.　　[2] *Ibid*.　　[3] *Religion and Science*, 230.
[4] *Ibid*, p. 232.　　[5] *Ibid*, p. 237–8.　　[6] *Ibid*, p. 243.

jectively valid. " Organic life," writes Lord Russell in this connection, " has developed from the protozoon to the philosopher, and this development, we are assured, is indubitably an advance. Unfortunately, it is the philosopher, not the protozoon, who gives us this assurance, and we can have no security that the impartial outsider would agree with the philosopher's self-complacent assumption."[1] That is to say, it is merely our human prejudice in favour of ourselves which makes us judge a protozoon less valuable than Socrates. Of Lord Russell's many *saugrenu* judgements this is the most *saugrenu*. It is also the *reductio ad absurdum* of his position. We perceive that a man, and *a fortiori* a wise man, is more valuable than a protozoon with the same immediacy and self-evidence with which we perceive that ten is greater than two. Ethical perception is at bottom the perception that certain values are intrinsically higher than others, and therefore that the lower values ought when necessary to be sacrificed to the higher.[2] Nor can Lord Russell maintain the logic of his immoralism. " In so far," he writes, " as acquiescence, in the universe is a cause of faith it rests upon *moral discipline*, a suppression of self and its demands which is necessary to any life in harmony with the universe."[3] If morals are essentially the desires of the human self, how can the suppression of selfish desire for the sake of harmony with the universe be a *moral* discipline ? Moreover, Lord Russell often speaks in tones of warm indignation against beliefs or acts which are opposed to his moral code or even his political creed. Such moral condemnations—for such they are in substance if not in form—are meaningless if morality is only what men desire. Nor in fact does Lord Russell in practice regard ethical differences as simply questions of taste like conflicting tastes in food. He does not, for example, think the difference between Hitler and Einstein akin to that between

[1] *Mysticism and Logic*, 106.
[2] See Max Scheler, *Der Formalismus in der Ethik und die materiale Wertethik.*
[3] *Essence of Religion.*

the man who likes oysters and the man who hates them. The former definitely represents values which Lord Russell regards as evil, not merely unpleasant, the latter values he considers good, not merely pleasant. He does not simply happen to have a personal taste for Einstein's moral and political views, a distaste for Hitler's. And if moral values are but human desires, what becomes of the conflict between the finite and infinite self, described with such noble eloquence ? For it is not a conflict of one man's desire with that of his fellows—to be harmonized as far as possible by some utilitarian ethic—but a conflict of values respectively lower and higher in a self-evident hierarchy of value. The logic of Lord Russell's system forces him to deny the validity of ethical values ; his heart and even his common sense compel him to affirm it. The inconsistency for being creditable is not the more tenable.

Nor is it even true that differences of taste are solely expressions of divergent desires. The conflicting opinions that oysters are good and bad express genuine apprehensions of truth about the flavour of oysters. The former expresses an apprehension that their flavour is pleasant at least to one human palate, the latter an apprehension that it is unpleasant to at least one human palate. And together they express the objective truth that the taste of oysters is pleasant to some human palates, unpleasant to others, though for all we know the former or the latter may be in a minority of one. And this truth in turn signifies that in the order of physical-pleasure values oysters are valuable for some men but not for others. And since, in fact, many men pronounce oysters good their judgement proves that they are objectively valuable in the order of gustatory values for a large number of human palates, a truth as objective as the fact that the planet Mars has two moons. Moreover the pleasant flavour of oysters to many palates is as much an aspect of their nature, of their form, as is their whiteness to normal human eyes.

Lord Russell attempts to evade the consequences of his purely subjective ethics by distinguishing between " purely personal " and " large impersonal desires " and by telling us that the latter must be encouraged as against the former because " The sort of life that most of us admire is one which is guided by them."[1] How does he know that the sort of life most of us admire is in fact admirable ? In the Middle Ages and in the modern totalitarian state the majority approve the persecution of obnoxious beliefs. Lord Russell strongly disapproves of it. Moreover, the vast majority of the human race have believed in God. Lord Russell is certain that they have been wrong. He does not therefore value opinions by counting heads. What he really means is that the impersonal desires and the life they produce are not simply admired by the majority, but are in fact admirable, therefore objectively valuable. He cannot, however, admit this. For it contradicts his subjective view of ethics. He therefore seeks to escape the issue by stating that objective desirability, value is simply the fact that subjectively most men desire, value a particular object or type of conduct. Fortunately, this mental sleight of hand is easier to detect than the conjuror's physical tricks.

If there is nothing in ethics except the fact that most men desire and admire a certain kind of life, ethics cannot exist. For no kind of life can be objectively desirable. Nevertheless Lord Russell, like every one else, is convinced that a certain kind of life, certain conduct is desirable and admirable. From the impasse created by his subjectivism he cannot escape by the back door of impersonal desires. For as soon as we open it, we are faced by objective desirability, objective ethical value. The impersonal as opposed to the purely personal desire implies the judgement that its object is desirable, valuable not only for the subject of the desire but in itself. When a desire is genuinely impersonal its object is

[1] *Religion and Science,* 240.

desired, not because the subject desires it as his private good, but because he regards it as desirable, that is valuable, even though his personal good must be sacrificed to its attainment. Obviously no man can desire a value which he does not desire. The mere judgement that something is desirable is not enough. He must desire what he judges desirable. But the fact that we may desire something only because we regard it as desirable, though our personal desire may run wholly counter to our impersonal desire; and *a fortiori* that we can judge something desirable without desiring it at all, as when we judge a course of conduct morally right but cannot desire its accomplishment because it is opposed to our private wishes: is a self-evident proof that we distinguish between subjective desire and objective desirability that is, between subjective valuation and objective value.

3. *Perception through the Senses not the Sole Apprehension of Objective Truth.*

IN his latest book *Science and Religion*, Lord Russell states plainly the fundamental reason why he refuses and must refuse to accept the testimony of ethical and religious intuition to objective truth. " Science cannot decide questions of value, because they cannot be intellectually decided at all, and lie outside the realm of truth and falsehood. *Whatever knowledge is attainable must be attained by scientific methods, and what science cannot discover mankind cannot know.*" I am grateful to Lord Russell for this plain statement. It expresses the basis of modern agnosticism and atheism. If we agree with it we are logically compelled to be agnostics and for all practical purposes atheists. For the sciences are of their nature confined to sensible phenomena and moreover to their measurable aspect, mathematically determinable quantities. Obviously within this sphere of reference there can be no evidence of God. He cannot be a scientifically determinable fact. If, therefore, our knowledge is confined to the conclusions of science, it is impossible to know whether He exists. When Sir James Jeans argues from the mathematical order of the universe to a cosmic mathematician, he is going beyond the sphere of science, which can inform us only that this order exists, and is offering us a metaphysical interpretation of this scientific result. He is speaking as a philosopher not as an astronomer.

This confinement of truth to the mathematico-quantitative sciences is, however, nothing better than an epistemological prejudice Why should we restrict truth to these quantitative data? If it is argued that we can trust the evidence of the senses and that alone we reply that the senses witness to qualities as well as quantities. That one flower smells sweeter, one food has a more acid flavour than another may indeed depend upon factors capable of quantitative determination. But the sweet scent and the acid flavour are objective facts, which are not themselves quantities. Nor are the ultimate data of science purely sensible. In and through sense stimuli which of themselves could not afford more than a chaos of atomic sensations if as much, the mind apprehends the outer forms of objects. And the outer forms with which science is concerned are quantities mathematically determinable. If however we accept as we must intuitions of these quantitative forms, as apprehensions of objective reality, on what ground do we refuse to accept intuitions of qualitative forms as the apprehension of objective truth? Not because the former intuitions are infallible, the latter fallible. For this is not the case. " Because the former are more definite and unlike the latter can be employed to construct a vast edifice of scientific knowledge." This fact, does not affect the reality of the more indefinite intuitions. It merely excludes their employment in the mathematico-physical sciences. And to regard this scientific inutility as a sufficient reason for denying their objective truth, is simply to assume the issue in question by asserting *a priori* that scientific knowledge is the sole knowledge possible.

If however we accept as objectively valid the intuition of non-quantitative forms in sensible objects there is no reason to deny the objective reference of the forms apprehended by metaphysical, aesthetic ethical and religious intuition. The intellectual gymnastics to which Lord Russell is driven in his attempt to explain away our apprehensions of moral, aesthetic and religious values, that is of moral aesthetic and religious form, gymnastics which involve him, as we have seen, in self-contradiction, are superfluous. Moreover, we cannot apprehend even the outer forms, including the quantitative outer forms of objects without apprehending metaphysical forms. Time, space, quantity, sufficient reason, not to speak of the fundamental laws of thought, *e.g.*, the logical axioms of identity, contradiction and excluded middle are mental forms immediately apprehended in all categories of human experience. This fact was emphasised by Kant, who perceived that knowledge is impossible without mental categories not themselves sense data. We cannot indeed follow him in his contention that these metaphysical categories are imported by mind into an order to which they do not objectively belong. It was an unnecessary concession to the sensual empiricism of which Hume was the most thoroughgoing exponent. Nor of course would Lord Russell accept Kant's semi-idealism. We must therefore regard these categories as apprehended in the sensible order though not confined to it. And although they are presupposed by science they are not established by it.

Lord Russell it is true makes a valiant effort to reduce these metaphysical presuppositions of science. He will not admit true causation but merely what he misleadingly calls causal laws, which he defines as "rules connecting events at one time with events at another." Since the sciences are confined to the mathematical forms of sequences, the purely formal and static aspect of process and cannot deal with the concrete process itself, we may grant that for the purpose of scientific description nothing more than these orderly connections are

required. An order, however, connecting events experienced
at different times is not itself an object given in the experience
of its individual constituents. It is a form of the series apprehended as a whole, as a tune is apprehended in the entire
song, not given in the successive apprehension of the individual notes. It is plainly a supersensible form apprehended by
the mind. Why then should we accept its objective reference
and yet deny the objective reference of such a supersensible
form as the beauty of a flower [1] or the moral value of a human
act ? The supersensible apprehension of objective form has
been in principle admitted. Moreover, the occurence of events
in an orderly sequence is not purely accidental. If it were,
there would not be an orderly sequence, a " rule," a " law."
That is to say the fact of an order implies a sufficient reason
for that order. Even if the mathematical sciences, owing to
their intrinsic limitation, cannot discover what that sufficient
reason is, by the very fact of establishing an order, a law of
sequence they imply the existence of a sufficient reason
for it. Moreover, since these ordered sequences are as
sequences the product of a process their sufficient reason cannot
be static. It must be dynamic, causation in the strict sense.
That is to say though the mathematical sciences owing to
their necessarily formal character cannot attain causation,
because they cannot attain process in the concrete, they imply
its existence, as their establishment of the abstract form of
process implies the existence of the concrete process, whose
quantitative form they describe. Thus the casual laws
admitted by Lord Russell imply the existence of true causation.

And in fact Lord Russell is unable to confine himself to
the abstract truth of mathematical science. He is compelled
to accept in practice the objective reality of genuine causation.
He informs us for example that Carlyle's misanthropy was
caused by his dyspepsia. This clearly does not merely

---

[1] Beauty, the quality of outer form, as significant of inner, ideal form, though having
a sensible ground, the outer form perceived, is supersensible in this ideal reference.

mean that the phenomenon of misanthropy followed the phenomenon of dyspepsia but that the latter actually produced the former. And this is genuine causation. One of the main themes of *Religion and Science* is the historical interaction between them, not a mere statement of the temporal sequences obtaining between religious and scientific phenomena. That is to say, as soon as he exchanges abstract science for concrete reality, Lord Russell, like everyone else, has to accept the fact of genuine causation. Thus not only does the mathematical science which he accepts as knowledge of objective truth involve apprehensions of metaphysical form, but these have to be increased when he comes to deal with the concrete problems of human life. If, however, the validity of any metaphysical apprehensions is admitted it is illogical to rule out of court unexamined those metaphysical apprehensions which involve an apprehension of the existence of God, *e.g.*, the apprehension of Absolute in contingent being, of Necessary Being in possible, of a First Changer (Mover) in change. And these apprehensions, metaphysical proofs, or monstrations of theism are simply excluded *a priori* by Lord Russell, nowhere, so far as I know, discussed on their merits.

Lord Russell therefore denies the objective reference of religious and moral intuitions and thus the objective truth of religion and ethics, only by an epistemological exclusion which implicitly rejects the objective reference of those metaphysical forms, which, as we have just seen, are involved not only in the concrete knowledge of daily life and historical events, but even though to a lesser extent in the conclusions of the mathematical sciences to which Lord Russell would confine our knowledge of truth.

"Philosophy," he wrote " is ' a science of the possible,' an inventory of possibilities, identical with logic whose function it is to provide a repertory of abstractly tenable hypotheses." It ' must therefore ' make only such assertions as would be equally true however the actual world was constituted.

This is as much as to say, we can make no assertions as to the nature of the universe. How then can Lord Russell be even practically certain that mind is no more than an accidental product of a mechanical universe?

Moreover if the mathematical and quantitative scheme established by the sciences is true even formally, its truth implies an epistemology which in turn establishes the truth of other forms of knowledge. Though the fundamental metaphysical truths would indeed be true whatever the nature of the created universe they imply the existence of an Uncreated Being and, given the empirical fact of creatures, truth as to their nature as such and their relation to Uncreated Being. Philosophy therefore cannot be indifferent to concrete reality. Indeed the very existence of logic involves the existence of thought. And thought is a reality beyond the mathematical measurements of the quantitative sciences.

As we have already seen Lord Russell denies the permanent identity of the individual. A man is not even himself till death. On the contrary, what I experience as my abiding self is in fact simply a sequence of atomic point-selves or psychoses whose continuity and rapid succession produce the illusion of a permanent self. Not only does this contradict the self-evident testimony of introspection aware of an abiding self, it renders all knowledge, therefore scientific knowledge, impossible. A complicated chain of reasoning must be held in a mind which continues in existence far longer than the atomic point which is the sole duration admitted by Lord Russell. And how does the knowledge of point ego A pass through to point ego B who being totally different must be wholly unconscious of it—or to point ego Z in whom it appears as a recollection?

And in fact we may be sure that Lord Russell's just antipathy for Herr Hitler is not directed to millions of atomic Fuehrers, a Hitler nebula. It is one definite and enduring person whom he has in view.

Thus from the standpoint of the knower as well as the object known, Lord Russell is unable to maintain his exclusive validation of scientific knowledge. His atomic psychology has destroyed it with other categories of knowledge.

Lord Russell's denial of religious truth rests therefore upon an epistemology which is logically incompatible with any knowledge of truth, and involves pure scepticism. And by the very fact that he is not a pure sceptic but accepts scientific truth as objective Lord Russell implicitly accepts, as we have sought to shew, the objective validity of apprehensions of form and moreover of forms which are not the quantitative forms of the sciences. His refusal, therefore, to admit the evidence of metaphysical and religious apprehension is unwarranted and illogical, a positivist prejudice. That is to say the foundation of his denial of religious truth is unsound and the entire edifice therefore collapses.

Finally it appears that after all Lord Russell does not consistently admit that science attains genuine knowledge. " Science," he writes, " encourages abandonment of the search for absolute truth and the substitution of what may be called ' technical ' truth, which belongs to any theory that can be successfully employed in inventions or in predicting the future. ' Technical truth ' is a matter of degree : a theory from which more successful inventions and predictions spring is truer than one which gives rise to fewer. Knowledge ceases to be a mental mirror of the universe, and becomes merely a practical tool in the manipulation of matter."[1] This utilitarian view of knowledge whose barbarism would have profoundly shocked the great thinkers of the past, whether philosophers or savants, measures the degrading effects of secularism upon a mind inspired by a noble love of knowledge and truth for their own sake. And it is inconsistent with the statement that science

[1] *Science and Religion*, p. 15.

gives objective truth. For all truth is as such absolute, not indeed in the concrete, but in its abstract character as truth. One proposition can, to be sure, contain more truth than another and be in that sense truer. But the truthfulness of the truth contained in both is the same and is absolute. If Lord Russell meant merely that science cannot attain ultimate truth but merely truth as to the mathematically determinable quantities of objects I should heartily assent. But he clearly means more than this, that its truth is simply pragmatic, what works. How astronomical truth about the remotest stars is a practical tool in the manipulation of matter is difficult to see. Comte was more logical in denying the scientific claim of such astronomy, though it involved him in the unfortunate statement that we could never discover the chemical composition of the stars. On examination indeed it is clear that even pragmatic or technical truth is knowledge of the nature of reality and therefore " a mental mirror of the universe." If I know that a given tool physical or intellectual successfully manipulates matter, I must know something of the nature of that tool and of the matter it manipulates, and the metaphysical implications of this knowledge, something therefore of the nature of the universe to which the tool and the matter belong. A purely pragmatic truth is self-contradictory. This indeed was obvious to Lenin, who was therefore unsparing in his criticism of attempts to found Communism upon a pragmatist ideology. That Lord Russell should champion a view so untenable suggests that he is aware that scientific truth, if it is to be more than merely pragmatic, involves apprehensions of objective truth which cannot be admitted without the admission of knowledge other than the quantitative measurements of natural science, and the mere determination of mathematical sequences. This pragmatism is in short the *reductio ad absurdum* of his positivist epistemology which, as I have shewn, is the foundation and substance of his denial of religious truth. His attempt to confine truth to the sciences has ended, as it must end, in the denial even of scientific truth.

F. FALLACIES IN "RELIGION AND SCIENCE"

I WILL conclude by dealing with some of Lord Russell's statements, in his recent book on *Religion and Science*. For both from its popular, though not superficial, treatment and its low price—it is published in the Home University Library —it must be widely read.

The opening chapters deal with the historical relations between science and Christianity, Catholicism in particular. At the very outset the sweeping statement is made that "religious men and women, in the present day, have come to feel that most of the creed of Christendom as it existed in the Middle Ages, is . . . a mere hindrance to the religious life." No branch of science could admit for a moment such gross inaccuracies. Are the millions of Catholics throughout the world non-existent or not truly religious ?

Much is made of a few unwarranted attempts to determine scientific issues by religious authority or to employ exclusively religious methods, where scientific measures should also have been adopted, *e.g.*, in fighting smallpox. Nothing is said of the scientific work accomplished by Catholics, of the scientific investigations of Albertus Magnus, of the discoveries of Pasteur and Abbot Mendel, or the prominent part played by Catholic priests such as the Abbè Breuil in a field in which Christians are supposed to be particularly obscurantist, the study of human prehistory. Nor is the reader told how medieval Catholic thinkers, in deference to what was errone-ously regarded as the scientific truth that the heavenly bodies are incorruptible explained away the plain statement of Scripture, now known to be astronomical truth that "the heavens," *i.e.*, the heavenly bodies, "wax old as a garment." Instead the case of Galileo is brought up once more, as if it were typical of the relations between the Church and science.

On the other hand, Lord Russell actually refers to this doctrine of the incorruptibility " of everything above the earth's atmosphere " as an example of obscurantist theology, the result of a doctrine of Creation. Not a hint that it came from Aristotle who did not believe in a creation! He proceeds to expatiate upon the tenacity which clung to the theory and employed it to deny that comets were heavenly bodies, quoting a seventeenth century Jesuit astronomer. He overlooks the obvious fact that the conflict was between antiquated and more modern science, not between science and theology. Even the angels to which the Jesuit appeals to explain the motion of comets are adaptations of the Aristotelian movers of the spheres, not derived from the authoritative Biblical angelology. And even as regards Galileo it is certain that if he had been content to propound his Copernican theory as hypothetical, not as absolute, truth he would not have been condemned. This indeed was precisely the point of Pope Urban's objection that Divine Power could have produced the actual astronomic appearances without an actual revolution of the earth around the sun, the argument which Galileo foolishly ridiculed, thereby incurring the Pope's anger. Lord Russell himself points out in his last chapter that Einstein has proved that Galileo was wrong as well as the Inquisition. Personally I must confess to a doubt whether this latest view that the motion of the planets is merely descriptive, will be found tenable. It seems rather a *tour de force*. If, however, it is true or, if Lord Russell's pragmatic view of scientific truth were correct, the Inquisition rather than Galileo would have been defending the truth. Lord Russell cannot have it both ways. And when he tells his readers that " The Church forbade," apparently till the nineteenth century, " the teaching of the Copernican system as true," there is a serious suppression of truth. What was forbidden was to teach the Copernican system as " Simply," *i.e.*, absolutely and not merely hypothetically

G

true. If however Einstein's, not to speak of Lord Russell's more radical, view of astronomic truth is correct the Church was right in this attitude as against a world committed to error. In fact her sole mistake was that she withdrew her prohibition instead of waiting until it was scientifically justified by Einstein. I have not made these observations to justify the encroachment of ecclesiastical authority into the domain of science. They are merely intended to shew how Lord Russell has misled his readers, and on his own theory is not justified in condemning the attitude of the Church as erroneous.

Another statement equally wide of the mark is that " in the orthodox view the world had been created in six days." Neither St. Augustine nor the Cappadocian Fathers believed in the literal truth of the Hexemeron. But their orthodoxy is unquestioned. And though Origen, who treats the literal interpretation as absurd, was indeed condemned later, it was not on this score. Even his bitter enemies raised no objection on this point. To make these sweeping statements in defiance of indubitable facts is both unscientific and disingenuous. Most readers of *Science and Religion* will, however, swallow them wholesale on Lord Russell's authority and draw the intended conclusion that Catholicism has persistently opposed the progress of science in the name of theology.

The resistance to evolution which Lord Russell also emphasises is certainly discreditable. But the teaching authority of the Church has maintained a significant reserve. When Lord Russell is in search of an official condemnation he has to go not to Rome but to Tennessee. And even the opposition of private theologians, though it cannot be justified, is to a certain extent excused by the materialistic inferences unwarrantably drawn from the fact of evolution. The latter has been presented as a process by which being of a lower order produces *out of its own resources* a higher order of being, an effect exceeding the cause. In fact the theory does and can do nothing more than describe the order in which the higher forms of being have appeared and explain the mechanism by which the advent of higher forms was made possible. The misinterpretation of a scientific hypothesis by a false philosophy not unnaturally, though deplorably, led many representatives of religion to deny the hypothesis itself. The fault was not, as Lord Russell represents it, only on one side. It is amusing to note that he concludes these chapters by denying the nineteenth century faith in automatic and inevitable progress, thus defending against nineteenth century enlightenment, one of the most decried statements in the Syllabus of Pius IX, the proposition that the Pope must reconcile himself with progress. The latter has received many hard knocks since 1864. And now Lord Russell must add his blow—Et tu Brute.

The chapter on demonology and medicine contains the most serious charges against religion. But they show only, what we all know or should know, that a concrete religious system inevitably gathers a crust of popular superstitions, and that there is a most unfortunate, though very understandable tendency to invest the externals of religion with the absolute value and the divinity properly confined to the Divine Reality which is the object of religion as such.

Lord Russell concludes his criticism of religion by challenging believers to point to any advantage conferred by theological creeds upon the human race comparable to those conferred by science—of which he seems to regard as chief, improved health and increased longevity. It would be easy to reply that science has invested war with such powers of destruction that it will most considerably shorten our lives and that a plentiful supply of healthy bomb and gas fodder is not much to boast of. And it is the advance of science that has made our roads as slaughterous as medieval battlefields.

We might also reply that it is the organisation effected by applied science which has permitted the growth of those totalitarian tyrannies, Fascist and Communist, which enslave men body and soul, as no tyranny of the past was able to enslave them. Lord Russell devotes his last and his best chapter to lamenting this danger to intellectual freedom. There he himself points out that it is the development of scientific technique which has made possible these totalitarian states and indeed the destructiveness and comprehensiveness of modern war. If, however, science has conferred such evils upon man they must be weighed against its benefits.

It is true that Lord Russell rightly distinguishes between the scientific temper of mind and scientific technique, ascribing to the latter as contrasted with the former the evils he deplores. But if these material evils are justly attributed to scientific technique, not to scientific theory, the material benefits, such as better health and increased longevity, should equally be attributed to the former. And the specific benefits of scientific theory and the temper of mind which it demands, increase of knowledge, habits of accurate observation and unbiased judgement are intellectual not physical, therefore of a higher order than the health and longevity which Lord Russell regards as their choicest fruits.

But the entire challenge is misconceived. The benefits conferred by religion cannot be compared with those bestowed by science. They belong to another order. In fact they can be summed up in one word, God. Religion brings God to man. Incidentally it may confer other benefits, even, as at Lourdes, bodily health. But these are incidental and can be fairly offset by the evils caused, not indeed by religion as such, but by its imperfect human embodiments and expressions. If God did not exist religion would be a mischievous illusion. In drawing this conclusion the Godless League in Soviet Russia is more logical than Lord Russell's attempt to conserve a purely subjective religion whose object of worship has been reduced to the mere size of the universe. To ask religion for benefits of the same order as health and long life is a practical materialism, in harmony with the emphasis laid on magnitudes of time and space, for all their vastness of inferior value and lesser reality than a solitary thought, or act of love.

We could continue this examination of Lord Russell's fallacies to the end of his book. Prominent among them is the argument that if and in so far as science can prove that life or mind supervene upon a given material complexity they are thereby shewn to be the products of the latter, therefore of purely mechanical forces. It has always been known that the physiological and mechanical process of fertilisation and conception is followed by the production of a rational man, possibly a genius or a saint. But this fact has not been held to prove that mind is simply the product of the physiological factors involved in the process of generation. And if purely physical antecedents could be shewn for the first appearance of life or mind, generic as well as individual, it would not reinforce the argument for materialism. Life and mind would respectively represent something of a higher order than these antecedents, which therefore they could not produce by their unaided operation. Let us for the sake of argument suppose that a man could be produced in a laboratory instead of by sex union. His soul would necessarily be given from without. In neither case could the mere sum of physical operations produce it.

With the attack upon objective moral truth we have already dealt. But there is no space to continue further the discussion of Lord Russell's fallacies. They render *Religion and Science* an extremely misleading book.

It would, however, be unfair to conclude this criticism without expressing appreciation of Lord Russell's final chapter. Unlike many of the Left Wing he does not attempt to whitewash persecution and the suppression of intellectual liberty, when it flaunts the banner of a secularist enlightenment. On the contrary he warns his readers that the grave threat to freedom of thought which menaces the contemporary world comes, not from any Christian Church, but from totalitarian states making the absolutist claim of religious creeds. "The persecution of intellectuals in Germany and Russia has surpassed, in severity, anything perpetrated by the Churches during the last two hundred and fifty years." And he protests against the too common attitude which excuses the persecution conducted by a system with which we agree, while condemning the persecution conducted by a system to which we are opposed. Thus Fascists excuse Fascist intolerance, Communists and many adherents of a more moderate Socialism the intolerance of Soviet Russia, and the Spanish Reds. I am grateful to Lord Russell for this warning which, coming from him, may win a hearing in quarters otherwise deaf to it. His final sentence is worthy to conclude a truer book and expresses his noblest quality, his hatred of intolerance and tyrannical interference. "New truth is often uncomfortable, especially to the holders of power : nevertheless, amid the long record of cruelty and bigotry, it is the most important achievement of our intelligent but wayward species." Though we cannot endorse the view that the discovery of truth is man's highest achievement, for it is equalled by artistic creation and by moral action and excelled by the worship and service of God, this sentence expresses a valuation of truth in the noblest intellectual tradition. But it harmonises ill with Lord Russell's view that truth is merely technical, and the knowledge of truth but " a practical tool in the manipulation of matter." Such truth, could it exist, would be but the scientific technique which serves the tyrannical state, not the truth which defies its tyranny. I am, however, glad of the inconsistency. It does credit to Lord Russell's spirit, if not to his logic.

PROFESSOR HALDANE

SCIENCE AND RELIGION

THOUGH the relations between science and religion are no longer a problem which acutely torments our contemporaries, they continue to demand the consideration of all who care deeply for either. Professor J. B. S. Haldane's *Possible Worlds and Other Essays* invites us to review a problem on which clear thinking is not by any means so common as it is necessary. Professor Haldane's work, which aims at informing the public of " what is going on inside the laboratories "—in other words, at popularizing some of the latest scientific discoveries and hypotheses—is largely confined to the sphere of the natural sciences and their practical application. But the author is led to speak of religion, to which he thinks it is " vitally important that the scientific point of view should be applied, so far as is possible." The results to which he is brought are primarily contained in the essays " When I am Dead," " The Duty of Doubt," " Science and Theology as Art Forms." Further information as to the author's metaphysical and religious standpoint may be found in *Kant's Scientific Thought and Possible Worlds*. And what does it all amount to ? Nothing very definite. The efficacy of prayer can be scientifically disproved, there is very little ground to believe in personal immortality, we cannot tell whether or no there is a God. On the other hand, mechanism is inadequate to explain the universe ; some form of idealism—to which Kantism is the least inadequate approach made hitherto—is most probably the truest account of it, and if the human mind may perhaps be extinguished at death, it is quite as probable that it will be " merged into an infinite mind or something analogous to a mind which I have reason to suspect probably exists behind nature." And mystical experiences, despite the contradictory statements of the mystics, are genuine experiences of reality. For " religion is a way of life and an attitude to the universe. It brings men into closer touch with the inner nature of reality. Statements of fact made in its name are untrue in detail, yet often contain some truth at their core." As a creed to live by, this nebulous religion of vague probabilities cannot satisfy the needs of the human mind or heart. But it contains three implications, all extremely important : (1) The natural sciences have not disproved the fundamental principles of religion. (2) Their results are incompatible with an ultimate mechanism. (3) The natural sciences can give us no information as to ultimates—that is to say, they cannot tell us what in the last resort are the origin and nature of the universe revealed in our experience.

Professor Haldane does not claim that even personal immortality has been disproved by science. He is content to urge that no valid evidence can be adduced for it. Dr. William Brown and Dr. Driesch,[1] both professional psychologists, agree with Professor Haldane that personal survival of death can neither be proved nor disproved by scientific data. And, indeed, Professor Haldane himself suggests an answer, though for him it is a mere possibility, to the strongest arguments against immortality—the mental senescence which accompanies physical old age, and the mental derangement produced by injuries to the physical brain. " There is no reason why my present consciousness should not constitute one edge of a two-dimensional spirit. The chief reason against the indefinite prolongation of the series of specious presents which constitute my mind is not so much that they apparently end abruptly (for they might recommence elsewhere) as that if I survive beyond the age of sixty or so they will show a progressive deterioration. This deterioration is quite obviously related to that of my body.

[1] *The Crisis in Psychology*, by Hans Driesch.

If, on the other hand, the one-dimensional character of time is due to the nature of the ' material ' world rather than that of the mind, our desire for immortality is more likely to be satisfied in some other time series than in that associated with our bodies." Thus psychology not only does not disprove personal survival of death—indeed, the undoubtedly grave difficulties it raises against it do little more than confirm the obvious difficulty arising from the dependence of our mental on our bodily condition—it suggests—a suggestion confirmed by Dr. Driesch's view of the soul—that below the conscious life, so obviously conditioned by the body, is a deeper life more purely spiritual in its functioning, the Anima of Claudel and the Abbé Brémond, as opposed to the superficial Animus. If, therefore, we can hardly conceive that the Animus, a complex of the more superficial and sense-conditioned functions of the soul, can survive death, psychology has nothing to urge against a survival of the centre of the soul, the Anima, which even in this world is revealed by religious, and *a fortiori* by mystical experience, as transcendent of the time and space which condition the life of the Animus.[1] Still less has scientific research discovered any facts incompatible or difficult to reconcile with a belief in theism, or indeed with Christianity. True, Professor Haldane believes that the efficacy of prayer as a means of obtaining Divine assistance has been, if not actually disproved, at least rendered extremely unlikely by scientific experiment. Professor Galton, he tells us, believing, probably with truth, that more prayer is offered for sovereigns and the children of the clergy than for other classes of society, compared their longevity statistics with those of others living under similar conditions. He proved that their lives were on the average slightly shorter. Therefore, concludes Professor Haldane triumphantly, God does not answer prayers. Galton's experiment was grossly unscientific. For it implies that the

[1] The Animus, however, is not a soul distinct from the Anima but its superficial operation as the form of the body.

efficacy of prayer is in function of its quantity alone. The efficacy of prayer is, on the contrary, determined by the degree of charity which informs it. Prayers for an official ruler are not likely to be so fervent as prayers for a dearly loved relative or friend. This, it is true, applies only to the sovereigns. But in view of the large numbers of clergymen's children and the fact that they are merged with the rest of society, it is not easy to see how sufficiently reliable and exhaustive statistics of their comparative mortality are available. The criterion also implies that if God answers prayer, His answer must be automatic and must necessarily take the form of a fulfilment of the actual desire expressed. Such a grossly unspiritual view is, one need hardly say, not that of Christianity. If Professor Haldane wishes to contest on scientific grounds the Christian doctrine of prayer, he must adduce arguments against it as it is, not as he, or Professor Galton, supposes it to be.

If the present teaching of the natural sciences be as Professor Haldane represents them—and he is borne out by the contributors to *Science, Religion, and Reality*[1], as also by Professor Whitehead—it is certainly not incompatible with religion.

Even if this were all that could be said, the religious man could not be challenged by science in his beliefs. That conflict between religion and science which tormented so many of our Victorian fathers is, at any rate, imaginary.

Can we go further and affirm that the findings of science are incompatible with the mechanism which formed the philosophic background of nineteenth-century science? Professor Whitehead maintains that mechanism is no longer scientifically tenable.[2] The history of mechanism is related at length and its present scientific untenability is argued by Professor Whitehead in his *Science and the Modern*

[1] Edited by Joseph Needham.
[2] I supposed it myself when I originally wrote this criticism of Professor Haldane's book.

World.[1] A shorter statement of the same thesis—the bankruptcy of mechanism as a scientific explanation of the universe—is the subject of Professor Eddington's important essay in *Science, Religion, and Reality* : " The Domain of Physical Science." And if his language is less categorical, Professor Haldane is evidently convinced that mechanism is not the philosophy which science demands or justifies. No doubt a mechanical physics has explained a very wide range of phenomena. But its range is nevertheless limited. Where one should place those limits is still to a large extent a matter of controversy. If Professor Driesch and his followers declare a mechanical explanation of the living organism impossible, and to account for vital phenomena postulate a non-mechanical vital force, an " entelechy," Mr. Needham, a biochemist, sees no reason to affirm its existence, and is still convinced that a purely mechanistic biology is possible (" Mechanistic Biology and the Religious Consciousness "— *Science, Religion, and Reality*). Where doctors disagree, the layman, if he is wise, will suspend judgement. The problem is one for the scientific expert, to be solved by the progress of scientific experiment.

We must not however suppose, as Professor Haldane and others appear to suppose,[2] that if the vitalists prove right, biology *as a science* will have disproved mechanism and proved vitalism. The vitalists will have proved that biology can never be a complete science like physics but must be supplemented by a branch of philosophy, a philosophic biology which will be a department of cosmology. For they will have shewn that vital phenomena cannot be fully expressed by the quantitative formulae of material and mechanical processes and, in so far as this is the case are unamenable to the quantitative treatment distinctive of the sciences. Since the sciences are concerned with these quantitative aspects of

[1] Ably discussed by Prof. A. E. Taylor in the *Dublin Review* for July, 1927.
[2] *Science and the Modern World.*

reality, phenomena, aspects of reality, which are not quantitative are *ipso facto* removed from their province. With the
doubtful exception of the subatomic sphere physical and
chemical processes can be sufficiently described in these
quantitative terms. Though even inorganic objects are not
mere quantities their phenomena admit, for all practical
purposes at least, of a purely quantitative treatment, being
correlated *at every point* with quantities and quantitative
changes. If the vitalists establish their case and prove that
vital phenomena cannot be completely correlated with
quantities and quantitative process, biology as a science will
be confined to a partial treatment of organic life leaving the
residue to the unscientific, because inexact and non-quantitative treatment of philosophic biology. It is however unlikely
that biologists will resign themselves to this limitation. They
will probably persist in the attempt to correlate all vital
phenomena with quantitative relationships and changes as
chemists correlate all chemical phenomena with such relationships and changes. That is to say biology *as a science* cannot
disprove mechanism positively but only negatively by its
defect and surrender. For in so far as it abandons mechanism
it resigns its competence and transmits its subject, organic
life, to another discipline.

Even Mr. Needham, the thorough going mechanist, admits
that mechanism cannot explain mental phenomena. The
mechanistic psychology of association has, as Professor
Driesch shows, hopelessly broken down. It was always a
tour de force. A purely mechanist psychology is, we think,
practically confined to the Behaviourists, and no one who
is not prepared to deny what he affirms implicitly in every
action of his life can take the Behaviourists seriously. If not
in the biological, at least in the psychological sphere, mechanism
must be rejected. We mean, of course, as a complete explanation of the facts. The very language of common sense which
speaks of mechanical habits shows that it has its subordinate

place. But, as Professor Eddington points out, mechanism is obliged to deny that any physical effect can be produced by a mental cause. If I leave my chair to write an article, my mental purpose to write it has nothing to do with my rising. That is solely determined by previous physical changes and my consciousness of rising, because I will to do so, and to fulfil a rational purpose is sheer illusion. This *reductio ad absurdum*, though taken seriously by the Behaviourists, suffices to disprove a mechanistic psychology. That is to say, whatever may be the case with biology, psychology can never be completely a science, proceeding by quantitative methods, but must be largely a branch of philosophy.

Nor is it certain that even the ultimate constitution of matter is mechanical. Up to the present, at any rate, the internal composition of the atom, the mode in which the constituent electrons function, defy explanation in terms of the orthodox mechanical physics. And whatever be the ultimate nature of space and time—I should have said, of space-time—it is not what the older mechanical physics believed it to be. Mr. Haldane, indeed, regards space and time as Kantian categories imposed by the mind on the raw material of phenomena, and Professor Eddington would seem to agree with him. We are not prepared to accept this idealist position. Time and space are too obviously limits which condition the operations of incarnate mind to be its creations. If matter in its ultimate analysis and simplest mode, atomic radiation, should prove not to be subject to space-time, as it functions elsewhere, this only proves that space-time is the inherent form of matter at a specific level of complexity, the mode in which matter exists from the atom upwards. It does not prove space-time a mental category. Moreover, the alleged subatomic indeterminacy may well prove no more than a defect in our power of determination. If we cannot determine *both* the velocity and the position of an electron the reason is most probably not that both are not actually determinable but that we cannot discover both simultaneously. But the very fact that a scientist such as Professor Haldane can adopt the former view, shows the inadequacy of the absolute mechanism so lately regarded as the all-embracing law of being at every level and in every mode. [1]

And even if the mechanists prove to be right in their contention that life and even mind come into existence whenever a given complex of mechanical forces has been achieved, this will not prove the former a mere product of the latter. The effect cannot exceed its cause. It will prove merely that a higher form and therefore a higher life supervenes from the Divine source of Form and Life wherever its " matter " had been duly prepared to receive it.

Among the many phenomena which it was sought to explain mechanically was the descent of living species. A mechanistic theory of evolution rejecting all teleology ascribed the origin of every form of life to the mechanical action of natural selection upon chance variations. This was, on the whole, the view taken by Darwin. What is the view of modern science ? I am safe in saying that the unanimous consent of scientists accepts the descent of species from other species, of more complex and more highly differentiated forms from simpler and less differentiated. But if there is agreement upon the fact of descent, there is no agreement as to the factors which have caused or conditioned it. Professor Julian Huxley[2] and Professor Haldane[3] are inclined to follow Darwin in his emphasis on natural selection. Other scientists stress the importance of favourable mutations[4] while appealing to natural selection to account for their survival. Professor

---

[1] Indeed on analysis it becomes clear that the quantitative sciences are not in the full sense mechanical. For they do not deal with a mechanical process, since they are not strictly concerned with process of any kind. They are mechanical only in as much as they are concerned with the quantitative aspect of an object and its process abstracted from the latter, that is to say with mechanism as measurable.

[2] Art. "Evolution," *Encyclopaedia Britannica*, Thirteenth Edition.

[3] *The Future of Biology*.

[4] e.g., Professor Lucien Cuénot, *Le Transformisme et l'Inscription Patrimoniale des Caractères acquis d'abord par le Soma*, also Professor J. B. S. Haldane.

MacBride[1], on the other hand, decisively rejecting both the inheritance of chance variations and the importance of mutations, which are, he argues, abnormalities produced by an artificial environment, defends the Lamarckian theory of acquired variations due to use or disuse, which he claims can be inherited. And, indeed, even those who follow Weissmann in denying the heritability of characters acquired by the body-cells admit that, at least occasionally, the environment affects the germ-cells. Most biologists still hold that the development of the individual embryo recapitulates the stages of specific evolution, ontogenesis recapitulating phylogenesis, but Professor Vialleton, in his *Morphologie et Transformisme*, adduces an elaborate argument against the thesis. He also distinguishes between the formation of " types of organism "—*i.e.*, the main groups of animals and plants of which, he maintains, " the mechanism is still unknown "—and the formation of specific types which involve no " important changes in the character of the organism," and are therefore rather a diversification, than a " true evolution which implies an improvement or change of some considerable importance affecting the organism as a whole."[2] In face of such disagreement and uncertainty, not as to the fact, but as to the agencies and mode of organic evolution, the layman will be well advised to keep an open mind. We must, however, beware of deciding scientific questions on *a priori* grounds, and adopting an hypothesis not yet sufficiently established by the evidence because it *seems* more favourable than its rivals to our philosophical or religious beliefs. We should therefore be prepared for the possibility, however unlikely, that the more mechanical explanation, that which ascribes evolution to the action of natural selection upon mutations, accidentally and mechanically produced, may be true. But even in that event evolution could not be regarded

---

[1] *Zoology* in *Evolution in the Light of Modern Knowledge*. Repeated in art. " Evolution," *Encycl. Brit.*, Thirteenth Edition.

[2] *Le Transformisme*. (Cahies de la Philosophie de la Nature.)

as a purely mechanical process. For, as Professor Haldane points out, the subject of variation and selection is a living organism, not a lifeless machine.

Moreover, at least in the appearance of the great organic kingdoms, we should be inclined to say, even in the origin of a new species, a new value appears or, to use the phrase of Professor Lloyd Morgan, " emerges." This emergent value or quality, however, is not, Professor Morgan points out, the mere resultant of the forces, qualities, or values previously in existence. It is something genuinely new. It cannot be explained as a sum of forces, therefore, operating mechanically. Professor Morgan speaks of evolution as emergent—*i.e.* as a process in which new qualities emerge. But emergence is no explanation, and emergent evolution can be only the phenomenal appearance of values and qualities somehow already existent, and derived directly or indirectly from a source in which they were formally or eminently present. That is to say, even if mechanical factors determine the conditions upon which a new and higher form supervenes, emerges, in the phenomenal order, that form originates in the Divine Wisdom from which it derives upon and informs the phenomenal complex which is ready to receive it, is in fact its appropriate matter. These further considerations however take us outside the sphere of the natural sciences, which can state only the fact of emergence, leaving to philosophy its ultimate explanation.

But the denial of mechanism is not by itself the affirmation of theism. It leaves open many possibilities—for example, a purely immanental vitalism or energeticism, pantheism, or sheer agnosticism. Nor can we say that the natural sciences, prescinding from psychology, compel us to decide between these alternatives, and to decide in favour of theism. For these alternatives concern the nature of ultimate reality, and the natural sciences give no information as to ultimates.[1] They cannot tell us what matter is in itself, nor space, nor time,

[1] Moreover, only ontological, not phenomenological or empirical psychology deals with ultimates. And the former is rather a branch of philosophy than a natural

still less life. They can only provide abstract schemata and formulæ which, though enabling us with astounding accuracy and over a field unimaginably vast to predict material, spacial, and temporal phenomena—phenomena, that is to say, capable of a quantitative determination—reveal very little of the nature underlying these phenomena, in fact only its measurable and quantitative aspect. "Matter," Lord Russell has told us,[1] " may be reduced to a law according to which events succeed each other and spread out from centres. . . . The net result of relativity theory is to show that the traditional laws of physics, rightly understood, tell us almost nothing about the course of nature. . . . Physics tells us much less about the real world than was formerly supposed. . . . In the four-dimensional space-time frame there are events everywhere. . . . The abstract mathematical relations of these events proceed according to the laws of physics, but the intrinsic nature of the events is wholly and inevitably unknown, except when they occur in a region where there is the sort of structure we call a brain. Then they become the familiar sight and sounds, and so on, of our daily life. We know what it is like to see a star, but we do not know the nature of the events which constitute the ray of light that travels from the star to our eye. And the space-time frame itself is known only in its abstract mathematical properties ; there is no reason to suppose it similar in intrinsic character to the spatial and temporal relations of our perceptions as known in experience. There does not seem any possible way of overcoming this ignorance, since the very nature of physical reasoning allows only the most abstract inferences, and only the most abstract properties of our perceptions can be regarded as having objective validity." So limited is the sphere of physics, the science to which it was once hoped that biology and even

science. (See Joseph Maréchal, S.J., *Studies in the Psychology of the Mystics.* I. " Empirical Science and Religious Psychology.")

[1] " Relativity : Philosophical Consequences," *Encyclopaedia Britannica*, Thirteenth Edition.

psychology might be reduced. And the limitation holds over a wider field. Biology can tell us no more of the nature of life than physics of the nature of matter. " Science," writes Professor Haldane, ". . . is concerned with everything but the nature of reality. Statements of fact made in its name . . . can only reveal the form, and not the real nature of existence." It is true that these statements are excessive in their agnosticism. To know the quantitative properties of objects is to know something of their nature, therefore of the nature of reality. But it is not knowledge of the substance of which these quantities are but the accidents. If science tells us something about the nature of physical reality it does not and never can enable us to grasp that reality. To know the measurements of an object is to know something about it, but not to know it adequately.

From so limited and abstract a form of knowledge we cannot expect a revelation of the Ultimate and Absolute Reality. This is not to say that we can approve the gibe in which certain well-meaning but stupid supporters of religion indulge, that science is bankrupt. To talk of the bankruptcy of science at an epoch when the natural sciences are winning such stupendous triumphs and giving man such control over natural forces that his external environment is being revolutionized, at a period when he is learning to measure the stellar universe and determine the composition of the furthest stars, is midsummer madness. Science is not bankrupt because she cannot go beyond her own sphere and do the work of metaphysics and theology. And it is not from her failure but from her success that she has learned her limitations. Newman, to be sure, anticipating some eighty years earlier the language of Lord Russell, Professors Haldane, Whitehead, and Eddington, suggested that relativity of scientific statements which Einstein was destined to establish.[1] But Victorian

[1] Sermon preached before the University of Oxford, " The Theory of Developments in Religious Doctrine," 341, 346–8, 350–1 : " What if the properties of matter, as we conceive them, are merely relative to us ? . . . If so, it would follow

science was not likely to pay heed to the "obscurantist" cleric at the head of the Oxford Movement, and thought herself able to provide the sole philosophy of religion attainable by man. If she is more modest now, it is because she has learned so much more. And if the believer may not sneer at science because she has learned to be herself, he must not call upon her to outstep her boundaries in the opposite direction. He must not ask from the natural sciences, from physics or biology, a proof of theism. For evidence of theism he must look to metaphysics, religious experience, and positive revelation. Though God is everywhere, and everywhere active, He is not equally revealed everywhere.

> "La gloria di Colui che tutto muove
> Per l'universo penetrà è risplende
> In una parte più, e meno altrove."

The human body, taken as a whole, reveals the rational soul which informs it. What evidence is there of rational purpose in the individual cell ? No doubt that cell is informed by the soul, and unless it were the cell of a living human body it would not be what it is. Nevertheless, it does not reveal the rational soul to which it is in fact subject. And if we may imagine a soul attached to a cell—or *a fortiori* to the atom—that cellular or atomic soul could not, from the evidence afforded by the cell or atom, conclude the existence of the intellectual soul, which in fact informs the entire body and all its parts. *Mutatis mutandis*, for God is the Creator,

---

that the laws of physics, as we consider them, are themselves but generalizations of economical exhibitions. . . . Scripture, for instance, says that the sun moves and the earth is stationary ; science that the earth moves and the sun is comparatively at rest. How can we determine which of these opposite statements is the very truth till we know what motion is ? If our idea of motion be but an accidental result of our present senses, *neither proposition is true, and both are true; neither true philosophically, both true for certain practical purposes in the system in which they are respectively found.*" The words in italics are almost verbally identical with Professor Whitehead's judgement of the Galileo controversy in the light of relativity (*Science and the Modern World*). The entire passage should be compared with Lord Russell's words quoted above.

not the soul, of the universe, this is applicable to our soul
and its knowledge of God. The soul's transcendence of the
cell or atom of the body is not to be compared to God's
infinite transcendence of even His highest creation, and *a
fortiori* of those comparatively low levels of reality which
are the subject-matter of physics and biology. If we do not
expect to find evidence of rational human purpose in every
cell or atom of the body, why should we expect to find
evidence of Divine Purpose in the mechanism of inorganic
matter, or even in the development and functioning of living
organisms? Inasmuch as lifeless matter and living organism
are forms of being and activity, they afford a basis for metaphysical argument to a Divine Ground and First Cause. But
that argument is drawn by metaphysics, not by natural
science. Even the phenomenal course of evolution which is
all with which science can deal, can be described without
reference to a Divine Agent. It is philosophy not science
which shews us that this phenomenal description is not an
adequate explanation of the process. Newman was troubled
because, on turning to nature, he could not see the God so
evident and so present to him in his spiritual life. But is it
surprising that, if we look for the reflection of God in forms
of reality so deficient that they can mirror only the infra-
rational qualities such as energy and magnitude, contained
eminently in the Godhead, we should not see the face of our
Heavenly Father? Even human personality, which as the
highest value and most real being we know is our best mirror
of God, is infinitely below His Absolute Being. What
divinity, then, can we expect to learn from the composition
of the atom or the data of biochemistry? If the quantitative
data and methods of the natural sciences, the pointer readings
of which Professor Eddington speaks,[1] were man's only
source of knowledge about reality, we should be doomed to
agnosticism. We are glad that Professor Haldane admits other

---

[1] *Science, Religion, and Reality*—" The Domain of Physical Science."

forms of knowledge, and among them religious experience.
But he stops short too soon. Underestimating the actual
agreement—of meaning, if not of terminology—between the
mystics, and not even considering the possibility of an
historic revelation, he treats all and every expression of
religious belief as an art form conveying obscure feelings and
indefinite values. This vague religiosity he contrasts with a
Christianity which the Catholic theologian and mystic would
condemn as grossly anthropomorphic. If for a moment it
dawns on his mind that Christian theology does not regard
God as a glorified man, he concludes that He must be regarded
as a glorified society. And he thinks that the formulæ defining
the Incarnation are meant to explain how Jesus is God and
Man, whereas they were devised to safeguard what was
admitted to be an incomprehensible mystery against attempts
to make it intelligible by denying one or other of its elements.
Professor Haldane would be first to pour out the vials of
righteous indignation on any theologian who without expert
knowledge should make pronouncements on biochemistry.
Yet he himself will criticize without the least hesitation
doctrines of Christianity which he has never adequately
studied. He can even make the erroneous statement that
"the Catholic clergy claim a spiritual descent from the Jewish
priesthood." We might as well declare that water is composed
of oxygen, nitrogen, and carbonic acid gas. This may seem a
digression—the introduction of side issues. But it seems
necessary to point out that, though the application of science
to religion preconized by Professor Haldane and Professor
Julian Huxley is incompatible with the essential character of
both, a scientist is hardly justified in treating of religion
without that measure of scientific method it admits, a careful
accuracy in the statement of its doctrines.

If, as we have seen, the natural sciences, in consequence
of their intrinsic limitations, cannot teach philosophical or
theological truth—though metaphysics and theology may

and should utilize their data—the believer must not illicitly wrest their results to a theological conclusion they cannot yield, nor the scientist confine his belief to their legitimate conclusions. Nor must the latter, as I am sorry to say Professor Haldane and Professor Huxley have done, abuse his expert scientific knowledge to uphold, as somehow scientific, an extremely superficial metaphysics or theology. Professor Huxley indeed, in a passage to which I would invite careful attention[1] rejects metaphysics altogether and seeks to determine religious truth purely on grounds of empirical psychology. Because he finds, what the least reflection would have shown him, that our religious images and ideas are drawn from our actual experience and cannot be adequate to ultimate reality, he concludes that religion is and must be an attitude of reverence towards the objects of our experience—the forces of nature and the aspirations and ideals of mankind. St. John of the Cross, who realized at least as powerfully as Professor Huxley the inadequacy of all human images and concepts of God, drew a very different conclusion. He did not bid us worship what we can understand—the sub-human and non-moral forces of nature or our limited human ideals ; he concluded—a conclusion supported by metaphysical proof and all the higher forms of theology—that religious experience is essentially the experience of an incomprehensible Absolute which transcends all the limited objects of our clear experience. If historically religion has often identified its object with forms or concepts in which He is in varying measure present and revealed, that is an idolatry, gross or subtle, refuted by a more purified and transcendent experience, a metaphysical discipline of thought or a fuller and more adequate revelation of Divine Truth. Not science but the restriction of human knowledge to the clear levels and spheres with which the natural sciences are concerned, and to which for all their brilliant achievements they are essentially confined, is the foe

[1] *Religion without Revelation*, p. 738 *sqq.*

of religion. That restriction can lead only to an agnosticism which declares the knowledge of ultimate reality impossible or a vague pantheism which deifies the objects of scientific knowledge. Professor Haldane oscillates between agnosticism and an idealistic pantheism ; Professor Huxley bidding us worship, that is to say regard as adequate objects of that distinctively religious attitude which he accepts as an empirical fact, the forces of nature and the ideals of man, is practically a pantheist. In this they are not spokesmen of science but bad philosophers —bad interpreters, we may add, of the religious experience which they accept. True, Professor Haldane admits religious experience as a source of knowledge other than the data of science ; but only as a vague feeling that beyond the sphere of science there is a wholly unknowable Something. This agnosticism denies the deliverances of religious experience when it testifies to personal communion with a God who, if He transcends, includes the values of human personality. Professor Haldane's less definite position no doubt leaves open possibilities of a more satisfactory religion than Professor Huxley could without a radical change of position achieve. The obstacle to their realization is, I think, his bigoted hatred of the most adequate revelation and corporate embodiment of religion in human history—namely, Catholic Christianity. For Professor Haldane the Catholic Church is nothing but an extremely well-organized political society. Of her inner life he knows nothing. Where Christianity is concerned he loses every vestige of the scientific habit of mind.

I shall conclude by a summary of the situation as between science and religion. Though the natural sciences do not support the mechanical materialism they were once believed to establish, their subject-matter, if we except that ontological psychology which is a philosophical not a scientific discipline, is confined to such levels and aspects of reality that ultimate realities—even the ultimate nature of matter, *a fortiori*, therefore, the nature of spirit and the

Absolute Reality and Ground of being—lie outside their scope. Hence the natural sciences can neither discover nor judge religious truth. Metaphysics and theology must take due account of their data, which they must never attempt to influence or control. But those data must themselves be interpreted and completed by metaphysics and theology before they can be set in their due place within the total fabric of human knowledge. Those lower and vaguer forms of religious experience which cannot distinguish between the natural or human phenomena and the Godhead present but so inadequately manifest in them, tend, no doubt because they are concerned with the same empirical objects, to appeal as " scientific religion " to men of science. But the pantheism, more or less indefinite, which their very indistinction appears to support—seductive perhaps at first sight, but fatal to super-natural and distinctive religion in all its forms—must be rejected as incompatible alike with the conclusions of meta-physics and the higher deliverances of religious experience. A world view that shall do justice to man's experience as a whole, and it has to be truly " catholic," must include not only the facts discovered by the physico-mathematical sciences on the middle level of human knowledge, but the equally indis-putable facts experienced by metaphysics and religion in the profound depths of human knowledge. Made for the whole, capable of the whole and requiring the whole, the human spirit cannot permanently be content with less than the whole.

HAVELOCK ELLIS

TO THE UNKNOWN GOD

MANY, I expect, have formed a false or rather a grossly incomplete picture of Havelock Ellis. They think of him as exclusively a writer on sex and in particular on the pathology of sex. Certainly he has been a pioneer in the scientific study of sex and that study has led him to describe at length the most unpleasant and bizarre perversions of the sexual instinct. But these studies have not led him, as sexual preoccupation has led Freud, to interpret the whole of human life in terms of sex. Nor have they made him cynical. For he is first and foremost an artist and a religious man. Many of his books are not concerned with sexual physiology but with human life and achievement in various departments. From these books a volume of Selected Essays has been published in the Everyman Series. Of these the only one particularly sexual in its subject is a study of Casanova. And even here there is no sexual detail but a psychological study of his subject's character.

Together the essays shew us their author's outlook upon life. As I have said it is the outlook of an artist and a religious man. Not however of a religious believer. Havelock Ellis stands or rather kneels in the outer court of the temple looking through the open door into the sanctuary where God is worshipped. But he does not enter.

For he does not believe in God, and human immortality is for him a baseless dream which " testifies to a curious lack of imagination."

But if ever there has been an anima naturaliter religiosa it is his. In the essay entitled " The Art of Religion " he describes his personal religious experience. By the age of seventeen he tells us, he had lost the Christian faith in which he had been brought up, and accepted the secularist " scientific " outlook, popular with the more advanced intelligentsia of the nineteenth century. " There were, however, times when I became painfully, almost despairingly, conscious of the unsatisfied cravings of the religious impulse. These moods were emphasised even by the books I read which argued that religion, in the only sense in which I understood religion, was unnecessary and that science, whether or not formulated into a creed, furnished all that we need to ask in this direction. . . . I had the feeling that the universe was represented (by David Strauss) as a sort of factory filled by an inextricable web of wheels and looms and flying shuttles, in a deafening din. . . . That, it seemed, was the world, as the most competent scientific authorities declared it to be made. It was a world I was prepared to accept and yet a world in which I felt I could only wander restlessly, an ignorant and homeless child."

Then at the age of nineteen he reads James Hinton's *Life In Nature* and he finds religion never to lose it again. " While Hinton saw the world as an orderly mechanism he was not content . . . to stop there and see in it nothing else. As he viewed it, the mechanism was not the mechanism of a factory, it was vital with all the glow and warmth and beauty of life : it was, therefore, something which not only the intellect might accept, but the heart might cling to. The bearing of this conception on my state of mind is obvious. It acted with the swiftness of an electric contact ; the dull aching tension was removed ; the two opposing psychic tendencies were fused in delicious harmony, and my whole attitude towards the universe was changed. It was no longer an attitude of hostility and dread, but of confidence and love. My self was one with the Not-self, my will one with the Universal Will. I seemed to walk in light ; my feet scarcely touched the ground ; I had entered a new world." And " the effect of that swift revolution was permanent." Here is a religious conversion, as authentic if not as profound, as Pascal's. Pascal found God. What of Ellis ? If we are to accept his own explicit statement, he did not find God. " Neither was I troubled about the existence of any superior being or beings, and I was ready to see that all the words and forms by which men try to picture spiritual realities are mere metaphors and images of an inward experience. There was not a single clause in my religious creed, because I held no creed. I had found that dogmas were . . . but the mere empty shadows of intimate personal experience. I had become indifferent to shadows, for I had the substance. I could face life with confidence and joy, for my heart was at one with the world, and whatever might prove to be in harmony with the world could not be out of harmony with me."

So understood religion becomes purely subjective, an attitude towards the empirical universe. In fact Ellis declares that the " Quintessential core of religion " is " the art of finding our emotional relationship to the world conceived as a whole." And he agrees with Edith Simcox that the result of religious conversion is that " the universe is apprehended no longer as hostile but friendly," with Hinton's definition of religion as " the home-feeling of the universe " and with Bosanquet that its " elemental assertion is that we are at home in the universe." Here is no room for the Transcendent and Absolute Creator whose apprehension is indeed the essence of religious experience. There is nothing but a subjective emotion entertained towards the finite and defective world of our experience. How then can the experience be authentically religious ? But if not, can we trust the testimony of any religious experience ?

The dilemma is due to a failure to distinguish between the religious experience itself—a union-intuition which transcends conceptual formulation—and its inevitable interpretation in the categories of conceptual thought.

Havelock Ellis experiences a transcendent Reality. Therefore he experiences God. But for lack of an adequate philosophy and theology he misinterprets this Reality and his experience of it. Because he apprehends the Object of his experience as exceeding all intellectual formulas, in which he is supported by the Christian mystics from the Areopagite to St. John of the Cross, he concludes that dogmas must be empty shadows. He does not see that any attempt to state the relationship between the data of our ordinary experience and the Object of religious experience—and without such statement we could literally say nothing whatever about a religious experience—involves dogma in the wide sense, *i.e.*, intellectual doctrine about the ultimate Reality. When he identifies the object of his religious experience with the world apprehended as friendly and good he commits himself to a dogma about it. If he contrasts it with religious dogmas as the substance with shadows he again commits himself to a dogma about it. Indeed this distinction between substance and shadow, between what is more and less real, is logically inconsistent with his identification of the Object of religious experience with the world as a whole. For the shadows—be they dogmas or anything else—are part of that whole. If, however, we admit as Ellis implicitly admits, degrees of reality and declare that the object of religious experience is the most real of these, we have admitted by implication that it transcends at least some of the data of experience and therefore at least some part or level of the universe as we experience it.

And when Mr. Ellis terms the religious Object " the Universal Will " he has gone far in the direction of a theistic interpretation. For the universe as we know it and the sciences study it is not a rational will but a complexus of energies mostly unconscious and all, below humanity, subrational. If then the Object of religious experience is a Will it cannot be identical with the subhuman universe. Nor certainly would Ellis identify it with humanity, whose heart-breaking stupidity he deplores elsewhere and which obviously presents us not with one will but a multitude of conflicting wills. The Universal Will must therefore be a superhuman superwill, what theists know as the Divine Will identical with the Divine Being.

It would seem as though Ellis identifies the Substance apprehended by religion with a superspiritual reality of which the universe, as experienced by our normal consciousness and its scientific prolongation, is an appearance. If this is so, and it is suggested by a note in this essay, the Object of religious experience is in fact conceived as an absolute reality transcending the data of ordinary experience—substantially therefore as God. But the latter are falsely regarded as His necessary appearances. This interpretation is confirmed by a passage in *The Star in the East*, in which we read " Illusion and reality are both part of life, each supporting the other," and Reality is explained as the Divine Sphere, as opposed to the superficial order of experience—" God's sphere as contrasted with Caesar's." Here obviously the Object of religious experience is the ultimate Reality underlying the level of superficial experiences. But it cannot then be the universe as a whole. Moreover, if the appearances are necessary they cannot be contrasted with an underlying Reality as Caesar's sphere in contrast with God's. For it must be the nature of that underlying Reality to produce the appearances as its expression. Caesar's sphere is thus God's sphere made manifest —incidentally a doctrine welcome to the supporters of the Totalitarian state. There can be no genuine contrast between them, no escape to the latter from the restrictions and evils of the former. Nor can the necessary appearance of reality be correctly termed illusion. Unfortunately Mr. Ellis' epistemology is frankly subjectivist. " Every one defines the ' Universe ' in his own way and no two people—not even the same person long—can define it in the same way. We have to recognise that even the humblest of us is entitled to his own

' universe.' " If, however, we can know nothing of the nature of the universe and every man's view of it is merely his arbitrary and purely subjective choice we cannot know that it is at one with man or with any particular man. We cannot know whether we are really in harmony with it. Still less can we know that it is marked by a " general rhythm " as Mr. Ellis says elsewhere. In fact we can know nothing whatever about it. Probably nothing more is meant than that the ultimate nature of reality is unknowable, not literally that we can have no knowledge whatever of the world. This, however, is an ambiguous statement. Ultimate reality is indeed unknowable in the sense that it infinitely transcends our knowledge. But it is knowable in as much as it contains and infinitely exceeds the utmost of finite being and value we can experience or possess, while admitting none of its limitations and defects, and is therefore the infinitely transcendent cause of the universe we experience and wholly distinct from it.

His rejection of metaphysics and positive religion has left Mr. Ellis unable to state consistently the relation between the rest of human experience and its data and religious experience and its data. He is aware of having apprehended something wholly good and satisfying and that this something is the most real, the most substantial object of his experience, somehow the ultimate truth and value behind and within the world. That is to say, he is aware of having apprehended what theists know to be God. But he is quite unable to state what it is. He does not know that it is God. He thinks that somehow it must be the cosmos as a whole experienced as good and beautiful and in harmony with his own spiritual nature and its needs. But at the same time he is well aware that the empirical universe, so far as humanity is concerned the realm of Caesar, is far from Divine. Therefore the object of religion must be a profounder reality behind the superficial illusion. There is a confusion here which he cannot clear up. The reality, the non-self, the universal will or in short the universe apprehended in religious and pre-eminently in mystical experience (for, as he truly points out mysticism is the fullness of religious experience) is at once the universe and is not the universe but an underlying and transcendent reality. What Mr. Ellis has in mind, I believe, is the beauty of the universe to which, as an artist, he is so keenly sensitive. What he regards as Divine is the rhythm which determines the life of the cosmos. That is why he regards the dance as the specifically religious cult, " the supreme symbol of spiritual life."

For dancing is the imposition of a delicate and subtle order, a rhythm upon bodily motions which threaten at every moment to break that rhythm and degenerate into a chaos of unregulated movement. And as such it symbolises and represents the cosmic rhythm imposed upon the forces of nature as they strive to break away into the corruption of lawless anarchy. There is here a most welcome denial of energeticism, an assertion of the primacy of form as the determinant of life and positive being. There is a perception of the Word in His cosmic function as the world artist incarnate in the universe, as the artist in his work. So far Ellis's religious insight is in agreement with Berdaiev's vision of the cosmic art of the Word Incarnate. " Beauty is the Christianised cosmos in which chaos is overcome ; that is why the Church " (His mystical body with its cosmic extension) " may be defined as the true beauty of existence. Every achievement of beauty in the world is in the deepest sense a process of Christianisation. Beauty is the goal of all life ; it is the deification of the world ; an integral conception of the Church is one in which it is envisaged as the Christianised cosmos, as beauty."[1] Unfortunately Ellis unlike Berdaiev cannot attain a clear view of the relation between this cosmic order or rhythm and the energies which it determines. He tends to regard the actual form as it is in the universe, as Divine. That doubtless is

[1] *Freedom and the Spirit*, Eng. Trs., p. 332.

the reason why he identifies the object of religious experience with the universe. Since however the evil, the enmity, the mutual destructiveness, in short the tendency to chaos, are undeniable facts of experience, he is obliged to regard the actual universe of daily experience as an unreal appearance, not the object of religion.

In fact, however, the actual form of the universe, therefore its rhythm and beauty, is inseparable from its defects, its mutual oppositions, its tendency to chaos. The forms which determine its concrete energies are essentially bound up with those energies and as realised in them, are subject to their limitations. It is the nature, that is to say, the form of a beast of prey to devour its victim, of a disease germ to cause plague. The actual order of the universe is not perfectly good. Nor is it perfectly beautiful. There are many stunted and distorted trees in the forest. A crowd is not a beauty chorus.

So long as the Object of religion is regarded as bound up with the universe either as the reality of which the universe is the appearance or as its formal factor, the rhythm actually existing in the universe, the evil in the world, not least the human evil, must be attached to that Object. Either as part of Its necessary appearance or as inherent in the deficiency of the form which ex hypothesi is Itself it belongs to the Religious Object, be it the " Not-self " or its Universal Will. Religion therefore cannot produce perfect harmony with this object. For there can be no perfect harmony with what is not wholly good. Under the influence, probably, of the world war, when for four years the majority of the human race behaved like the inmates of Broadmoor—for there are many bitter allusions to it—Mr. Ellis has reached, in certain moods at least, at a Swiftian contempt and loathing for mankind. Concluding one such passage he writes : " The God that made this thing (Mankind) hides His shameful face and can nowhere be found." This cry is the nemesis of an unintellectualised religion.

There is no harmony here with the non-self or the universe, nor even with the rhythm of the universe to which the form of man, naturally so far from divine, must belong. If the Object of Religion is a Reality whose necessary appearance is humanity or an immanent form of which it is part, it must be guilty of the human evil which, if here depicted too exclusively, is all too real. It would seem that in face of the spectacle Ellis' religion with its fundamental optimism had been overclouded. And he has no support under the cloud. For only if the Object of religious experience be a God wholly transcendent of the universe and of man, whose evil therefore is no necessary expression or result of His nature but arises in the last resort from the inherent limitation of created being, can religion hold fast to its Object in face of the spectacle of evil.

It is indeed as impossible to be in harmony with all natures, that is with all forms, as it is to be in full agreement with opposing armies. Therefore the form of the universe, as concretely embodied, cannot be divine, cannot be the perfect and ultimate reality. It cannot be the Logos. It must be the imperfect and contingent reflection and expression of that divine Reality in an order of being outside Itself, the reflection and expression of the Word not the Word Himself. Of this too Mr. Ellis is aware when he regards the object of religion as a mysterious reality underlying the universe. He cannot however clear up the confusion and achieve consistency, because he will not accept a Deity wholly transcendent of the universe and its created beauty. Strangely enough, since he is well read in the Christian mystics, he seems to have no notion of the Christian doctrine of God. If he had grasped it, he could hardly have dismissed theism so light-heartedly as belief in "the existence of any superior being or beings." And elsewhere he dismisses with an equal light-heartedness "faith in gods." The Christian God is depicted here by implication as nothing more than a supreme spirit among others, a sort of superman or angel. God, gods, finite spirits evidently, of whom there may be a multitude. For theism the existence of *many* gods is an intrinsic impossibility. The theism therefore rejected offhand is not theism but the anthropomorphism with which a child's conception of God must begin but which is too often never outgrown. If our conception of God is this childish anthropomorphism, we must reject belief in God. Such a Deity does not and cannot conceivably exist. And if Mr. Ellis's knowledge of Christianity were confined to what he was taught in the Sunday School religion of his childhood his misunderstanding and therefore his inevitable rejection of Christian theism would be only too intelligible. But how is it he has learned nothing better from the mystics? He refers to St. John of the Cross. How any reader of the Ascent of Mount Carmel can continue to think of the Christian God as no more than a superior being is difficult to conceive? Perhaps Mr. Ellis imagines, like Baruzi, that there is a contradiction between St. John's theology as a mystic and as an orthodox Catholic. If so he might do well to study St. Thomas. But since he refers to St. Thomas in terms of appreciation he is presumably acquainted with his thought.

In a passage, however, where he points out the distinction between the aesthetically and the sexually attractive he adds : " They are two different substances as the mediaeval metaphysician would have said." This confusion between substance and quality proves that although he has a nodding acquaintance with scholasticism he has apparently failed to understand it.

Or it may be that he has not found himself able to reconcile the transcendent Absolute beyond concepts with the apparent anthropomorphism of the Heavenly Father and Lord.

In any case it is clear that like Richard Jefferies, Mr. Ellis has rejected not the true God but a more or less anthropomorphic and in any case finite conception of God falsely supposed to be the God of Christian theism. Like Jefferies he has found God in actual religious experience. But whereas out of his very experience Jefferies formulated as a personal discovery the transcendent theology of the Areopagite Ellis achieves no consistent intellectual interpretation of his experience. He confuses the God he has found with the universe while yet distinguishing Him from it. That is to say his spirit has found God but not his intellect.

At the beginning of this essay I spoke of Ellis as a man kneeling in the outer court of the temple unable to enter the sanctuary. This is indeed, true of his intellectual position. When however we penetrate deeper to the central depths in which the soul of man meets the Divine Spirit the picture proves false. He is worshipping in the sanctuary but he is blind. And his blindness is not only that blindness common to all who find God, the blindness of human vision dazzled by the excessive brilliance of the Divine Light. His mental vision is blind to the identity of Him whom he adores. He does not see that He is the God who made man and the world, the God of Abraham and the God of Jesus Christ. He cannot clearly distinguish Him, from the world which He has made but whose comparative nothingness is revealed by defects and evils infinitely remote from the Divine Perfection. For having rejected revelation, reduced therefore to his personal religious experience, he also rejects metaphysics by which alone religious experience and its data can be integrated with the rest of human knowledge in a complete and consistent Weltanschauung. Even the deliverances of common sense are refused as "a hardened mass of dead metaphysics." "There are no metaphysical formulas to suit all men, but, every man must be the artist of his own philosophy." This pragmatism fatal to objective truth and therefore to the science in which Mr. Ellis believes and to which he has himself contributed so much, makes a consistent intellectual interpretation of his religious experience impossible. Happily it does not, it cannot, invalidate that experience. We cannot follow Mr. Ellis as a religious teacher ; indeed he takes us nowhere. But we can and must reverence him as a religious man and value his personal testimony to God, though he is unable to give it a satisfactory intellectual statement. No believer who reads these essays with the least care can fail to perceive the depth of their author's religion. It is at the core of his art, and of his appreciation of natural beauty, the cosmic rhythm dimly but powerfully envisaged as a Divine artistry. And Catholics in particular should read these essays with sympathy. For the writer has clearly found God in their holiest rite.

" As the gracious spectacle of the Mass is unrolled before me, I think, as I have often thought before, how much they lose who cannot taste the joy of religion or grasp the significance of its symbolism." He proceeds, it is true, to tell us that the value of the Mass does not depend on " faith in gods or immortal souls or other such figments of the intellect." And elsewhere he says that even when the end of Christian faith has made the Mass impossible as an act of religion it could and should still be celebrated as a work of art. But his appreciation of the Mass is notwithstanding religious, not merely aesthetic. " It may," he writes, " bring joy and peace to the heart." This indeed it might do as an artistic spectacle, though when a work of art produces such an effect it is at least pointing above the aesthetic to the religious level. But this is not all. The Mass is " the embodied presentation of the soul's great adventure, the symbolic initiation of the individual into the spiritual life of the world." It " is a function, at once dramatic and *sacred* which culminates in a *spiritual communion* with the Divine." This initiation into the spiritual life of the universe, this communion with the Divine is not aesthetic, not art. It is religion. Not only has the spirit of Mr. Ellis found God, though his mind has not, it has found God in the Mass.

Nor was it the pursuit of a purely aesthetic satisfaction which led Mr. Ellis to Monserrat. Our misguided British Liberals who in face of the plainest evidence to the contrary regard the nominally democratic Spanish Government as representing the cause of liberty and civilisation could not do better than read Mr. Ellis's account, which they cannot ascribe to clerical prejudice, of his visit to the shrine now a third time violated and ruined by a militant irreligion. After recalling with evident sympathy the great spiritual history of this mountain shrine of Our Lady he continues with a flat denial of the " Liberal " lie about Spain. " It was not alone in the spiritual sphere that Monserrat stood forth resplendent above the world around. Like *every great Benedictine monastery* it was a focus of work and enlightenment." (Which no doubt is the reason why the apostles of enlightenment and progress suppress monasteries.) "Its abbots were sometimes fine architects" (modern enlightenment is more expert in destruction than in building) ". . . and they knew also where to find the best sculptors and craftsmen in Spain. . . . They founded a school of music. They set up a famous printing press when printing was still a novelty in the world. If men brought here in profusion their precious things for love of the Virgin, the guardians of her shrine in the days of its prosperity were never unmindful of their own responsibilities. The gifts of natural site and scenery, antiquity and legend, the adoration of a large part of Europe, the skill and energy of its own monks, thus combined to render Monserrat a shrine of almost unparalled magnificence."

And it was in a religious spirit that Mr. Ellis arrived. " I stepped into the train . . . somewhat awed at the prospect of at last visiting a sacred spot towards which my thoughts had so often been set." His sense of an awful mystery deepens when he visits the Church where " a light subdued to gloom, befits the attitude of prayer . . . an atmosphere of mystery . . . the attitude of approach to the supreme mystery." This is not aestheticism but an authentic apprehension of

Godhead, the Divine Mystery in its shrine. " Truly God is in this place."

But the awful mystery is fascinating also. " Sounds of youthful laughter " on the mountain strike no discord " for the note of Monserrat is one of laughter as well as of prayer." " For many a weary and sensitive soul, we may be sure, it was not the thirst for suffering but the thirst for joy that led them to Our Lady of Monserrat. When they let the heavy burden of the world slide from off their shoulders . . . and climbed to a new home in this mountain it was not with a sinking but with a rising heart, with the exhilaration of St. Francis, with the glad new sense of delicious freedom which once filled the men who went into the Thebaid," men regarded as lunatics by the enlightened secularist.

A man who could enter thus into the spirit of a Catholic shrine is indeed not far from the Kingdom of God. Or rather he is within the Kingdom though he may fail to recognise the King.

Invincible ignorance of the intellectual interpretation and implications of religious experience has indeed as we have seen led Mr. Ellis into a bitterness about humanity, its history and its destiny, which admits little hope for man. And it has made him alternately deify and condemn the nature of which mankind is part. But it has not deprived him of the experience itself, union with God, even though the Unknown God, in the centre of his spirit. And this after all is " the one thing necessary "—absolutely and unconditionally—the heart of religion. If inculpably Mr. Ellis's mind is closed to his Maker, " heart speaks to heart." And that converse is not, as Mr. Ellis believes, interrupted by death. For it is the speech of the Immortal to the Eternal.

GEORGE SANTAYANA

THE BEST IN THIS KIND ARE BUT SHADOWS

THE majority of philosophers have exercised, directly at least, but a narrow appeal. Their language is too technical, their thought too abstract. But Professor Santayana is also a literary artist of rare skill and charm—an artist of the impressionist school. Had he never written a line of formal philosophy, he would have made his mark by such brilliant characterisations of nature and human life as we find in his *Soliloquies in England*. Those who regard his philosophy as radically unsound may wish he had confined himself to a sphere where his accomplishment can be heartily applauded and enjoyed. But a formal philosopher he also is, with a philosophy which, if deliberately incomplete, is drawn in firm, clear outlines and with a measure of internal consistency which, though far indeed from flawless, is, under the circumstances, a surprising achievement of hard thinking. This philosophy, presupposed at every turn in the *Soliloquies*, is explicitly, if in parable, enunciated in several places of that book. It inspires the criticism of American philosophers in *Character and Opinion in the United States*. It is the theme of the Lucianic *Dialogues in Limbo*. The heart of it is poetised in the Sonnet Sequence entitled " 1895." Its main position is defended against Dean Inge—in his *Platonism and the Spiritual Life*. And its formal exposition is the theme of the work which may be taken as the representative expression of his thought, *Scepticism and Animal Faith*. He who has mastered this work—commendably short for a philosophic treatise—may claim to understand its author's philosophy. The five volumes of the *Life of Reason* published years earlier are in part a less developed statement of the same doctrine, confusing rather than helpful towards its understanding, in part its application in the spheres of art, science and religion. Professor Santayana's view of religion can be further studied in the collection of essays entitled *Poetry and Religion.*

Three main ingredients have gone to the making of Santayana's philosophy: (1) Epistemological Scepticism; (2) Materialistic Positivism; (3) Platonic Idealism. Strange bedfellows, one might think, not easily to be reconciled. Though it cannot be said that Professor Santayana has succeeded in effecting a reconciliation, his ingenious attempt is an intellectual feat, calculated to give no little pleasure to those who are willing to forget facts for a moment and let their thought wander in a realm of pure concepts. To this realm, indeed, he invites us, not, as we might gladly do, to make a passing visit, but to emigrate. But I am anticipating.

The Epistemological Scepticism relentlessly prosecuted throughout the earlier chapters of *Scepticism and Animal Faith* leaves us not even Descartes' *cogito ergo sum,* but a realm of essences—the forms we perceive, imagine, or conceive—devoid of existence and unrelated to each other. Once admit that we can be certain of, can know only, that which, without logical contradiction, cannot be denied, and there is no escape from the ruthless scepticism of Professor Santayana's argument. It is the old scepticism of Descartes and Hume and the Associationists more consistently carried out. This epistemological scepticism can be refuted only by taking a firm stand on the bed-rock of any sound philosophy, the self-evidently objective reference of knowledge.

Having fully elaborated his scepticism, Professor Santayana introduces the two remaining materials of his philosophical edifice. The result is a dualism. In so far as the essences can be related directly or indirectly to anything which in reality, or in Professor Santayana's belief, can be explained in physical and mechanical terms, they are allowed to give us knowledge of real existences. But it is only in virtue of an act of faith, to be sure inevitable, posited by irrational instinct—" animal faith " Professor Santayana terms it. Thus positivist Materialism finds its justification. But the essences themselves—the forms with their qualitative characters—have no objective existence. They belong to a world of unsubstantial forms, infinite in number and deriving their degree of value or unvalue from our needs, and appear because the blind mechanism of existence has chanced to exemplify them for a moment, as it grinds out its aimless changes. Professor Santayana thus introduces in a modified form the realm of Platonic ideas. Fortunately among the products of this purposeless machine is a quality, peculiar, so far as we know, to man, the power to apprehend and contemplate the essences for their own sake. This quality, which Santayana terms " spirit," can alter nothing in the world of existence. For it is an unsubstantial epiphenomenon of the mechanical process which has given it birth. This aspect of Santayana's philosophy is strangely loyal to the crudest materialism of the late nineteenth century whence he adopted it. It is, however, taken for granted as the final deliverance of science. (One might imagine that Professor Santayana had never heard of the objections to this mechanistic epiphenomenalism raised by such men of science as Professors Eddington and Whitehead.) Spirit can, however, enjoy a disinterested contemplation of the essences as they pass before it. And for Santayana this contemplation is the true spiritual life, nobler far, he thinks, than the unfounded belief that the essences *exist* in some better world, are thoughts in the mind of a substantial Divinity, Ideas of the Divine Wisdom. This, indeed, is the theme of *Platonism and the Spiritual Life*.

This philosophy obviously involves a radical dualism. If there is no common ground which connects the realm of Essence with the world of actual Existence, how is it that the existences always embody an essence—can, indeed, be known to us only because they do so—and that the essences in turn are such as to be capable of this incarnation and revelation by existences ? It may, perhaps, be argued that the essences are mere reflections of existences, and indeed for a consistent epiphenomenalism spiritual ideas must be mere reflections of mechanical processes. But Professor Santayana shrinks from saying this. The essences are an eternal cosmos, though it is difficult to see, how, if they are not intrinsically interrelated, they can form a cosmos of any kind ; a cosmos independent of the existences which happen to embody some of them. And if it be argued that, since the existences must have some determinate character, they must therefore embody some essence—and this Professor Santayana admits—it surely follows that the essence, embodied by a particular existent, is a true character of that existent, *which is therefore not a mere existent which happens to embody it.* For if the nature of the individual existent be such as necessarily to embody and express an essence, the essence must exist, at least as a quality of that existent. The essence, therefore, must give us true information about the existent which embodies it. The dualism of essence and existence is thus transcended, and we are left with three possible explanations of the relation between the kingdom of essences and the order of existences. (1) The latter, conceived in purely mechanical terms, may totally determine the former. But how, then, can the realm of essences, as Professor Santayana holds, transcend the order of existences and be the object of a worshipful contemplation ? If spirit and its objects are nothing but illusions arising, no one knows why or how, out of a mechanical process which is the sole reality, the spiritual life is at best an inevitable illusion which cannot possess the value attributed to it by Santayana. Nor can spirit be a rebel against the mechanical life of physical desire and need which has given it birth.[1] For that which is totally determined by another cannot be in any respect independent of, far less in opposition to, that

[1] *Soliloquies in England,* XLIX. *The Psyche,* 223–4.

from which it derives its being.[1] Neither can the essences, spirit, or the spiritual life, which is spirit's contemplation of essence, have any value other than that possessed by the mechanical existents. And in fact, Professor Santayana admits that the essences are intrinsically valueless and derive their values from actual human needs. Thus the disinterested contemplation of essences prescinding from human needs, in which he finds the highest form of human activity, is, after all, a contemplation of the valueless. (2) The world of existences is totally determined by the essences. Experience, however, shows that actual objects do not perfectly express their ideal natures, the forms which they embody. We must therefore admit in their constitution a material as well as a formal or ideal factor. Pure idealism is false. (3) Essences partly, but only in part, determine existents. The problem then arises of the respective contribution due to either factor. If in the last resort a mechanical process of existents be the concrete reality and the predominant factor, we are brought back for all practical purposes to the first, the purely mechanistic and epiphenomenalist position. If the preponderance of power and reality be reversed, we have a position such as is represented by the ideal realism of Christian philosophy. But we are remote from Professor Santayana.

For Professor Santayana, while reducing spirit and the essences it perceives to shadows of the mechanical process, renounces in theory all attempts to unite the realms of existence and essence in a higher synthesis. He is content to affirm both, the latter given immediately but non-existent, and the former believed inevitably by " animal faith," but substantially real. Their actual co-existence and co-operation he ascribes to " chance." No wonder that, in spite of his over-subtle

---

[1] Sinful wills are not in rebellion against God as such but against a finite good which He wills. The beatific vision excludes the possibility of sin. Nor could sin be possible if creatures were not essentially defective, half beings with a factor of nothingness in their composition. Were they what they cannot be, divine emanations, they could not oppose God's will.

speculations in the realm of epistemology, in the Introduction to *Scepticism and Animal Faith* he disclaims metaphysics. To appeal for explanation to chance, as he so often does, is to renounce explanation. No doubt we must accept much that we cannot explain. But before we will admit with Professor Santayana that experience is radically inexplicable, we must be sure that all alleged explanations have been disproved. The explanation given by subjective idealism is certainly refuted. But no serious attempt is made to disprove the theistic explanation founded on an ideal realism and the affirmation of degrees of reality. Nearly always Santayana prefers to assume its refutation, to treat it as an explanation already so thoroughly exploded, that it deserves no serious discussion.

Moreover, the philosopher cannot logically assert an absolute dualism of existence and essence, since, as we have seen, the co-existence of both demands that one of three or four explanations of their relationship be true. He might indeed decline to decide between the competing alternatives on the ground of insufficient evidence. This, however, is not Santayana's position. For practical purposes he accepts a mechanistic materialism, but refuses to carry it to its logical conclusion, leaves subsisting though somehow not existing an independent realm of essences, and for the nexus between them appeals to chance. A connection however between two related facts or series of facts, in the present case between the existents and the essences, presupposes something common to both. If that common factor be a temporal-spatial mechanism of the existent, the relation of the essences to the existents must be explicable by that mechanism, must in fact be its product. That is to say on this hypothesis the mechanism determines the entire realisation of essences in the world of existences and therefore our knowledge of essences. We cannot rise above the order of mechanically determined existents to an objective and independent realm of Platonic ideas in which the human spirit attains liberation and a refuge from the cosmic machine.

Not only does Professor Santayana shirk the explanation of the relationship between existents and essences—his account of the actual nature of that relationship eludes close determination. The essences are, he tells us, " symbols " of the existents. The word " symbol " is ambiguous. There are symbols and symbols. There is the symbol which is purely arbitrary and conventional, revealing nothing of the object for which it stands. Such, now at any rate, are the characters we write and usually the sounds we utter. Neither the written character " MAN " nor the sound " Man " tells us anything of the human being for which it stands. But for the conventional agreement of English speakers " Pig " might just as well take its place. There are also symbols which are not purely arbitrary, in which the symbol and that which it symbolises possess some common quality or stand in some real relationship, in virtue of which the former is a natural symbol of the latter and possesses something in common with it—*e.g.*, a flaming heart as a symbol of love, water as a symbol of spiritual purification. When Santayana calls essences symbols of existents, he should explain to which category of symbols they belong. This he does not do. He often speaks as though the essence-symbol revealed nothing of the existent for which it stands. Yet, as we continue our reading, we discover that the essence-symbols manifest the existents in so far as they enable us to place them. They locate them in space-time, and relate them there one to another. Nor for the performance of this function are the essence-symbols of equal value. The abstract essence-symbols with which the scientist operates are the most accurately determinative of the true locus and inter-relationship of the existents. Thus for Santayana the essences are after all symbols of the second class, symbols which are symbolic in virtue of a character possessed in common with the object symbolised. Indeed, in the ordinary usage of language they seem to me hardly entitled to be called symbols. For the common quality in virtue of which essences symbolise the existents is no mere analogy founded in the possession of some common quality at different levels of being, as, for example, the heat of fire and love, but a character formally existent in the object symbolised—namely, the spatio-temporal position which the essence abstracts and reveals. This surely is the relationship between a map or plan and its object. A plan represents a building by abstracting and depicting the spatial position of its parts—a quality actually existing in the object represented. So for Santayana the essences are maps or plans which reveal the actual location of the existents relatively to the observer and to one another. It seems misleading to call them symbols—for we do not commonly call a map or a plan a symbol of its object. Moreover, if location in space and time or in space-time is a fundamental property of corporeal existents, and this location is determined by the essence, the essence determines at least a very important part of the nature of the existent. This view, however, of the relation between essence and existence amounts to an imperfect ideal realism for which reality, the order of concrete existence is largely determined by the order of essence, though not to the extent demanded by the thoroughgoing ideal realism of the Scholastic philosophy. But even this incomplete ideal-realism is incompatible with the purely casual nexus between the essence and the existent which Professor Santayana affirms elsewhere.

Accepting, however, this account of the bond between essence and existence—more explicit, I think, than any actual statement of Professor Santayana, yet the only possible interpretation of his language—we are at once faced with two questions. Does this local designation exhaust the function of the essence? Clearly not. Indeed Professor Santayana implies the contrary, though he maintains that the highly abstract essences formulated by the mathematico-physical sciences are better symbols of the existents than the essences of poetry, art, or religion. There is, therefore, necessarily in the essence a further function implying a further symbolism besides this symbolism of temporal-spatial location. And, indeed, it is precisely this non-locating function and quality, which the essences of art, poetry, and religion possess to a far greater degree than the essences with which the sciences operate, that Santayana in his Platonist aspect values so highly and offers as the supreme object of human contemplation in place of the spiritual existents which are the objects of religious faith. We are therefore brought back to the same unanswered question. How does this non-mathematical non-quantitative factor of experience arise? If only the quantitative aspect of the essences reveals existent reality, why do the essences possess any further quality or function? Until Santayana provides a satisfactory answer to this highly pertinent, indeed inevitable, question, he cannot complain if we persist in the traditional and commonsense reply that concrete existence is not confined to its mathematico-quantitative aspects, but does actually possess the further qualities which experience reveals, and therefore that the forms of experience—Professor Santayana's essences—manifest reality, not only in their spatio-temporal locations, but in their other and, as even Professor Santayana admits, higher and richer qualities.

What epistemological justification can Professor Santayana claim for treating the locating, mechanical spatio-temporal qualities of the essences as veridical, designating actual existence, while refusing to admit the same of the more spiritual qualities? Animal life, he replies, compels us to posit with an inevitable faith actual existents corresponding to the former qualities in the essences perceived. For, though theoretically we are not obliged to accept the reality of such existents, the objects designated by the essences do, in fact, act on us coherently and compellingly as mechanico-physical units. Hence animal faith rightly accepts the mechanico-physical aspects of the essences as manifesting objective entities. Professor Santayana misinterprets as faith a combination and confusion of two intuitions. One is the intuition of a concrete order in our experience of the world as involving an objective reality as its ground. This intuition however is compatible with an objective idealism. Berkleian idealism or the Kantian metaphysic also accounts for, indeed demands, a coherent experience of what appears to be an external corporeal order. And there is a direct apprehension of corporeal reality in the compelling pressure of physical objects, as they act upon us. This is an immediate and self-evident manifestation of external objects directly apprehended by the subject of their action and in and through that action. Self-evident apprehension however is the very reverse of faith, being certain knowledge.[1] I experience a network of spatial and temporal relations mechanically juxtaposed and determined, and I therefore know as an experienced fact—Santayana would say believe—that this mechanico-physical system exists outside my experience. This system however is not experienced as a system of abstract relations or phenomena but as a system of properties inherent in concrete substances, energy-objects. But, we must insist, why, while accepting the mechanico-physical aspects of experience as objectively valid, does Santayana exclude other aspects of experience ? Because—here again I compress and render explicit what he implies—these other aspects, the spiritual qualities, do not and cannot conceivably act on the mechanically determined system to which they admittedly belong. The answer involves the position, often indeed explicitly stated by Santayana, that no immaterial force— e.g., human thought and will—does or can act on matter. Certainly, as Professor Eddington has pointed out [2]

---

[1] For the difficulty arising from hallucinations, see my *Philosophy of Form* pp. 91-2.
[2] *Science, Religion, and Reality.*

from the purely mechanical standpoint all action of mind on matter is impossible. If I rise from my chair because I know a friend is due—the physical movement thus partially caused by the mental fact of my knowledge—the occurrence, from the standpoint of mechanical materialism, is as miraculous as the multiplication of loaves and fishes. Logical materialists have therefore striven desperately to explain away, in fact deny this obvious fact of experience. The entire and complete explanation, they tell us, of my rising from my chair is a series of previous physical changes. My undeniable impression of rising because I know my friend is at hand is an illusion. Such is the philosophy of the American Behaviourist. Santayana accepts this defiance of experience : he is, in fact, on this fundamental matter a Behaviourist. But he never produces a shred of evidence to show why we should accept the deliverance of experience—in his terminology, the perceived essence—when it testifies to mechanico-physical units ; and refuse to accept it when it testifies, with equal immediacy, to the causal efficacy of mind. *No philosophy can hope to stand which is not broad-based on the acceptance of all forms and levels of experience.* Santayana's philosophy begins by squeezing the data of experience into the narrow shoe of a mechanical hypothesis which represents the abstraction of certain, real no doubt but partial and comparatively super-ficial, aspects and levels. And inasmuch as he regards the acceptance of even these aspects, as in the last analysis, an act of faith, it is, if possible, even more arbitrary to refuse credit to others at least as immediate persuasions of experience and common sense. As I cannot accept his scepticism and fideism I would not press the point. I would, however, urge that since the mechanical properties which are the subject-matter of physics are mental abstractions, they have, on Professor Santayana's hypothesis, no claim to be regarded as truer pictures of existents than essences of a more qualita-tive and ideal character. Why should we regard the noumenon

K

(the existent) as more akin to the quantitative and mechanical phenomenon (essence) than to the qualitative and non-mechanical? "Because of the coherence and the compelling force of the quantitative and mechanical aspects of our experience." But its qualitative and mental aspects, though less accurately determinable, are just as coherent and as compelling in their immediate self-evidence.

In place of a philosophy which, while admitting that our experience eludes on all sides our comprehension—God alone can possess the perfect philosophy—accepts frankly all the deliverances of experience, Professor Santayana has offered us an artificial scheme constructed out of three factors of disparate provenance and mutually irreconcilable.

Of these, one, epistemological scepticism, through a radical error of method, is largely neutralised by the acceptance on faith of a real objective universe. The second, mechanistic materialism, as the exclusive interpretation of concrete reality, is a dogma accepted without proof. The apparent proof offered is, as I have shown, simply the acceptance theoretically on animal faith, in fact, as we have seen, by self-evident intuition, of those data of human experience which correspond with that interpretation, while the irreconcilable data are relegated to a realm of pure essence devoid of substantial reality. And the third factor, the Platonic idealism demanded by Professor Santayana's personal temperament, is introduced by regarding this residue of essences, neither existent nor reflecting existence, as a world of ideas whose contemplation is the noblest function of the human spirit.

Not only is this denial of existence to the essences except in so far as they manifest mechanical properties, arbitrary; a further objection can be brought against it. Essence without existence is meaningless. Every essence involves some degree and kind of existence. That is to say, every object of imagination or thought must exist somehow and somewhere. The fairy-tale dragon, for example, exists both as a mental modification of those who imagine it and as a combination of forms actually present in nature. Every sensation, every imagination, every thought raises the question, not of existence, but of location. We must enquire not whether it exists; but in what order of being it exists. As regards the quantitative aspects of essence, Professor Santayana, as we have seen, accepts their existence, thus admitting by implication a partial identity between existence and essence. What, of course, he really means and at times says, is that the qualitative non-mechanical essences have no substantial existence—exist only as embodied by the passing collocations of mechanical existences. But the mechanical factors of experience are far indeed from substances—mere abstractions from substances which possess also non-mechanical properties. And if the non-mechanical qualitative essences do, in fact, cause human action—and when off his guard Professor Santayana is himself insistent that the moral and rational ideas which we contemplate should move us to improve the actual world—they must be either substances or qualities of a substance which comprises and therefore transcends them, manifestations in either case of the substantial reality to which our experience as a whole refers. Thus on examination the shadow world of non-existent essences proves intrinsically untenable, and we are led to posit, instead of Professor Santayana's artificial dualism, what I may term a higher monism which, whether we interpret it as Christians theistically or in terms of a spiritual pantheism, is inconsistent with the philosophical edifice, erected, to be sure with a deft hand, by Professor Santayana on an artificial foundation.

We may ask in conclusion why Professor Santayana in spite of his Platonism has accepted the fetters of mechanical materialism and been content to satisfy his spiritual needs by the contemplation and worship of shadows. To understand this shadow worship we must read the *Dialogues in Limbo* and the Sonnet-sequence, " 1895." The sonnets provide, I think, the psychological explanation. They tell the tale, whether literally true or only symbolic, of the poet's Platonic love—as Platonic as Dante's for Beatrice. With this he is satisfied. No return of love does he need, not even that the beloved should know of his love. His subjective love suffices. In the case of Dante this is intelligible, for he hoped for an eternal union of spirit with Beatrice in their common vision and love of God, the Substance of all that is lovable. But in Santayana, who looks for nothing save the passing and barren love, whether it be of woman or ideal essence, beautiful form, or noble conception, this satisfaction betrays a temperament strangely lacking in grip of the actual, devoid of the strong desire that wills and must will the concrete fruition of good. " The best in this kind are but shadows." If this be the last word of Shakespeare's philosophy, it is a confession of failure, and, in any case, as Professor Santayana himself notes, Shakespeare stands alone among the supreme poets of the world in his apparent lack of religion. Santayana may be content with the doom imposed by his philosophy on the human heart—the curse of the Lady of Shalott gazing all her days on the reflection in her magic mirror of realities she may never behold. Mankind cannot be content, but will rise in revolt, and, like the Lady herself, utter the protest, " I am . . . sick of shadows."

Professor Santayana's contentment with shadows—non-existent unsubstantial forms of beauty and truth—explains the arbitrary distinction he makes between the quantitative and non-quantitative data of experience. The former he accepts, for he has what he terms animal faith, in fact immediate intuition, whereby to apprehend them. But he lacks the super-animal—the human—and above that the supernatural apprehension which grasps with certainty the things of the spirit. " The animal man," the man whose faith, whose insight—is but animal, " perceiveth not the things of

the spirit, neither can he." To be sure—and here is the
perplexing feature of Professor Santayana's mentality—he
does apprehend spiritual and even distinctively religious
facts in an exterior way as phenomena. But he lacks
the intuition, or rather the central combination of intuition
and vital union, which grasps them as realities. Unhappily
this function—the sovereign function of man in whose
exercise intellect and will are blent, and in which man enjoys
immediate contact with God—is apparently wanting or
undeveloped. Santayana is content to look on the revelation
of spirit as on a painted beauty, and is not aware, does not
even desire to be aware, of a living Countenance. " My soul
is athirst for the strong, the *living* God." That profound cry
of the human soul he cannot understand. Indeed, he can
even explain away the loving communion of an Augustine
with his God as a contemplation of abstract ideas,[1] and
he misses the intensely religious experience of Socrates
and Plato. He lacks their spiritual will. For this living
experience is not only intuition but also, and indeed primarily,
union, a contact of the concrete spiritual energy of the soul,
in its fundamental volition, its radical will with the Divine
Superenergy. On this factor of will, of union by love, the
mystics have always laid stress. As his *Sonnets* (1895) suffice
to prove, Professor Santayana will not exercise this spiritual
energy, this will by which concrete vital union is effected.
Hence, in defiance of the evidence, he excludes will and action,
therefore vital union, from the sphere of spirit which he confines to pure contemplation. Nevertheless—as, for example,
against Dean Inge in his *Platonism and the Spiritual Life*—
he holds up this sterile shadow worship as the true spiritual
life, besides which the demand for actual fruition in time and
eternity of objective Truth, Beauty, and Goodness—that is
to say, of God—is an impure and materialistic self-seeking.
The lover enjoying the returned love of his bride will not

[1] *Reason and Religion.*

be inclined to think the unknown and unrequited love of the Sonnets a happier or worthier lot; still less will the religious man, and least of all the most perfect example of the religious man—the mystic—be impressed by the proposal to substitute the worship of spirit-shadows for communion with the Living God. Indeed, Professor Santayana himself feels that mystical experience is the most powerful witness against him. He is never tired of denouncing mysticism as illusion. " Mysticism is not a religion, but a religious disease." [1] It is, he explains, no perception of spirit, but the weary relapse of the tired soul into the primaeval sense of undifferentiated being with which consciousness began. [2] That this vague animal consciousness exists I do not question. It may perhaps enter into dark ecstasy of sense in which D. H. Lawrence sought the consummation of human felicity. That it is an adequate account of all and every form of mystical experience can be maintained only if we run flatly counter to the obviously truthful descriptions given by the mystics themselves, and moreover shut our eyes to the intellectual, moral, and spiritual values bound up indissolubly with their experiences. Indeed, Lawrence read into the ecstasy of animal instinct the desire and doubtless some actual experience of spiritual ecstasy above not below the plane of normal reason. Santayana's criticism of mystical experience, as of religious experience in all its forms—indeed, of all forms of qualitative and of immaterial experience—is like the criticism of solid forms by an imaginary observer whose organs of perception revealed only the dimensions of surface. Superficial in the ordinary sense, it would be ridiculous to call Professor Santayana's philosophy; superficial in a more fundamental sense it is. A superficial vision blind to spiritual solids, united with a dogmatic presupposition of the epiphenomenalist materialism fashionable when he began to philosophise, is not the founda-

---

[1] *Poetry and Religion*, 105.

[2] It is true he excepts from this condemnation the intellectual contemplations of an Augustine, but only by a misconception of their nature.

tion on which even so skilful a craftsman as Professor Santayana can build an enduring edifice. We may enjoy its tasteful decoration and beautiful furniture, and the vistas so pleasantly arranged here and there. For Professor Santayana is an expert craftsman of letters whose writing is accomplished art. In fact it may be questioned whether, since Plato, there has been such a combination of the philosopher and the artist. But we cannot take up our dwelling in a house built on foundations which cannot bear the solvent of critical thought and reared high with unsubstantial pinnacles of no stronger substance than lath and plaster mimicking more solid material. Wisdom, declared by Professor Santayana impotent to move even a finger, " hath built her a house " set fast on foundations of adamant—the total experience of the human race—and lifting proudly heavenward firm walls and battlements. There let us dwell.

PETER WUST

DIALECTICAL IDEAL REALISM

THE basis of our knowledge of physical objects is perceptions of sensible objects, immediate apprehensions or intuitions of outer form in and through sense data. From these the intellect abstracts their quantitative aspects and with them builds up the edifice of physical science, which, though in its own sphere of reference true to the reality it professes to represent, ends, as Professor Eddington and others have pointed out, with abstract mathematical equations. This method we may call the analytic method. For it analyses quantities.

Mental forms or ideas and among them the inner forms, the ideas, behind external forms are apprehended by the intuition of a mental object, as its counterpart sense perception is an intuition of a physical object. From these intuitions the structure of metaphysics is built up. The method of metaphysical enquiry is the method which contemplates a mental fact, an idea until its significance is intuitively apprehended. We may therefore term it the contemplative method. Nevertheless, the enormous advance of empirical science, and the rationalist mentality which has accompanied it, have led to the belief that the sole method by which valid objective knowledge can be obtained is that employed by the physical sciences. Metaphysics has been either rejected as empty verbiage, or distorted into a positivist " analysis " which apes the analysis proper to quantitative science and explains away its specific object. This analysis instead of accepting the ideal datum as a whole and in its distinctive quality as such seeks to explain it by analysing it into the factors which condition its appearance. For example the distinctive form of an aesthetic style is explained by an analysis of the economic and social conditions under which it arose or the technical processes employed. A metaphysical system is similarly explained by economic and social or by psycho-physical conditions concomitant, or alleged to be concomitant, upon its formulation. And a religious intuition is explained by the psycho-physical condition and antecedents of its subject. It is as though it were sought to explain the distinctive nature and properties of water by its analysis into its component gases. And the objective is always to explain spiritual forms and the realities they determine by the abstract quantitative forms with which the physical sciences are exclusively concerned.

A reaction, however, has begun against this exclusive analysis which " murders to dissect," and among its leaders the German Catholic philosopher, Peter Wust, has merited a high place. Hitherto he is known chiefly by two works, *Naivität und Pietät* (Naivety and Piety) and *Die Dialektik des Geistes* (Dialectic of Spirit or Mind.)[1] Since the former will, I hope, become accessible in English, and moreover is in many respects a preliminary and partial treatment of the ground covered in the later and larger work, I propose to confine this essay to a study of the *Dialektik*.

Professor Wust approaches his subject by what I have called the contemplative, he terms the speculative, method. " In our opinion," he writes, " it is the distinctive method of philosophy. Perhaps an analogy may help us to understand it. It is akin to the method of the archaeologist who from the study of a few fragments does not piece together a picture of the whole, but, certainly not without hard labour, sees it so clearly that he is able to make others see it " (*D.G.*, 73). This is not explanation by dissolving the object to be explained into the factors which it has integrated into a

---

[1] Like the French *esprit*, *Geist* is partially coincident with both these English terms—denoting both the " spiritual " and the " intellectual " aspects of man's higher psychical activity.

distinctive and novel reality, but the conveyance of a vivid intuition of that object in its distinctive quality.

This method Wust applies primarily to the fact of the human spirit.[1] The nucleus of his metaphysics is a metaphysical " anthropology "—if you prefer, a metaphysical psychology, which, however, is found to involve a metaphysical cosmology, biology and sociology, and above all a theology. Indeed, as we shall see, the theology is rather a concomitant than a consequent of the anthropology. " Philosophy," writes Wust, " may be compared to an ellipse with two foci, in which from one point of view everything depends on speculative theology, in the other on speculative anthropology." Nevertheless, as he proceeds to point out, since man is nearest to man from the point of view of knowledge, and also, as we shall see, the metaphysical centre of known reality, the metaphysical microcosm ; metaphysical anthropology *i.e.*, the study of the human spirit is, strictly speaking, the centre of metaphysics.

Wust has divided his work into three books. The first deals generally with nature and spirit laying the metaphysical foundation of his edifice. The second is concerned with the " Fundamental Essence of the Human Personality "—a metaphysical psychology of the higher functions. The third book, passing from the individual human spirit to the society, deals with the " Phenomenon of the Collective Movement of the Spirit in Human History."

Wust begins by applying his speculative or contemplative method to four fundamental concepts : *nonentity*, or sheer *nothingness ; entity* or *something ; chaos ;* and *order.* The contemplation of sheer nothingness as a possibility leads to the perception that the existence of anything at all requires an absolute being—which alone could overcome utter nonentity. " The least minimum of being involves a will to posit

---

[1] I shall use the term " spirit " in the wider sense of the German *Geist* and French *esprit.*

being : the first origin of a positive production signifies in the
contest between nothingness and being the complete defeat
of the former." Hence " the most insignificant being reveals
a wholly mysterious primordial will to production, which is
thus the first and most profound of all ontological mysteries "
(*D.G.*, 38). This " absolute positivity " must " be absolutely
concrete and eternal." It is an absolute energy. But this
energy must also be order. A study of a supposed " sheer
chaos " displays its intrinsic contradiction. Being, energy,
and order are correlative. This strict correlation of form and
energy is indeed a fundamental principle of metaphysics,
reconciling, as Wust shows in a later passage, the philosophies
of action and flux with the philosophies of duration and
objective intelligible form. In creatures the energy whether
material or volitional is determined by the order, the form
which actualises a potential energy, its matter.[1] And " in the
absolute being of pure reality form as the absolute order must
be identical with the aspect of prime energy " [2] (*D.G.*, 45).
" There must be a reality which is absolutely concrete and
in which the primary dynamic of being is united with the
primary order of being to constitute the most perfect concrete
form " (*D.G.*, 47).

But is this absolute Energy-Form personal or impersonal ?
To answer this the speculative method must be applied to
" spirit " as manifest in man. We must discover what is the
distinctive quality which distinguishes the human spirit from
the impersonal life or being below it. Primarily the presence
of intellectual " distinction " and the power of volitional
choice. The appearance on the scene of the human spirit
is the appearance of an intellectual will, the intellect represent-

[1] In my explanation of Wust I have inevitably stated what I understand to be
his meaning in terms of my own thought—thus making explicit what is implicit
in his own statement.

[2] On the higher planes of being the form is so perfectly unified that strictly it
can no longer be called an order but is rather the principle of the order produced
by its presence and action. In the wider sense however it is the most perfect order,
being the internal integration of the entire order it implies and produces.

ing the formal aspect of being, the will its dynamic. We have thus reached the notion of a *personal self* distinguished by its power of rational choice from all below it, as " an absolutely new domain of reality." But the existence of this relatively independent personality—as we see it in man—implies an absolute personality whose knowledge and will are not dependent upon anything outside Himself and that personality is in turn identical with the absolute being and energy which we have already found ourselves compelled to postulate.

This proof of theism, by applying the speculative method first to " being " in general, then to the distinctive phenomenon of human spirit, is, as Wust himself points out, a special application of the traditional proof from the graduated perfections of being—*perfectiones entis*—the fourth of the five Thomist proofs.[1]

Wust shews that man, standing as he does on the frontier between impersonal nature, where every operation is predetermined and rigid law prevails, and the domain of free intellectual activity, is the metaphysical centre of reality and mirrors every level and form of being from inanimate matter to God. And although I cannot agree with the exclusion, which he seems to imply, of the possibility of rational animals elsewhere in the universe, I can at least agree that man is the centre and focal mirror of all *known* reality. In so far a theological anthropomorphism is justified. " Simply in virtue of his nature man is the highest of all conceivable theomorphic productions, the noblest copy of the primary Divine Form, and therefore the exemplar and centre of all beings and forms, the mirror of all forms in the universe, in whom meet all the lines specifically relating nature with spirit." Thus from the relative independence, or aseity, of man we conclude the absolute independence of God, from his relative unity as one

[1] These metaphysical proofs of theism are applications of the speculative or contemplative method. A particular characteristic of created being, a particular metaphysical form which it displays, for example contingency is scrutinised and seen to imply an Absolute and Uncreated Being as its source. Contingent Being for instance is seen to imply Necessary Being.

person, God's absolute Unity. Man's personality shows that any notion of God as somehow an impersonal substance, even of a spiritual nature, as, for example, an impersonal idea or consciousness, must be rejected. And his relative creativeness points to the absolute creativeness of God, undetermined by anything outside Himself and therefore creating from nothing.

Reality is now seen to fall roughly into three levels: impersonal or unspiritual nature, the relative spirit of man,[1] God the absolute Spirit. They constitute a ladder of increasing reality which passes from the negative pole of pure nonentity to the positive pole of God's Absolute Being. As we mount the ladder, form or order and energy manifest themselves more perfectly. For, as we have seen, form and energy are correlative with each other and with positive being. Content to describe the differentiating qualities of these distinctive orders of being, Wust never, so far as I know, grapples with the fundamental relation of the material to the spiritual. There are gaps in his statement which his interpreter must fill, yet is afraid of filling incorrectly. It seems impossible to regard matter as possessed of any positive quality not present formally or eminently in spirit. In mathematical formulation, matter is spirit minus. Does Wust hold this view, which would reduce the difference between spirit and matter to a difference of degree in the scale between non-being and Being? I do not know. That he regards " first matter " as an " energy-substrate " analogous to the " energy-substrate " of volition, and everywhere finds in non-spiritual nature reflections and analogies of spiritual phenomena, points in this direction. On the other hand, had he held this view explicitly he would perhaps have recognised more adequately than he has put the element of evil and therefore " disorder " within the sphere of impersonal nature—the inevitable effect of its intrinsic

---

[1] Though Wust, far from rejecting the existence of created discarnate spirits, good and evil, finds their operation, at least indicated in the history of mankind, he leaves them out of account here as neither accessible to direct observation, nor like the existence of God, capable of proof.

privation of being. And if he had clearly seen that the qualitative difference between matter and spirit, however unbridgeable by development from below, is ultimately one of ontological degree, he might have been more ready to recognise the intermediate position of the animal—below the spiritual person, but *above the pure object.* He seems to me to exaggerate the orderliness of impersonal nature and to minimise the intelligence and volition of, at least, the higher animals. Both indeed are questions of emphasis; and as regards the former Wust is the first to insist that the order of nature is an externally controlled anarchy, in which the blind impulse of the individual to unrestricted self-assertion is subordinated by the inherent law of its nature to the order of the whole. But is the order of nature as a whole perfectly satisfying to reason? Is the anarchy totally subordinated to order? Or, owing to the low degree of being possessed by matter, is the subordination only partial, merely sufficient to prevent the chaos which, as Wust has shown, would be the equivalent of nonentity and to allow of the appearance and development of human spirits? Is not this lower world after all what Lossky has termed a kingdom of enmity? In his battle against the absolute pessimism into which so many modern thinkers have been led by a one-sided rationalism and its consequent lack of religious faith Wust has, I think, over-emphasised the order and rationality of the infra-human world.

Hitherto he has sketched the first outlines of his picture : God, the absolute Spirit, Person and Creator; Man, the relative spirit, person and creator; infra-human Nature, an impersonal createdness. He will now study in greater detail the central of these three realities. To man God is chiefly known in and through man, and nature possesses significance only as known and interpreted by the human spirit. Thus, as we have seen, a metaphysical " anthropology "—" speculative anthropology," is Wust's term—constitutes the centre of metaphysics. And this in turn will be sub-divided into individual and social "anthropology." First of all we must study by the contemplative or speculative method (whichever you prefer to call it) the spiritual and, that is, of course, the distinctively human aspects of man, man as a relative spirit.

This study is the more necessary because the decay of metaphysics has led to the denial of man's profound spirituality, and his reduction to the purely vital level as an animal provided with a rational instrument to subserve his vital self-maintenance. But man has, in fact, a dual nature. If in part he shares the vital sub-personal life of the animals, he rises above it as a centre of intellectual action. With the vital impulse of the animal he unites a spiritual will, and if, like animals, he perceives the outer forms of things, by thought he is able to penetrate beyond these external forms to that inner form of which the outer is but the physical and superficial expression. By abstracting the universal from the particular he can distinguish between "the sensible form" and "the supersensible idea."[1] "For every form points inwards, inasmuch as that which is extended in space and time rests upon its own inner content invisible to us." In man, indeed, perception of sensible form and intellectual apprehension of ideas are always combined.[2]

Every form of expression, whether concept, word, work of art, tool, social organisation, or culture, is "a significant product," the "focusing of significance at one point." A single intellectual act abstracts from the concrete reality certain significant aspects, and simultaneously recombines them in a novel fashion. "At one and the same moment the old form is thus released from its concrete bondage and a new form created. The form is divorced from its foundation

[1] For a further distinction between the concrete universal or idea and the abstract universal, see my *Theism, Atheism and Agnosticism*.

[2] I should except from this rule the direct intuition of God and the soul, though even here sense perception is a necessary occasion and a more or less immediate concomitant.

in objective reality and moulded into a representative form in a new ideal kingdom, the world of significant form which man the body-spirit places between himself and nature, between subject and object." The new form thus created, whether purely mental, like the concept, or embodied in some external shape, the "schema," to use Wust's term, is a characteristically human product.

The schema is a "concept in physical form, a medium between the spheres of sense and spirit " (*D.G.*, 160). Gradually from the rudest sign the entire world of human expression develops. Always inadequate to the objective reality, it invites unending improvement—the never ceasing progress of human culture. Man is thus essentially the artist, and his art significant form, which, however, is also representative. And it is only by man's interpretative art that the forms implanted in nature by God realise their content. "The moment a single form has been released by a being that can understand meaning and produce significant form, life and movement enter into the entire multitude of these forms implanted in nature. . . . Offspring of the primary Spirit, all forms of being desire to return to spirit. Products of that Spirit, they would be recognised and understood by spirit as children of spirit." And man, as Nature's artist-priest, must, by his interpretation and reproduction, make all her forms appear in their inward beauty and power to offer homage to his and their God. "The form will thus be glorified in the halls of science, will blaze forth in the temple of art and stand before God as a symbol in the sanctuary of religion " (*D.G.*, 166).

Wust proceeds to argue against those who see in man's reason only the tool of a purely vital purpose. How then, he asks, could it have arisen, and what benefit has it brought to compensate for the loss of sound animal instinct ? A healthy beast is better fitted to obtain a purely vital goal than reasoning man, who must painfully grope his way—whither ?

Moreover, man has actually attained a supervital zone, a sphere of spiritual-intellectual values. His arts and crafts are more than simply utilitarian. They reveal a delight in the contemplation and reproduction of significant form for its own sake. " This un-utilitarian delight in the quality of things, in form as such, a love of pure contemplation disinterested of vital aims, is the feature which primarily makes man human and distinguishes him from the animal " (D.G., 178). Moreover, human love transcends vital selfishness. Wust is indeed mistaken when he identifies " attraction " as opposed to " unselfish giving " with vital as opposed to spiritual love. The highest love of all, the love of God, is not only a devoted self-donation to Him, nor even exclusively an adoring contemplation of Him as transcendent and utterly other than ourselves—it is also a passionate desire for union with Him, a supervital desire far more intense and more passionate than any vital desire for union with a fellow creature. But this qualification does not affect the self-evident difference between spiritual and vital love, and its proof that man's goal cannot, like the animal's, be found in the merely vital order. Moreover, Wust proceeds, a spiritual love is operative from the first in human nature, impelling him inward and forward to the spiritual and eternal. " Already in the root of the self vital lust is transformed by a different principle into a restless craving of a *higher order*. Nor does human nature hunger and thirst simply for physical food. Far stronger is its hunger and thirst for the eternal. Of its very nature it hungers and thirsts for truth, beauty, goodness, and holiness (D.G., 186).[1]

But whereas natural law, as we have seen, subordinates individual impulse to the universal order, man's will is free to assert itself against that order as it manifests itself through the spiritual impulse of cosmic and transcendental love.

---

[1] This passage surely is incompatible with the confinement of " attraction " to " vital love."

L

Objectively man cannot resist the universal order which will assert itself against him; but subjectively he may, thereby exchanging the interior harmony with which he began for an inner disharmony between self-will and the radical impulse and need of his nature, " the desire for light and love " that arises from the depths of his being.

But before it can provoke this disharmony, the self must awake from the state of mere potentiality with which it begins. Its first awakening is expressed by the dual phenomenon of *wonder* and *reverence*. In this emotion the self first begins consciously " to see " and " will "—awakening " from the deep slumber of unconsciousness to the first faint dawn of consciousness." Still unreflecting and inevitable like the operation of a natural force, it is in fact the activity of a spiritual self. For Wust this decisive moment in the soul's history, when it awakens to enter upon the long and dangerous journey of conscious rational life, is symbolised in Michelangelo's Sistine fresco of the creation of Adam. In this wonder and reverence, philosophy and religion have their root. Not, as Descartes maintained, by a doubt of reality, but by a wondering and reverent acceptance of it does man begin to philosophise, where also he begins to worship. And the positivism which vaunts a cold scientific disinterestedness is radically vitiated because it starts by denying or doubting the positive value of the reality which, because it is given from the outset, philosophy must accept and interpret.

But however psychology may reveal a tension between the impersonal forces in the soul, the vital force below and the spiritual love-energy above, and the self-conscious reasoning self placed thus between both, the spirit is essentially one. It manifests its unity in memory, which, whatever the mechanism of its activity, represents in its objective content the fundamental duration of the self transcending the superficial flux of time, the " noumenal," as opposed to the " phenomenal," man. Memory thus displays the formal and durational aspect of man's being, which corresponds to the durational and formal aspect of God, who is thus in a sense the "absolute world memory." But whereas in God the durational and formal aspect is identical with the active and dynamic, in man they are distinct, if inseparable. And if objective memory, the entire content of intellectual cognition, never adequately represented by the intermittent flashes of subjective memory, witnesses to our self-identity as a being of such and such a nature, the "ethical memory" of conscience witnesses to our self-identity as a being whose will is or is not in harmony with the universal order. Conscience thus watches over the ethical integrity of the self as a volitional unit in the universal order of wills, revealing and rebuking any breaches of that order produced by the inharmonious self-assertion of the free rational will. "Thus memory and conscience not only make us aware *subjectively* in all our mental acts of the essential identity of the self, they *objectively* constitute that identity in the depth of the personal centre, and throughout the process of its temporal development guarantee and maintain it ontologically and ethically" (*D.G.*, 249).

At the beginning we saw that the data on which the reason works are twofold, material facts apprehended by the mind through the senses by the intuition of outer form, and immaterial facts apprehended by the intellect in its intuition of inner form, of ideas. This distinction corresponds, on the whole, to the two faculties which Wust now distinguishes as *Sinnlichkeit* and *Vernunft*. By the former, sense perception, man perceives the exterior form; by the latter, intellect, the interior idea. Both, however, co-operate in every act of human knowledge. The animal, on the contrary, only perceives those outer aspects of things which are of value for its vital purposes. Wust argues at length that the activity of *Vernunft* implies an illumination which is a divine gift to the soul and operation in it, and that it is thus the subject of "an epistemological mysticism." The "metaphysical ground of the soul is the portal through which God exercises a peculiar and mysterious operation in the depths of our spirit " (*D.G.*, 270). But the spirit is never a merely passive recipient of that operation any more than its part in sensation is merely passive. So far I am in entire agreement. On the other hand it will be clear from what I have already said that I think Wust is mistaken when he confines the intuition of *Vernunft*, as apparently he does, to the " primary intellectual principles," the "*prima principia intelligibilia*," and more seriously when he denies, as he does elsewhere in this book, the possibility of a direct contact, above the ordinary operation of *Vernunft*, between the soul and God, a contact to which the mystics bear such abundant witness.

Between the perception of sensible form and the ideal intuition of *Vernunft* mediates the discursive reason, *Verstand*. From the senses and the outer forms apprehended in and through their data and from the vital life to which they belong man receives knowledge of the physical world; from the intuitions of *Vernunft* and from the metaphysical-spiritual life to which they belong he receives knowledge of intellectual and spiritual ideas and values. To relate these data and at the same time to analyse and set in order the obscurity and confusion of their original apprehension is the function of the discursive reason. From the particular forms given in perception it abstracts the universal, and it clarifies the apprehensions of *Vernunft*.

In the last analysis, and this Wust does not, I think, perceive, the *Verstand*, the discursive reason, is not a function opposed to intuition but a particular type of the latter. It is the intuition of clear abstract forms, in particular those of a mathematical and quantitative kind, and as such is the function which discriminates clear and abstract aspects implicitly contained in the integral and concrete but obscure intuitions of sense perception and *Vernunft*. To it is due, when applied to the data of perception or *Vernunft*, the creation of those forms of expression of which we have already spoken. Here Wust points out the essential inadequacy of its abstractive concepts to the data from which they were taken and the constant and endless necessity to correct and supplement them. They are never, however, wholly false to the reality—as the sceptic alleges—being necessarily founded upon its self-manifestation. In relation to the data of *Vernunft* the *Verstand* exercises a control—a " police function." " The intuitive disposition lights up as it were with an enormous flashlight the landscape to be explored, and it is the function of those dispositions in which the *Verstand* dominates to investigate by laborious work of detail the field thus illuminated by the ideas apprehended by the *Vernunft*" (*D.G.*, 603). The temperament in which *Vernunft* predominates operates by flashes, misses detail, and is liable to be carried away by its emotions in ethical or intellectual unrestraint. Without the control of the *Verstand* the spirit would be overwhelmed by the obscure data presented by the intuitive intellect, " a stream from the infinite depth " of spirit. It would be carried away blindly by an intoxication of vague ideas unrelated and uncriticised. Or it would accept some particular idea as the entire and absolute truth. Blake's later development bears witness to the necessity of this rational control—as indeed do the host of fanatical and unbalanced religious enthusiasts whose vagaries have done so much to bring religion itself into discredit.

After these distinctions Wust finds it necessary to reaffirm that personal unity of the soul, already witnessed, as we have seen, by memory and conscience. He shows how every faculty presupposes and is conditioned by the others, and that every act of human sense-perception, not to mention any more spiritual activity, implies the identity of the perceiving subject—a memory of his past, and a will, or at least an urge, to truth. Moreover, the tendency to specialisation manifested in turn by any particular faculty is compensated by a counter-tendency to restore the equilibrium and harmony of the entire soul, a law of differentiation and reintegration which Wust will later find decisive for the social history of mankind. And the human spirit is endowed in principle with a universal determinability to any direction of its powers and the operation of any faculty, a determinability which the one-sided specialisation inevitably produced by inheritance, education and environment cannot totally destroy.

Wust now discusses the will, " that enigmatic substratum of our ego and intellect." He refutes the identification of will with sheer power, since " its inner essence is spirit, order, measure, intellect; in a word freedom " (*D.G.*, 329). Here, indeed, there is a certain laxity of expression. If the will is the substratum of the intellect, intellect cannot be its essence. But his meaning is clear and correct enough. Unformed will, which in the pure state cannot exist, being a merely potential energy, is the substratum, the matter of the intellectual form which constitutes the essence of the will as formed. The identification of unformed and potential energy with metaphysical matter—of order with form, in spiritual being the conscious order of reason and objective memory, is here as elsewhere implicit in Wust's philosophy, though never explicitly worked out. In God, as we have seen, absolute order and energy coincide. Therefore He is the pure will which, because perfectly actualised, is perfectly free. In man, because the form of the known object is never adequate to the ultimate Object to which his volition is directed in the obscure impulse of spiritual love proceeding from the depth of his being, the conscious will is free with a preliminary freedom to accept or reject the Good to which that impulse tends. If it accepts, it will finally attain the freedom of inevitable adherence to that Good—the *beata necessitas boni* which reflects the freedom of God and is the creature's perfect freedom. Incidentally Wust disproves the thesis that man's final freedom, and, *a fortiori*, the Divine Freedom, involves a possibility of evil choice. This, he shows, is excluded by the will's absolute adherence to the Good, and in God by its perfect identification with the Good. Meanwhile the human will as created must reckon with exterior forces acting upon it. These are three : Fatality, God and Good Spirits, Evil Spirits. Fatality is represented by man's environment, also by the effects of past choice. An extreme tension may be set up between an external situation demanding the exercise of some undeveloped faculty, whereas the individual has developed another. Yet such is the power of the will that it can in principle rise to the occasion and develop triumphantly the faculty which the situation demands. The irrationality, however, presented by the disharmony between will and environment exceeds our limited knowledge to comprehend. The mysterious power of wickedness operative in the evil spirits entices man's will to assert its autonomy against the urge and order of cosmic love. It might be argued that " the serious metaphysical reality of wickedness, as a real kingdom of spirits inspired by hate," is not provable by philosophy, but is a theological belief only. Wust would reply that philosophy discovers in its contemplation of the depths of human evil the phenomenon which he calls " the awful mystery of iniquity."

The interplay of these forces within and without the human spirit sets up in it an oscillation, an interior dialectic, which from the individual extends to society and becomes the endless oscillation and dialectic of human history. Within the individual and the society alike the centre of gravity, the emphasis, shifts constantly from one faculty to another, with a corresponding attention first to one, then to another aspect of external reality. And always the totality of the one person within, of the universe without, tends to restore the balance by counter-specialisation and reaction to the opposite extreme. Moreover, the one-sided and inadequate concepts and symbols created by each of these specialisations of faculty and insight press, as we have seen, by their very inadequacy and limitation to be completed and balanced by supplementary concepts and symbols. And through all this web of action and reaction runs the warp of the fundamental dialectic of individual and social man—the self-assertion of a rational will formed by the clear intellections of abstract reason, representing and expressing the conscious ego, but only to identify itself with the lower vital urge within the soul, and to be finally repressed by the triumphant return of that spiritual urge of cosmic love which objectively can never be resisted because it is one with the order of God and His universe. Yet the assertion of the rational will was not in itself evil. It was inevitable if the vital instinct with its sense perception was to be subdued by the rational spirit, and the spiritual instinct with its obscure intuition be transmuted into the possession and act of the self-conscious and rational self. Only its revolt against that which it should accept and make its own is evil, the insolent pride of a self-willed rationalism. How far in view of the necessary onesidedness and "jerkiness" of human development this divorce and revolt are an inevitable aspect of human self-realisation is indeed a question which, in my opinion, Wust has nowhere satisfactorily answered. He might, perhaps, agree that it is mysteriously both inevitable and guilty. Given human liability to sin, Fr. Joseph Rickaby has taught us, if Adam had not sinned, his posterity certainly would. Yet Adam was guilty. And Wust himself points out that, owing to the necessary intermixture in human acts of value and worthlessness, " every positive production involves the simultaneous production of a negative effect which checks the operation of the positive " (*D.G.*, 437). Along these lines I should look for the solution Wust never explicitly gives us.

But the objective order of love finally makes the evil, the revolt, the instrument of good. It affirms itself through the very denial. *O felix culpa—O certe necessarium Adae peccatum!* Rationalism prepares and purifies with the *Verstand* the categories by which the data of *Vernunft* are necessarily mediated. The Sophists are precursors of Plato—the self-assertion of Caesar and his Empire prepares the way for Christ and the Church.

So impressed was Hegel by this dialectic, the thesis, anti-thesis, and synthesis of human history, that he extended it to reality as a whole. Wust, however, maintains that in the lower sphere of impersonal nature we find only its shadow. For the forces of nature are always rigidly bound by their intrinsic laws. And in God the dialectic is at rest in the perfect and simultaneous actuation of all the possibilities of being. While agreeing with Wust that the dialectic can have no application to Absolute Being, I regard it as the law of development in the subhuman, equally with the human order. Though free will can play no part here, the intrinsic deficiency of matter, the metaphysical subject of form, involves a successive embodiment of complementary and contrasted forms through which a synthesis of the contrasting forms is finally achieved. The same deficiency of matter which necessitates this dialectic, however, prevents its complete and perfectly logical realisation as also do the conflicting forces which cut across and deflect any particular dialectical development—a conflict itself due in the last resort to the deficiency of matter.

This study of the individual human spirit and its dialectic has thus laid the foundation for the study of that historical dialectic of collective humanity which occupies the concluding half of Wust's treatise. It has indeed brought us to its very threshold. Wust begins by discussing the solidarity of mankind as the subject of this historical process. As a preliminary he rejects the Averroistic thesis, which in one form or another exaggerates this solidarity into a universal spirit of which the individual is but an organ. Such a doctrine contradicts the personal character of individual spirit, which has already been established. " Individual personality alone is the true integer of history, the atom of all historical reality " (*D.G.*, 403). Every individual is at once a " closed " and an " open

unit." The transcendent Divine Unity of an infinite Multiplicity is revealed, reflected and approached by " the co-
essence and co-operation " of " all finite spirits existing and
working in mutual interrelation in the solidarity of a ' universal
Kingdom.' " The centre of this universe of spirits is God
Himself in His absolute unity, fullness, and rest. For the
" total community of spirits constitutes a *corpus mysticum*, of
which the primary Divine Will is the absolute centre of
activity " (*D.G.*, 429–30).

But this total solidarity of mankind is built up of subordinate groups bound together by various factors and in
various ways. The fundamental principle of these groupings
which " articulate " the structure of human history is the
" field of action." Every act produces a positive form, as
such claiming universal and final validity, and in so far
uniting those who accept it. But that form also possesses
its negative limited and temporal aspect which invites rejection. Thus " every personal work, as it affects the environment in virtue of its finite-infinite and temporal-supertemporal
character, proves at once a factor of separation and union "
(*D.G.*, 440–1). The effect of this joint separation and union
is a circumscribed " field of action "—larger or smaller
according to the positive value of the act, also no doubt to
its accessibility by others. Geographical situation, temporal
situation, blood relationship, and in and through these the
power of the spirit to create and demarcate form, are the
fundamental factors which articulate the solidarity of mankind. Wust points out the radical significance of sex. Man
more correctly, I think, masculinity, since both psychological
factors are present in either sex and differ simply in their
proportion, represents the abstract thought and rational activity
of self-conscious spirit with its tendency to revolt ; woman,
or rather femininity, the instinctive natural energy, vital and
spiritual, whose organs are sense perception and concrete
spiritual intuition and which conserves the forms impressed by

the rational activity of the conscious mind. Hence anarchy is avoided by the return of man from the perilous adventure of his rationalising self-will to the conservativism of woman hallowing sound tradition, "the abiding and the constant."

The solidarity of human spirits, the *nexus animarum*, is effected by three media. The first of these is that world of "expression" already discussed, which by outer forms—language, gesture, work of art, institution—communicates "significance," the "inner form or idea," to individuals, groups and generations. This is the *commercium spirituale* of human intercourse. The formal permanence of the expression guarantees mankind against the anarchy of sheer change, while its inadequacy secures it against stagnation. Here also we find that beneficial co-operation of motion and rest, stability and flux, form and energy, which belongs to the very essence of created being and reflects the absolute unity of both factors in God. The expression is an "objective spirit" in itself dead, but as the product of living spirit revivified by the contact and interpretation of living spirits, whose inner form is in turn modified by this "spiritual wedlock" with the form laid down by spirits of the past. For the old form never simply revives, the old is never merely reproduced. Every individual spirit possesses its distinctive style, the expression of its personal character—its "formal predestination" Wust calls it—and a distinctive style belongs by extension to every group and period even when it reproduces the past.

But this *commercium spirituale* is not the sole medium of human solidarity. Indeed, it cannot be, since man is not merely intellect. As an embodied spirit he is physically related to his fellows acting within and acted upon by the same physical environment. This is the *motio physica* which erects the outer framework of human history. He is also a will interacting with other wills. This volitional interaction constitutes the *motio metaphysica* which is the interior motive force of history. The universal drama of human history, therefore, like the artificial drama which reflects it, consists in the interplay of these three factors, each apt to attract the one-sided attention of individual spectators : the *motio physica* of the material scene and movement, the *commercium spirituale* of expressed and interchanged ideas, the *motio metaphysica* of conflicting or co-operating wills. Thus the realists who see history as the interplay of physical and vital factors, and the idealists who see in it the predominance of spiritual ideals—the advocates respectively of power and love as the key to human history—are both partially right. " Throughout history the great adventurers of power and the great adventurers of love succeed each other in turn, and by their one-sided activities keep the mutual interplay going " (*D.G.*, 530). Moreover, as is shown in a later passage, a pure realism and a pure idealism are alike impossible, for the realist claims the ideal sanction of truth, the idealist seeks to embody his ideal in real life. But the goal is a spiritual kingdom of love.

Wust now discusses the differences of temperament, slow and quick, narrow or wide in their range of interest, and the differences of type produced by professional specialisation, as further determinants of human grouping. And he takes occasion to show how original width, originality, and freshness inevitably become canalised, overcrusted, and withered as specialised routine and the imitation and interpretation of past achievement accumulate their pressure, until finally the forces of a humanity bound by its very nature to safeguard its own integrity burst forth from the depths and shatter the prison walls thus erected. Other differences arise from the preponderance of one or another of the forces and faculties which we have observed in the soul. Thus arises the opposition between the realist, whose centre of gravity lies in the vital and animal instinct, and the idealist, for whom it lies in the higher spiritual love. There is the antithesis between power or energy and form as each predominates in the disposition of an individual or group—each pole, however, requiring the other and tending therefore to pass into its opposite. There is the predominantly subjective and the predominantly objective temper, also manifest in particular societies or epochs. There is the contrast between the active and the contemplative nature; also the kindred contrast between the reasoners of *Verstand*, who seek to reduce everything to the clear categories of discursive reason, or, as I should term it, clear and abstract intuition, and the intuitionists of *Vernunft*, who despise the detailed analyses of ratiocination and have eyes only for the forms dimly visible by obscure but concrete intuition through and beyond the detail. And this in turn leads to the contrast between the rationalist, the " gnostic," Wust calls him, and the believer. Temperamentally these two opponents represent respectively the abstract reasoner and the concrete intuitionist; but the difference of temperament has issued in an attitude towards the universe, on the one hand of a critical scepticism which will accept only what can be demonstrated by abstract reasoning, by which in the last resort, it must be added, is meant the apprehension and manipulation of quantitative relations and what is deducible from these ; on the other, of a trusting acceptance of mysteries beyond conceptual explanation but guaranteed by their appropriate evidence. The rationalist deifies the human reason as the function that abstracts and handles distinct concepts abstracted from sense-perception and regards these concepts as the sole truth accessible to man, if not indeed the absolute truth. His counterpart, the fideist, having proved their inadequacy, rejects them as wholly untrustworthy, despairs of knowledge, and seeks refuge in a blind faith which affirms a Deity conceived as totally unintelligible.

These, then, are the factors which determine the never-ending dialectic of human history. But the historical process is not, therefore, as the historicist sees it, a chaos of conflicting values and forces without objective and abiding significance or fixed goal, in which every estimate can be but relative, and an historical personality or phenomenon can be judged solely by its adaptation to the situation in which it occurs. Human nature on the one hand, God on the other, set the poles and standards of the historical movement. Every one-sided development must be judged and corrected by reference to the " mean," the golden mean of human nature in its integrity. And above human history, as its invisible and transcendent goal is God, in whom the infinity of differences observable in creation are united in a perfect unity, and the values which appear successively in the flow of time coexist in an eternal present. The progress of man is from " animality," in which his vital nature predominates, to " sacrality," in which that higher spiritual nature which directs him to the Divine Eternity has become the realised understanding and possession of a society whose members coexist and co-operate in God. The intrinsic laws of God, of impersonal nature, of human nature itself, set bounds to every subjective revolt and excess. Movement pushed to its utmost in one direction is automatically compensated by a movement in the opposite direction, as the mechanism of a clock makes the pendulum swing back. That human mean of which we have spoken is the centre and regulator of the movement. And the worst excesses of evil reveal most clearly the majesty of Good. The *mysterium iniquitatis*, as it appears throughout the course of history, is the abiding manifestation of God on the Sinai of His objectively inviolable law. And the end of all is an ἀποκατάστασις παντῶν, a restoration of all things, in which every spirit by free obedience of love or enforced submission to an omnipotent law subserves the order of God's Kingdom.

Is there, then, a progress observable in history? There is certainly no rectilinear progress such as was taught by the optimism of eighteenth- and nineteenth-century " enlightenment." The sole rectilinear progress consists in the constant increase of souls, each a unique mirror of the Divine and an additional member of the human solidarity, and in the accumulation of positive human achievements, of " objective spirit." Otherwise there is decadence as well as progress. The line of development, when a certain measure of explicit sacrality has been reached by a culture which consciously expresses a spiritual faith, turns backward, as that faith is undermined by the excessive pride of a self-willed rationalism, towards the animality from which it began. Here, however, I feel that Wust has left his work incomplete. If the goal of human history is indeed this process from animality to sacrality, this establishment of a kingdom of spirits consciously realising the spiritual possibilities of human nature, or, as Dante put it in his *De Monarchia*, " the actualization of the whole capacity of the intellect," the backward swing of the pendulum cannot simply take us to the original starting-point. That is to say, the metaphor of the pendulum is not altogether accurate. The movement of humanity is rather a succession of *ascending* spirals in which each revolution is above the former. Even the scheme of pre-human evolution seems to have displayed this spiral pattern. Indeed, the conjunction of the pendulum swing, which Wust has described so well, from the naivety of the primitive child of nature to the self-conscious civilised man and backward to the disintegrated post-rationalist of the decadence, with the rectilinear advance of accumulated experience must produce a spiral movement of this kind. For the individual, Wust finds the mean in his nature as dimly expressed by his dispositional capacity (*D.G.*, 682)— the ideal of what he could be. Therefore the regulative mean of humanity must be the ideal of which mankind is capable —a point, that is to say, above the swinging pendulum of action and reaction. But if the regulative mean of ideal humanity is thus *above* the dialectic movement, that movement must on the whole be in an upward direction. And actually such a spiral is discernible in recorded history. Wust would admit that the sacred culture of Christendom, destroyed by the rationalism of the Enlightenment, was superior to the sacred culture of Greece undermined by the rationalism of the Sophists. And further, if that sceptical movement of antiquity can be shown to have contributed unintentionally to the higher and purer sacred culture of Christendom, we have every reason to expect the same positive result from its modern successor. I am therefore unable to accept as finally true Wust's picture of human history as a sea tossing everlastingly between the shores set by God, humanity, and nature. It is indeed inconsistent with his own doctrine of compensation and the final " restitution of all things." I would replace it by the images of a tide which, despite the ebb of every advancing wave, is slowly advancing, or a river which for all its meanderings gradually approaches the sea. The element of irrationality undoubtedly present in the order of natural forces as the result of its defective being, the fact of free will, the inherent limitations of human wisdom and knowledge, in particular the limitations set by physical obstacles, diseases and disasters, combine to make the progress of history extremely slow and its course so complicated that even the spiral progress can only be very dimly descried and at a very long range. But it exists nevertheless. And the counterplay of the two ultimate metaphysical factors—duration and movement, as represented in man, the former by his vital and spiritual natures with their subjective expressions, sense perception and concrete spiritual intuition, the latter by his self-conscious will with its cognitive counterpart, abstract conceptual reasoning, that is, as we have seen, clear and abstract intuition and its analysis—must be increasingly integrated as socially and individually man draws closer to God, the absolute identification of both. And such indeed is the conclusion to which Wust's profound study of the dialectic of the human spirit decisively points, if it fails quite clearly to enunciate. Wust is in short a pioneer of the dialectical ideal realism which is the approaching and victorious synthesis of dialectical idealism and dialectical materialism.

This sketch of so vast a theme has of necessity been reduced almost to the baldness and dogmatism of a synopsis. Moreover, Wust's speculative method by which he returns again and again to view the same phenomenon from a different angle, or to continue it more profoundly in another context, may well seem, in such outline, mere repetition. If so, I would ask the reader to remember that the way of knowledge, where the profound ultimates of reality are concerned, is not the accumulation and arrangement of diverse phenomena, but a patient gaze at a few simple realities of inexhaustible significance; in other words, the contemplative rather than the analytic method. To reject the former is to reject metaphysics. And for those who reject metaphysics Wust has no message.

PLOTINUS

PLATO'S INHERITANCE

THE influence of Plotinus upon Catholic thought is universally admitted. Its extent is not always realized. In the first
place Plotinus is a very difficult author. The *Enneads* are
an ill-arranged assortment of unrevised lecture notes written
without pretence at style and even faulty in grammatical
construction. Only when a wave of religious or metaphysical enthusiasm seizes the writer does he rise above
the involved tortuosities of a debate in monologue to flights
of sustained eloquence. If he is to receive his due, a
selection should be made of these "inspired" treatises or
passages. Only under their influence will the average reader
have the patience to mine his other writings for the ore
concealed in their dark labyrinth.

But this obscurity has not only discouraged the study of
Plotinus, it has led to the most serious misconceptions of
his work. He is regarded either as a pantheist or as an acosmist
whose extreme transcendentalism completely severs God
and the world and leaves only the irrational plunge of an
ecstasy stultifying the intelligence—imported, in despair of
Hellenic rationality, from Oriental mystery cults. He has
been regarded not as a genuine philosopher, but as a
mystic who under the garb of a philosopher built up a dream
palace of religious phantasy and mysticism in reason's despite.
The tide is now turning at last. Plotinus' claim to rank
in the genuine succession of Greek philosophy is, I think,
generally admitted. And the breadth, subtlety, and profundity of his system are widely acknowledged. But Catholics
are still loth to acknowledge their debt to a thinker who,

ell acquainted with Christianity, chose to remain a pagan.
is intelligible enough. But debts of honour should be
aid.

On the other hand we must not imagine that whatever
atholic theology and philosophy have taken directly or
directly from Plotinus is necessarily his original contribu-
on or of purely pagan origin. Trained as he was in the
chools of Alexandria of the third century A.D., Plotinus
herited an eclectic and syncretist philosophical tradition.
he Platonism of Alexandria, a current of thought rather
an a fixed system, embodied large elements of Stoic and
ristotelian provenance. Only of the Epicurean philosophy,
ith its mechanistic atomism and hedonist ethics, was it
e uncompromising foe. From Socrates downwards the
rphic " theology " had formed an integral part of Platonism.
n a lower intellectual level, but of kindred inspiration,
ligious syncretism, more or less Gnostic in character,
rrounded and influenced the Platonic tradition, coloured
e milieu in which it was taught. A typical product of this
tellectual current in its more popular form is the *Corpus
ermeticum*—the writings which bear the name of Hermes
rismegistus. Whether written before or after the age of
otinus or during his lifetime, they represent a crude, ill-
rmulated, and popular neo-Platonism. Moreover, even
fore the Christian era Jewish religion and Platonic philos-
phy had met and intermingled at Alexandria. Already the
isdom-literature of the Old Testament bears an Hellenic
print, and to formulate the doctrine of the Incarnation
. John employs terminology of Stoic-Platonic origin. This
wish Platonism is pre-eminently represented by Philo
daeus, whose doctrine shows considerable affinities with
at of Plotinus. The Syrian neo-Pythagorean Numenius
the second century—a forerunner of the later neo-Platon-
n which valued and utilized his work—represents a blend
Platonism, Gnosticism, and Judaism. It was he, not, as

one might suppose, some Hellenist Jew, who first terme
Plato an atticizing Moses. Moreover, it was in Plotinu
Alexandria that Christians first utilized Hellenic speculatio
on a large scale to formulate their theology. In the Ale
andrian Catechetical School, Clement and his greater pup
Origen wedded Christian faith with Greek thought. An
the Greek philosophy utilized was, as we should expect, th
eclectic Platonism current in Alexandria. Plotinus, as hi
biographer Porphyry tells us, after a considerable searc
found the teacher of his predilection in Ammonius Sacca
He became his ardent disciple. Among his fellow pupils wa
Origen. Plotinus and Origen were thus disciples of th
same philosopher, and, if we are to trust Porphyry, Orige
was no less enthusiastic than his friend. Evidently the syste
of Ammonius must have entered profoundly into the philos
ophies of both. We are also told that Ammonius was
Christian who had left the Church. Though the statemer
is generally accepted, it is not free from difficulty. It is no
easy to imagine such an ardent, almost fanatical, Christia
as Origen sitting at the feet of an apostate teacher and recei
ing his instruction as a sacred deposit. According to Por
phyry, Plotinus, Herennius, and Origen bound themselve
not to reveal it to outsiders. Was Ammonius still a Christia
at this time ? Was Plotinus himself attracted to the Church
What was it that made him unable to deliver his usual lectur
in Rome when Origen visited him and pressed him t
speak ?[1]

In view of the fact that Plotinus was more concerned t
attack Gnosticism than genuine Christianity it is possib
that Ammonius had belonged to some Gnostic sect rath
than the Christian church. Origen would hardly hav
refused to be the pupil of a man who had exchanged n
truth for error but one form of error for another.

There is, however, another possible explanation. In th

[1] Porphyry, *Life of Plotinus*, p. 14.

rst book of his Periarchon Origen writes, " There are many mong Greeks and barbarians alike who promise us the uth, *and yet we gave up seeking for it from all who aimed it for false opinions after we had come to be-eve that Christ was the Son of God and had become nvinced that we must learn the truth from Him.*" ince the context makes it plain that the ' we' is rigen himself the obvious meaning of the passage is that e had not always been a Christian but had sought truth sewhere. Was not this search for truth from pagan teachers is studies under Ammonius as Plotinus' fellow pupil? 'hat he was brought up as a Christian, was indeed the child f the martyr Leonidas and as a boy had been so eager to aare his father's martyrdom that his mother had to keep .m at home by hiding his clothes, does not disprove this ypothesis. When the social environment is predominantly nchristian many who as boys were fervent Christians abandon eir religion in youth. Soloviev, brought up by a devout hristian father, succumbed in his youth to the fashionable tionalism of his intellectual milieu. And Soloviev had uch in common with Origen. Moreover, it is evident from s writing that the unintellectual and naïve religion of e average Christian was distasteful to Origen whose ith demanded an intellectual expression. What more atural than that he should revolt against it and turn to the latonism which always appealed to him so strongly? Indeed, e may well have been influenced by the teaching and example f Ammonius, whose permanent abandonment of Christianity ay well have been the cause or occasion of Origen's tem-orary lapse. Moreover his self-mutilation may perhaps be tributed to a period of temporary paganism, when he lopted an attitude of extreme hostility to the flesh. Even hen convinced that a Christian Platonism was possible he was ever able to reconcile completely his Platonism with his Chris-anity in spite of his powerful efforts to achieve a synthesis.

This is shown by the hesitation and uncertainty which he di
plays in the Periarchon in regard to the Resurrection of t
Body, that permanent stumbling block to the Platonist.[1] A
in his theories of the angelic nature of the heavenly bodies
precosmic fall and metempsychosis, he also agrees with t
neoplatonists as against the orthodox Christian doctrir
though he could do so uncondemned, since they had n
been officially rejected. In view of these facts I a
strongly inclined to the view that when he sat side by si
with Plotinus at the feet of Ammonius Saccas he had tempo
arily abandoned his Christian faith. And he probably ow
his return to the Platonic Clement who must have shew
him that beside and beyond the simple Christianity he ha
rejected there was room for a higher and more intellectu
presentation of the Christian faith, the Christian Platonis
of the true gnostic such as he was teaching in the scho
of Alexandria.

Finally, what was Ammonius' system? Presumably h
relation to Plotinus may be compared with that of St. Albert
Magnus to St. Thomas. Nor is there any hint that his pu
seriously diverged from his master's doctrine. Further tha
this we cannot go. *Ignoramus et ignorabimus.*

This at least is certain: neo-Platonism was no creation
Plotinus' brain, but a continuation and more systemat
formulation of an Alexandrian neo-Platonism already
intimate proximity to Jewish and Christian thought. Orig
and his disciple, St. Gregory Thaumaturgus, may truly l
termed Christian neo-Platonists. Hellenistic-Judaism, tl
Christian Hellenism of Alexandria, and Plotinian ne
Platonism, represent a common tradition—neo-Platonis
in the wider sense. It was Plotinus' merit, or Ammoniu
to have reduced this floating tradition to a coherent syste

---

[1] Even in the fifth century the Platonist Synesius accepted the episcopate on
when he had informed his metropolitan that personally he did not believe in
bodily Resurrection though willing to teach the doctrine by way of accommodati
to his flock.

We might indeed almost term Plotinus the Aquinas of neo-Platonism. But we can hardly compare the rough notes of the *Enneads* with the elaborate construction of St. Thomas.

The philosophy of Plotinus may be succinctly described by the designation which his modern disciple, Professor Lossky, has given to his own restatement of neo-Platonism, a " concrete ideal realism."

It is an idealism because it affirms the primacy of mental or ideal being as more real than the material being apprehended by the senses. It is " realism " because this mental or ideal being with its intelligible order is not regarded as the subjective creation of the human mind, but as external objective reality, and because the subordinate and partial reality of the corporeal world is admitted. For intelligibility and being are correlative. In fact only the intelligible deserves to be called in the strict sense real. The sensible is but its shadow.

At the bottom of the scale is matter. What we call matter is due to the union of a formal principle, the reflection of an idea, in Plotinus' terminology a " logos," with a formless matter, which is mere indeterminate potency. Plotinus is clearly a hylemorphist—though Arnou considers that he failed to realize the substantial nature of the union between form and matter as Aristotle taught it.[1] Matter in its indeterminacy and constant flux is the source of evil, and the sensible world of which it is the substratum is defilement and bondage to the soul.

Above the world of matter is the soul, *psyche*—the principle of life. The soul mediates between mind or spirit, *Nous*, and matter, imprinting on the latter the *logoi* which inform and determine it. To the order of soul belongs the soul of the universe, its vital principle. In uninterrupted contemplation of the higher principle, the *Nous*, it draws

[1] *Le Désir de Dieu dans la Philosophie de Plotin*, pp. 70–3.

from it the ideal principles which it reflects automatically upon the material universe below itself. Immanent in the world soul and inseparable from it, yet distinct, are a host of souls—souls of stars, sun, and earth; god-souls; souls of men, animals, and all living things. Some of these, for example the gods and souls of the stars, live in unbroken connexion with the ideal world of *Nous*, and while moving cosmic bodies of incorruptible heavenly stuff are never immersed in the physical and sensible. The lower souls, among them our own, have been overpowered by the seduction of sense and become ensnared in bodies from which they must free themselves by ascetic purification and contemplative return to the world of spirit.

Above the Soul and its souls comes Spirit or Mind, *Nous* and its spirits. To *Nous* belong the ideas, *e.g.* Beauty in itself, Temperance in itself. In Spirit life has come to rest—the rest, however, of eternal activity—the activity of a perfect self-knowledge which is perfect self-possession above space and the flux of time. Mind knows itself, and knowing itself knows all true being—the ideas which are pre-eminently realities. The particular spirits are at once one with *Nous* and distinct from it. As in a perfect system of science one proposition implies all the rest, so every ideal being involves the intelligible order as a whole. Here there is, perhaps, some confusion between the ideas and subsistent minds. But the principle at least is clear. The intelligible world is a perfect organism. Every member implies all the rest. There is a perfect mutual interpenetration of all by all. Truth and positive reality—they are one—cannot be exclusive of truth and positive reality. It is the limitations due to material embodiment which produce mutual exclusion. Nevertheless truth is distinct from truth—mind from mind. Man is not only a soul, but also a mind—a spirit—for soul can never be separated from intellect. He can therefore, by turning his vision upwards and inwards to the spirit within himself, live in *Nous*, and, in virtue of that identity in difference of the intelligible world, he will be one with the divine *Nous*. *Nous*, however, is not the supreme reality. Above *Nous* is the Absolute One—strictly, therefore, Plotinus' God. He is beyond Spirit—for Spirit implies a duality—the dualism of self-consciousness, of knowledge and the object known. Both metaphysics, however, and the religious urge of the human soul demand an absolute Unity beyond all dualism. This is the One. It is by its contemplation and participation of the One that *Nous* is unified and is able in turn to reflect downward its light-shadow the Soul. And man, as participating in *Nous*, participates in the One. The centre or summit of his being beyond *Nous* is a likeness of the One, whereby he is able to enter into an ecstatic union with the One beyond the concepts of the intellect. Plotinus, according to Porphyry, attained this supreme ecstasy four times during the period of his acquaintance with him. It is mystical experience, but an experience integrated organically in Plotinus' philosophy. As Arnou points out, he does not base his affirmation of the One on his experience of the One, but on the metaphysical need of perfect unity.[1]

The One, the Spirit, and the Soul are the neo-Platonic Trinity. Plotinus' doctrine is not pantheism. The lower orders of being are not parts or substantial emanations of the higher. The higher produces the lower as its reflection by being what it is. The analogy employed is the sun and its light—the light not being regarded as by modern physics as an actual efflux of the solar substance. Nor is it acosmism. The lower orders of reality are real in their respective measures. Even the sensible world is but relatively unreal. It is at least the shadow of reality.

Set in the centre of this hierarchy, the starting-point therefore and ground of our knowledge of it, man may be compared to a church, whose parts in virtue of their composition

[1] *Le Désir de Dieu dans la Philosophie de Plotin*, pp. 265–71.

are in contact with different levels of reality. The nave is the soul on the biological level and as such apprehending the organic forms embodied in matter, reflections of the ideas. The choir is the spirit (*Nous*) in contact with the intelligible world and its ideas. The sanctuary is that higher point beyond *Nous*, the likeness of the One, the centre or apex of the Christian mystics, in contact with the One apprehended in the super-intelligible intuition of ecstasy.

It is a comprehensive and a profound system. Its two radical defects—the denial of creation *ex nihilo*, a denial which made the universe a *necessary* reflection of God, and the failure to distinguish in matter, its positive being which is good from its defect of being the source of evil—can be removed without prejudice to the structure. The latter defect indeed represents rather the exaggeration of a religious dissatisfaction with the flesh than a metaphysical demand. For the shadow of good is itself good, of beauty beautiful. Indeed, when Plotinus is speaking in the rigour of his metaphysics in face of the Gnostic denunciation of the material world as wholly evil, he adopts a more positive attitude towards corporeal matter.

The division of man into three parts, body, soul and spirit or rather into four, for above the *Nous* within us is the organ of union with the One, is but the misstatement of a very real and important distinction of levels in the human personality; body, biological life, metabiological spirit and its centre, the seat of mystical union with God. The subordinationist Triad misrepresents truths correctly stated by Christian mystics and theologians, the procession of the Persons from the formless abyss of Godhead of which Ruysbroek speaks, the Word as the Universal Exemplar, and the function of the Spirit as the source even of natural life. And on the other hand Plotinian neo-Platonism magnificently emphasises the hierarchy of being, the primacy of spirit over matter and sense, and the intrinsic religious reference both of the universe and the human soul. If the formulation of its hylemorphism is laxer than the Aristotelian, its intuitionist psychology is preferable to the empirical and rationalist psychology of Aristotle, and it explains and incorporates man's religious experience more satisfactorily and organically than Aristotelianism. No wonder it has made an appeal to Christian philosophers and entered profoundly into the structure of Catholic thought.

The first great Christian neo-Platonist indeed owed nothing to the *Enneads*, for he was, as we have seen, Plotinus' fellow disciple, Origen. His neo-Platonism therefore may fairly be taken to represent the teaching of Ammonius Saccas common to Plotinus and himself.

Unfortunately Origen's philosophy, so far as we can tell, was confined to the service and exposition of theology. He has left us no complete system which we can compare with that of Plotinus. But the philosophy which he employs to interpret and systematize the doctrines of faith is a thoroughgoing neo-Platonism. The supreme Being, God the Father, is the neo-Platonic One, beyond being, but knowable by man if he free himself from matter. Clement's doctrine of God was equally neo-Platonic—indeed ultra-neo-Platonic. God is not only beyond cause and thought, but beyond the One and the Monad.[1] Below the Father—for Origen's Trinity, like Plotinus' Triad, is subordinationist—is the Word —Plotinus' *Nous*—not the absolute God ὁ Θεός, but Divine, Θεός, a reflection of the Good (εἴκων ἀγαθοτήτος), not perfectly simple, because containing a multiplicity of ideas. Below Him in turn is the Spirit—though for Origen His function is not to be the soul of the physical universe, but the principle of supernatural life in the just. As with Plotinus, the souls are spirits fallen from the intelligible

---

[1] Clement also held Plotinus' trichotomy of the soul, in which he distinguished soul as the principle of life (Plotinus' *psyche*), spirit or mind (the *Nous*), and beyond that a σπέρμα πνευμάτικον, spiritual seed, which corresponds to the likeness of the One, by which the One is apprehended.

world into matter,—and he is even disposed, though tentatively, to accept metempsychosis. Souls may even perhaps be reincarnate in the bodies of animals. And as we have seen he cannot reconcile himself to the Resurrection of the body. If the perfect soul does not wholly discard matter, which so far as we can judge through the cloud of Rufinus's bowdlerisation he thought most likely, at least the Resurrection body is wholly unlike the gross flesh of our earthly embodiment wrought of some subtle and ethereal matter, rather spiritual than corporeal, and bearing no resemblance to the shape of our present bodies.[1] And, as is well known, he strongly inclined to a universal restitution by which all souls, including the evil angels, would finally return to union with God in the intelligible world of the *Logos*. Origen even seems to have regarded the humanity of Jesus as in some sense absorbed into the Word after His ascension. Moreover, he reckoned among the angels the spirits of the sun, planets, and stars. Plotinus' objection to the Gnostics, and implicitly to the Christians, that, mere men, they presumed to deny souls to the heavenly bodies, would have had no application to him.

Thoroughly Platonic is Origen's magnificent confidence in the power of reason, a confidence sanctioned by his Christian faith in the Divine Word that enlightens every man. " All things have been subjected to the Father through Jesus : for it is through wisdom, that is, by word and reason and not by force and necessity that they are subject. His glory, therefore lies in the very fact that He possesses all things ; and this is the purest and brightest glory of omnipotence, that the universe is held in subjection by reason and wisdom, and not by force and necessity." (Periarchon, bk. I, Ch. II.) Well would it have been for Christianity had Christians always held fast to the principle here so nobly expressed

---

[1] Both metempsychosis and the ethereal body reappear in the system of the contemporary Christian neo-Platonist Lossky. (See the *Organic World* passim.)

that power does not consist in physical force but in reason.

Origen is never more Platonic than when he regards understanding of the universe and human history as an important element of heavenly bliss. St. Paul " knew that when he had gone back to Christ, he would learn more clearly the reasons for all things that happen on earth that is the reasons which account for man, for his soul or his mind. . . . He will perceive what is the reason of souls and the meaning of the diversity among animals . . . and for what cause each genus is divided into so many species ; and what purpose of the Creator or what indication of His wisdom is concealed in each individual thing. He will learn the reason why certain properties are attached to certain roots and herbs. He will learn the judgement of divine Providence about each individual thing ; about things which happen to men, that they happen not by chance or accident but by a reason so carefully thought out. . . . When the Saints have reached the heavenly places they will see clearly the nature of the stars . . . why one star is placed in its particular position in the sky and why it is separated from another by so great an interval of space ; what would happen, for example, if it were nearer or farther away ; or if this star had been greater than that, how the entire universe would be changed into another form " (Periarchon, Bk. II, Ch. XI). This is the clearest statement known to me in Platonic literature of the ideal which haunted Plato of man's ultimate beatitude, the perfection of knowledge, a beatific vision of Truth in which the universe would be understood by final causes, the sort of knowledge for which Socrates vainly sought in the writings of Anaxagoras but which Plato hoped from a vision of the Good in which the religious hunger of the mystic and the scientific hunger of the seeker for truth would be gratified simultaneously. This hope can indeed never have been more than a remote ideal. Plato was aware that the clearest apprehension of ideal form was the aesthetic intuition of beauty and that " not by this is Wisdom seen." And his refusal in a celebrated letter to write a treatise on the Good is based on the fact that its experience is not scientific, an obscure consciousness not a distinct apprehension. That is to say he admitted, however regretfully, that a clear vision of Absolute Truth by mortal man is impossible. Perfect scientific knowledge is therefore reserved for spirits released from their fleshly prison. This scientific aspect of the Platonic ideal has indeed fallen into the background in Plotinus, who does not share Plato's enthusiasm for mathematical science and whose beatific vision of the One is more exclusively mystical, an ecstatic union beyond intellectual comprehension, not as with Plato and Origen, an understanding of man and the universe in its ideal ground, the Divine Reason. And Origen is even more remote here from Augustine's depreciation of scientific knowledge as superfluous to those who need no other knowledge than the knowledge of God and the soul.

In the infancy of Christian speculation Origen's Platonism overweighed in many respects his Christianity. Not to speak of his rash theories of metempsychosis and ultimate incorporeity, his view of Christ and redemption is too exclusively intellectual. Free will and rational illumination are pressed to an almost Pelagian neglect of grace. Christ is rather the teacher than the Redeemer. Origen lacks St. Augustine's profound sense of man's sinfulness and natural impotence in the supreme sphere of religion. But these excesses and mistakes are the inevitable falls of a Christian philosophy which is making its first steps. If Origen lacks Augustine's depth he is broader. And the union of Platonism with Christianity initiated in the school of Alexandria, for all its imperfect accomplishment, was the foundation on which Christian philosophy would be built up, an achievement to be completed but never undone.

This Alexandrian neo-Platonism, the first Platonic influx

into Christianity on a large scale, could not prevail in the
form Origen left it. Subordinationism, the fall of pre-existent
spirits, the denial of bodily resurrection as understood by the
tradition of the Church, and final restitution were abandoned
sooner or later by the heirs of Alexandrianism. But the tradition never died. Eastern Christianity had not to wait until
the Dionysian adaptation of Proclus for a neo-Platonic
exposition of theology. St. Gregory Thaumaturgus was
Origen's enthusiastic disciple. And in the fourth century
the Alexandrian tradition inspires the theology of the great
Cappadocian fathers, St. Basil and the two Gregories, of
Nazianzen and Nyssa. Their Hellenism, with its insistence
on the intelligible order and its humanism, to which Christopher Dawson has called our attention[1] is a Platonic, and
this means a neo-Platonic, Hellenism. When St. Gregory
of Nyssa sees in man the Godlike image of the archetypal
beauty, he states in his own terminology the doctrine of the
Enneads.[2] How thoroughly neo-Platonic is St. Gregory of
Nazianzen's magnificent apostrophe to God: " The end of
all art Thou, being One and All and None, being One Thou
art not all, being all Thou art not one ; All names are Thine,
how then shall I invoke Thy Name Alone Nameless ? "[3]
And St. Gregory of Nyssa's conception of artistic nature
($\dot{\eta}$ $\tau \epsilon \chi \nu \iota \kappa \dot{\eta}$ $\phi \upsilon \sigma \iota s$) is equally neo-Platonic. Nevertheless,
in the development from Origen to the Cappadocians the
detailed resemblances with neo-Platonism diminished, no
doubt in reaction from an assimilation which had compromised theological orthodoxy. It is the spirit rather
than the detailed framework that is common to both—a
genuine humanism, subordinated to an " overworldly and
ascetic " desire for union with a transcendent God,
an organic combination of intellectualism and mystical
religion.

[1] *Progress and Religion.*   [2] *Enneads,* i, pp. 6.
[3] Quoted in *Progress and Religion,* p. 91.

With St. Augustine there is a second and a more powerful influx of neo-Platonic philosophy and, moreover, in Western Christendom, hitherto little affected by Greek philosophy. St. Ambrose, however, had largely utilized and popularized the modified Alexandrian theology of the Cappadocian school—a fact of considerable significance when we remember that it was he who baptized the first great Christian neo-Platonist of the West.

As is well known, St. Augustine owed his conversion to a spiritual and transcendental theism to neo-Platonic writings —chiefly Plotinus—which the convert rhetorician Victorinus had translated into Latin. From them he learned his fundamental approach to God by the road, at once introversion and ascent, from the sensible and changing through the soul to the Divine Word within but above the soul. From Plotinus Augustine learned to set out from the soul in his search for knowledge of the intelligible world above it, indirectly even of the world of sense below it.[1]

It was the Platonists, *i.e.* Plato as interpreted by Plotinus, that saved him from a sensualist empiricism which had issued, as it logically must, in scepticism, by disclosing to him man's direct and certain apprehension of intelligible truth, the intelligible world, as the substance and self-sufficient guarantee of human knowledge. " After many centuries and many disputes at length a system of philosophy was discovered which, in my opinion, is most true. It is not . . . a philosophy of the material world " (*Contra Academicos*). This intelligible world is the world of the ideas, of the Plotinian *Nous*. But the truth of our intellectual knowledge presupposes a light, the Light of the Word above truth and the soul, in Platonic terminology the sun of the intelligible world whose image in the sensible order is the material sun. Here, too, Augustine is conscious of his debt to neo-Platonism. " Very often Plotinus affirms, explaining Plato's meaning, that even that

[1] *Enneads*, iv, pp. 2.

Soul which they consider the soul of the universe derives
its bliss from no other source than our own, namely the
light which is not itself but that by which it has been created
and by whose intellectual illumination it intelligibly shines."[1]
" I beheld, with the eye of my soul above the eye of my soul,
above my mind the Light Unchangeable . . . above my
soul because it made me." Neo-Platonic is the insistence
on the direct apprehension of truth by a soul illuminated by
the superior spirit or mind (*Nous, Logos*), Augustinian the
emphasis on the supreme value of truth. Plotinus had never
been a sceptic.

The fundamental Platonic principle of the correlation
between intelligibility and being is also the fundamental
principle of Augustine. It was for this reason that he sought
and found truth and God in the soul. The ascent from the
changeable apprehensions and objects of sense through the
intelligible world of conceptual truth to the Absolute Truth
which was relived by Augustine's vital experience at the
beginning of his conversion and in the famous colloquy
with Monica,[2] is Plotinus' ascent to God. Augustine's
description contains indeed verbal echoes of Plotinus. "If to
any the tumult of the flesh were hushed, hushed the images
of earth, and the waters, and air, hushed also the poles of
heaven." Before him Plotinus had written. "Let us suppose
the same rest in the body that surrounds the soul, that its
movement is stilled, and that the entire surroundings are also
at rest, the earth, the sea, the heaven itself above the other
elements " (En. V. I. 2). But whereas the goal of the spiritual
ascent, a mystical ecstatic union with the Absolute, was
regarded by Plotinus as union with the One beyond
Spirit, for Augustine the Word is Itself the Absolute.
Plotinus, portrays a gradual ascent from the World Soul
to the Spirit (*Nous*) and finally from Spirit to the One.
For Augustine, however, the soul is rapt immediately to

---

[1] *De Civ. Dei*, x, pp. 2.   [2] *Conf.*, pp. 7, 23, 9, 24–5.

N

the Eternal Wisdom who is the Absolute God, not, except in the fact of his procession, subordinate to the Father. Indeed it was Augustine who removed from Christian theology the last traces of the subordinationism found here and there among the earlier fathers. So far as we can judge—though of course Christian belief may have re-interpreted on this point pre-Christian experience—Augustine had never subordinated the Word to a higher God. The Absolute Object of Mystical Union, that which is attained " with the flash of one trembling glance," is " the *Light* Unchangeable above the Mind."

In Augustine's psychology we find a trichotomy of soul (*anima*, corresponding to Plotinus' *psyche*, the life principle of the body), ratio (discursive reasoning), and intellectus (direct apprehension of intelligible truth). Both the latter, however, belong to the spirit or mind, *animus* or *mens*, Plotinus' *Nous*. But for Augustine it is only a division of function, whereas Plotinus' language suggests a distinction of substantial principles, unharmonized with his belief in man's ability—surely as a unitary spirit—to identify himself at choice with a higher or lower level of knowledge.

Like Plotinus, Augustine will not allow that matter, the lower, can directly act on the soul, the higher principle. Therefore in sensation the soul is not moved by the physical impress of material objects, but merely stimulated by their impact on the bodily organ to apprehend the sensible object.[1] But the Plotinian-Augustinian account of sensation seems somewhat confused and incomplete. For a developed account of sensation on neo-Platonic lines we must go to the con-temporary neo-Platonist, the Russian philosopher Lossky. According to Lossky there exists what he terms an epistemo-logical co-ordination between the mind and objects. There-fore when physical impact awakes the attention of the mind

---

[1] See *Enneads*, iv, 326. In *Enneads*, i, 1, Plotinus attributes sensation more vaguely to a compound constituted by the body and an emanation of the soul.

it finds itself in contact with the object itself. The fundamental difficulty, however, remains : How can a spiritual being know a material object ? Perception, I would reply, developing this intuitionist epistemology, besides a sensible reception of sense stimuli, contains an intelligible factor—the apprehension of the form as distinct, but not separate, from the matter in which it appears. It is thus a sub-intelligence, intelligence at a lower degree, its percept apprehension of form as wholly immersed in its matter, as opposed to the concept in which the form is apprehended in itself. Matter as such is unknowable. This is the reason why physical science is confined to laws of numerical sequence. I may seem to have digressed far from Augustine. Yet this seems to have been *au fond* his doctrine of sensation. " The soul," writes Fr. Martin D'Arcy,[1] " in sensation is assimilated in its harmony of number to the excitations of the body by sensible objects. Wherever there are objects there is order and some kind of unity showing itself in equality, symmetry, beauty. . . . The mind recapitulates [apprehends] that order. St. Augustine does not claim for the human mind a knowledge of the essence [I would rather say matter. For there is a *partial* apprehension of the essence] of tables and chairs and other material things. His world is that of the intelligible, and he is content to find the trace of God in the order and unity of the world outside us, in the proportion and harmony of numbers." This surely means that for Augustine human sense perception comprises an inferior operation of the intellect which, in a higher operation, abstracts forms and apprehends intelligibles.

Though Augustine and Plotinus are alike in their hunger for union with God and His changeless Truth, St. Augustine's far keener sense of the weakness and malevolence of the human will led him to emphasize the volitional aspect of the

---

[1] *A Monument to St. Augustine : The Philosophy of St. Augustine*, pp. 177–9.

soul's purification and ascent where Plotinus had emphasized the intellectual. And whereas Plotinus in a Stoic self-sufficiency thought man had but to turn his spiritual vision Godward to receive His Light, Augustine was penetrated by the sense of man's utter impotence to rise of himself, his need of the Divine Condescension expressed by the Incarnation of the Word and the Aid of Divine Grace. As the doctor of Grace Augustine is the antithesis of Plotinus.

On evil Augustine speaks, not indeed with two voices, but with two accents. When he considers evil theoretically or is defending the goodness of creation against the Manichees, he insists, like Plotinus against the Gnostics, on the order of creation—that creation is a harmony in which evil is a necessary contrast. Indeed, he will even seem, like Plotinus, to minimize unduly its extent and significance. When, however, he considers the malice of human sin, the need of redemption and grace, his picture of evil is even too dark. There is no fundamental inconsistency of doctrine, for though evil is only defect, its extent and degree may be incalculably great. A famine is but lack of food; yet it may count its victims by the million. There is, however, a double emphasis. And only the former is neo-Platonic. Moreover, in his profound sense of man's need of the grace of Christ Augustine will come to deny that Plotinus and his fellow neo-Platonists attained the goal of their search[1] a denial based on the unwarranted pre-supposition that grace is given only to Christian believers, or in view of conversion to Christianity, refused to pagan seekers after God.

But the fundamental neo-Platonism remains to the end. Common to Augustine and Plotinus was the equation between intelligibility and reality, the scale of reality from matter to God, the ascent of that ladder therefore an ascent of increasing likeness to God, the soul as the starting-point, centre, and means for the apprehension of Truth and God, and the desire

[1] *Sermo* CXLI. M.A., 162.

for God as the guarantee of truth and the sole satisfaction of
the human spirit. And both insisted that man is not divided
from God by external barriers, for in the intelligible world
each is present to all and, *a fortiori*, God to all created minds.
It is the unlikeness of a spirit whose gaze is turned away to
the lower world of sense—for Plotinus through its weakness
and as the result of a precosmic fall, from the malice of a
depraved will for the more dynamic Augustine—which
separates the soul from its *summum bonum*. Augustine's
cry, "*Longe eram tibi in regione dissimilitudinis,*"[1] is a
verbal echo of Plotinus' ἐν τόπῳ ὀνομοιότητος. Like St.
Augustine, Plotinus turns away from the physical sciences,
with the exception, however, of astronomy, for the neo-
Platonist a sphere of intelligible order where the defective
and gross matter of earth has no place.[2] Whether Augustine
would, like Plotinus, have regarded them as affording only
opinion—not real knowledge—is more doubtful. In any
case perfect knowledge of any created object is impossible.
For no created object, since it is compounded of
intelligible form and unintelligible matter, can be perfectly
intelligible, therefore not perfectly knowable. And in the
case of inorganic bodies since they are lowest in the scale
of being, the factor of unintelligibility is at its maximum.
Hence possible knowledge of inorganic objects is less than
the possible knowledge of higher orders of being though
man's actual knowledge of them may be greater. Since,
however, this imperfect knowledge is within its limits
certain, genuine knowledge, Plotinus, and Plato before him,
were not justified in calling it mere opinion. Even Augustine's
celebrated observation, that he knows what time is until
he is asked, is substantially anticipated by Plotinus.
"We believe we have in our souls a clear impression of
these two (time and eternity) and speak about them

[1] I was far from Thee *in a region of unlikeness*.
[2] *Enneads*, 3. 8. 6., 5. 9. 7.

freely. But when we try to examine them closely and get to grips with the subject, we become embarrassed by our thoughts."[1]

To conclude, if in his profound realisation of the important part played by the will in the attainment of happiness—truth—God, the common goal of both thinkers, and of the need of supernatural grace to rectify it, Augustine departs widely from Plotinus, his metaphysics, epistemology, and what may be termed his metaphysical theology are neo-Platonic. In Augustine Plotinus is baptized and sits at the feet of Christ.

A third great influx of neo-Platonism was yet to come, this time once more from Eastern Christendom, in fact from Syria—the composition about the year 500 and universal acceptance of the pseudonymous writings of the monk who took the name of Dionysius the Areopagite. To expound his debt to neo-Platonism it would be necessary to transcribe almost in their entirety his *Divine Names* and *Mystical Theology*. It was not, however, from Plotinus that he directly derived his doctrine. It is Proclus, the fifth-century Athenian professor, who here assumes a Christian garb. Roughly speaking, Proclus elaborated or over-elaborated Plotinus' system and emphasized its religious aspect. Though Plotinus' philosophy was radically religious in its orientation to God and as culminating in ecstatic union with Him, a too abstract and impersonal conception of Deity, his inadequate emphasis upon the volitional factor, and, above all, a stoic self-sufficiency for which the attainment of bliss lay in man's unaided capacity, combined to impoverish his religion in its devotional aspect. Prayer, as a turning of the mind to God, he knew, though characteristically not by that name. Prayer, as humble supplication for Divine aid, he rejected. Proclus, on the other hand, practised devoutly the pagan cults, spending hours every night in prayer and sacrifice. Indeed, the better to honour

[1] *Enneads*, 3. 7. 1.

the gods he devised a place for them in his system above the *Nous* and immediately below the One. In other ways, too, he elaborated his master's system. At every stage of the ontological ascent he found a triad : an abiding in itself, a going forth, a return. His devotion, his emphasis on mediation and external cult, are reproduced in the *Heavenly and Ecclesiastical Hierarchies* of Dionysius. The triple motion reappears in the threefold motion of intelligence of which Dionysius speaks—the circular, rectilinear, and spiral—a triad which has its analogue in the Divine Life itself.

The necessary reflection of every degree of reality, save the lowest, upon that beneath it, which, though neither emanationism nor pantheism, involves the eternity and necessity of the universe, is for Dionysius replaced by the dynamic conception of the Divine Eros—imitated in turn by creatures, an overflowing love which compels God to go forth in the ecstasy of self-donation to create reflections and participants of His Divine beatitude. Moreover, since in accordance with Christian orthodoxy the Trinity is referred to the Absolute, the level of Plotinus' *Nous*, in so far as it is subordinate to the Absolute, is occupied by the orders of angelic intelligence, the level of his *Psyche*, in turn, by human souls. But the great merit of Dionysius was to have grappled more thoroughly than any of his predecessors with the radical problem of Christian Platonism : how to reconcile two presentations of God—the neo-Platonic Absolute, the Ineffable One without distinctive multiplicity, and the Father God of Christianity who knows, loves, and freely chooses. Metaphysics, in its inexorable demand for Unity, presses back to the former, religious experience and revelation demand the latter. St. Augustine had accepted both and embodied both in his richly concrete religion. But he does not seem to have explicitly investigated the problem of their theoretical co-ordination. Indeed, even to-day so profound and learned a student of Catholic philosophy as M. Gilson can write :

> The God of St. Thomas is not the God of Plotinus, but the Christian God of St. Augustine. It is not enough for St. Augustine to have been influenced by neo-Platonism for his God to be identified with that of Plotinus. Between the Plotinian speculation and the theology of the Fathers Jehovah is interposed, a personal God, acting by intelligence and will, who freely creates outside Himself the real world chosen by His wisdom. . . . How is it possible not to see that here we are at the very antipodes of neo-Platonic philosophy ?[1]

If this be so, it is indeed strange that St. Augustine, who criticized the neo-Platonists severely, indeed unwarrantably, for their inability to attain God, never criticized their conception of Godhead. He contrived to combine the alleged opposites.

Dionysius, however, addressed himself to the theoretical problem involved. His solution is the distinction between God as He is in Himself and God as He is in relation to creatures, or more accurately in their relation to Him. The Absolute beyond Being and Knowledge—the superpersonal " superessential super-Deity "—is the Godhead in its utter transcendence of all created being and its categories. The Personal God of revelation is His manifestation to man in terms of the highest categories of human experience, because He is more not less than they. Because He is superpersonal He can be personal to us. Because He is superessence, the higher the measure of being, the closer to Him, the brighter the reflection and the fuller the participation of His superessence. The *Mystical Theology* is concerned with God as He is—the Absolute and all-transcendent—the *Divine Names*

---

[1] *Philosophy of St. Thomas*, p. 354.

with His partial manifestations in terms of human experience. The distinction, indeed, would seem to be identical with the distinction of Hindu metaphysics between the undifferentiated Absolute Brahman and the manifested Brahma or Ishvara—that is to say, if Ishvara or Brahma is regarded only as a relative manifestation of Brahman, not His real internal self-development. Admittedly Plotinus' apprehension of the manifested personal aspect of God was inadequate. He did not indeed deny it, but his understanding of it was insufficiently concrete. For he did not see it in Christ. But to deny or obscure the unmanifested superpersonal aspect, and therefore to denounce Plotinus' profound presentation of that aspect as pantheist, agnostic, or in contradiction with its complement, is to deprive theology of its metaphysical foundation and substitute for the Absolute Godhead, in which metaphysics and religion find their common goal, the conception of a superman or a superspirit, chief among other spirits, a conception justly open to the charge of an untenable anthropomorphism. And if the Christian God is thus presented to the educated Hindu, he will be rightly unable to accept Him. Truth and expediency alike demand that Dionysius should accompany the Gospel.

The Western and Eastern representatives of Christian neo-Platonism—Augustine, who realized it in a profound vital experience, as a personal religion, and Dionysius, who, though his scope was more limited, and his personality deliberately obliterated, worked out the theoretical Christian presentation of its metaphysical theology—together determined the Catholic philosophy of succeeding centuries. The neo-Platonic current was further reinforced by Boethius, not only by his translation of the *Timaeus*, but by his popular *De Consolatione Philosophiae*, translated into English by Alfred the Great. The latter was a practical application of neo-Platonism, a book of moral edification based on its fundamental principles. The scale of reality, the primacy of the intelligible and ideal world, the supremacy and identity of the Good and the One, the deification of the soul by her participation of God, are the neo-Platonic themes which determine Boethius' lessons of practical morality. It is to this treatise that we owe the celebrated definition of eternity, *interminabilis vitae tota simul et perfecta possessio*, the simultaneous and perfect possession of boundless life—which in one lapidary sentence expresses the comprecence and interpenetration of spirit and its intelligible content and sums up Plotinus' description of eternity. " *Nous* possesses in itself all things abiding in the same place. It is, ever is, and nowhere becomes, nor is ever past, for here (*in Nous*) nothing passes away but all things are eternally present." [1]

In the West Dionysius was, as we should expect, a later arrival. Though known and accepted—in virtue, we must admit, of his pseudonymity—by Pope Martin in 649, it was only when translated by John Scotus Eriugena in the ninth century that his writings became generally known. Though an Irishman, Eriugena belongs in his thought to oriental Christianity. He is preoccupied with the ideal being of creatures in God and his place is therefore with those Russian thinkers who profess with various nuances a metaphysical theology of the Divine Wisdom, Sophia, and a corresponding devotion, and have therefore been termed sophiologists. Such are Soloviev, Bulgakov and Berdaiev. Of these sophiologists indeed Eriugena may be regarded as the first. Thus paradoxically, this Irish philosopher was the first of the Russians, a Russian before Christian Russia had come into existence. This enigmatic Carolingian thinker is often dubbed a pantheist. This, however, is the inveterate misunderstanding of neo-Platonism. In reality he based his system closely on Dionysius, and his condemnation for unorthodoxy is sufficiently explained on other grounds. He revived Origen's universalism though

---

[1] *Enneads*, 5. 1. 4.

it is partial and inconsistent. For the empirical or phenomenal self of the unrepentent sinner will somehow be eternally punished, at least by an everlasting frustration, while his inner, his noumenal self is reconciled and reunited with God. And he adopted from St. Maximus the Confessor the doctrine that sex differentiation is the result of the fall and will finally be abolished. Indeed the resurrection body is not more corporeal than Origen's, so far as the latter admitted it at all. Eriugena also, like Origen, regarded the fall as precosmic, the cause of this present world of gross matter and human bodies as we actually possess them. Moreover his doctrine of the Trinity is economic. Departing from his master and returning consciously or unconsciously to Plotinus, he reduces the Trinity to the level of manifestation and relativity, its Procession being but the first stage of the world process. But there is no reason to suspect a fundamental divergence between Scotus and Dionysius, who, indeed, has been termed a pantheist often enough. Since, like Eckhart later, Eriugena does not distinguish sufficiently between the uncreated ground of creatures in God, their super-reality, and their distinctive reality as creatures, he uses language which if pressed, would indeed be pantheistic or rather acosmic, as though creatures are Divine essentially, in their distinct being unreal. When, however, we take his system as a whole, and bear in mind his dependence upon Dionysius we can hardly doubt that he meant no more than a strong assertion of the truth that the ground of created being is GOD's idea of it which because Divine is more real than the creature itself. There is vagueness and pantheistic language not pantheism. On the other hand he seems to revert to the most unsatisfactory aspect of Plotinus' cosmogony by regarding the process of creation as an emission or externalisation of its ideal being in God, rather than a creation *ex nihilo*. But like Plotinus he did not realise the pantheistic implications of this conception. He did not intend to reject the Christian doctrine of creation, which presumably he regarded as a popular expression of this emanation. Nor is the latter conception wholly false. Creation is indeed an external projection of the ideal order eternally present in the Divine Wisdom. But Eriugena is a confused and obscure thinker wrestling with conceptions he cannot think out, much less state, clearly. He glimpses the vast and inspiring perspective of a universe expressing God on the lower plane of created being and as such issuing from Him to return to its Divine Source. But he is unable to achieve a clear or harmonious vision of it. In this vagueness and inconsistency also the Irish Eriugena is typically Russian. Like the Russians he loves vistas of thought, magnificent and far-reaching but wrapped in mist and impossible to fix clearly. Nor did his intellectual environment assist this lonely thinker to clarify and order his insights. We should therefore rather admire him for his bold design than condemn him for his failures in executing it. Did he identify religion and metaphysics, *vera theologia vera philosophia?* He can hardly have regarded such doctrines as the Incarnation as metaphysical. If we are to intepret him, as we reasonably should, in his context we must suppose him to have meant no more than a partial coincidence between the two disciplines, the doctrine of God in Himself and of the relation of the universe to God as its Source and End. On the other hand he would presumably have regarded the doctrine of the Trinity as coming within the scope of philosophy. This, however, it can only do if it comes within the sphere of cosmic manifestation— for a Trinity within the Absolute would as such be above rational apprehension. Hence no doubt his subordinationist and economical view of the mystery.

If, however, these unorthodoxies did not render Eriugena's system pantheist, they undoubtedly deprived it of the influence upon the development of Catholic philosophy which it would otherwise have possessed. His translation of

Dionysius spread knowledge of his writings, but it was not in Eriugena's presentation that neo-Platonism remained the philosophy of the Catholic schools during the succeeding centuries. Nor was it based on direct knowledge of Plato or Plotinus. Only Boethius' translation of the *Timaeus* and the Proclian *De Causis* were read in the West. It was the Augustinian-Dionysian adaptation that formed the groundwork of Catholic philosophy.

In particular, as Durantel points out, the hierarchy of being—the lower the reflection and participation of the higher—dominated the thought and imagination of the Middle Ages. The hierarchical principle embodied in all the greatest medieval achievements—the cathedral with its symbolism of spiritual truths sensibly embodied, the hierarchical arrangement of the *Divina Commedia*, the philosophical and theological Summas, the very scheme of education, the arrangement of the sciences worked out so elaborately in Dante's *Convito*—expressed the hierarchy of less and more perfect being between matter and God, of the sensible and intelligible orders, which was the fundamental principle of neo-Platonism.

St. Bonaventure is a typical representative of this neo-Platonic tradition. For him the soul is the centre and starting-point of human knowledge. He formally excludes knowledge of the soul and God from the Aristotelian doctrine that all knowledge originates from sensation :[1] " *Necessario oportet ponere quod anima novit Deum et seipsum sine adminiculo sensuum exteriorum* " (" It must be stated that the soul knows God and itself without the assistance of the outer senses "). And knowledge is impossible save by the illumination and direction of the eternal ideas (*rationes aeternae*), through whose operation on the mind we indirectly apprehend their source, the Divine Light itself—thus attaining what St. Bonaventure terms a contuition of God : " The apprehension

[1] See Gilson, *Philosophie de St. Bonaventure*, p. 361.

in an effect of the presence of a cause of which we lack intuition."[1] The ascent to God is through intelligibles—reflections of the Divine Ideas, aspects of the Word, displayed to the mind in creatures. There is a hierarchy of reflections of the Divine Light, in which every degree is a symbol and analogy of its superior. And at the top of the ladder, where human reason fails, there is the mystical apprehension of God, substantially as in Plotinus, but now clearly recognized to be the gift of God's free grace beyond man's natural power to attain. Even the details are neo-Platonic; for example, the acceptance of a spiritual matter whereby even the disembodied soul is a complete substance. Behind and beyond St. Bonaventure's immediate master Augustine we behold, changed and dim, but still powerful, the figure of Plotinus.

But was not the reign of Platonism or neo-Platonism over at last? Did not St. Thomas strike its death-blow to replace it by the comparatively rationalist and empirical Aristotelianism? The answer is not altogether easy. For some interpreters of St. Thomas, e.g. Rousselot and Durantel, he appears a neo-Platonist with a strong admixture of Aristotelianism, for others, e.g. Maritain and Gilson, he is an Aristotelian embodying a remnant of Augustinian neo-Platonism. Both quote his text abundantly. One has the impression that it is the case of an object regarded from two points of view; that Thomas is both Platonist and Aristotelian. This, of course, does not solve the question as to the relationship between both factors in his system. That, however, can be answered with any approach to precision only by the experts—and they disagree.

What I wish to emphasize here is that Aristotelianism and Platonism must not be opposed too strictly. Aristotle, after all, had been Plato's disciple, and retained much of his teaching. For instance, the intelligibility of form, the indeterminacy and therefore unknowability of matter, the supremacy

[1] Op. cit., p. 385.

of contemplation, God as the supreme object of desire, are
Platonic doctrines. Moreover, neo-Platonism was itself a
fusion of Platonic and Aristotelian elements. In this Plotinus
was truly a predecessor of St. Thomas. Augustine indeed
regarded this reconciliation of Platonism and Aristotelianism
as an essential characteristic of his philosophy.[1] To Aristotle
he owed two fundamental principles. One is hylemorphism
—though understood otherwise and perhaps less rigorously
than Aristotle understood it. For example, Plotinus departs
from Aristotle advantageously in his acceptance of spiritual
matter and of forms, and therefore ideas of individuals
(e.g. the form or idea of Socrates, αὐτοσωκράτης), disadvan-
tageously if, as Arnou thinks, he failed to realize the complete
potency of " matter." The other is the more general principle
on which hylemorphism is ultimately based, the distinction
between potency and act. Plotinus even formulates the principle that potency can only be brought into act by that which is
itself in act,[2] which for Fr. Aelred Whitacre is the essential and
fundamental principle of Thomist Aristotelianism.[3] He also
accepts and enumerates the Aristotelian doctrine of four
causes. Any further introduction of Aristotelianism
could therefore be only a matter of degree, a shift of
emphasis, not a change to a radically different system of
philosophy—as if a Scholastic were to become a Kantian or
Pragmatist.

That St. Thomas did incorporate into his system whatever
he could of Aristotelianism is a commonplace. It may be
that in certain points—e.g. in the exclusive derivation of
knowledge from sense data, and the denial that the human
soul is a complete substance apart from the body, he made
excessive concessions to Aristotle. Yet his *intellectus agens*
is at least susceptible of an Augustinian interpretation as
being the direct apprehension of intelligible truth. And
M. Gilson tells us that for Thomas matter is not the *exclusive*

---

[1] *Contra Academ.*, 3. 19.   [2] *Enneads*, 4. 7. 7.   [3] *E.R.E.* Art. " Thomism."

individualizing factor.[1] It may be that his doctrine of universal and particular, by a too rigid and exclusively definite system of abstract concepts which concretized unduly the necessary definition by thought of aspects of reality in themselves organically united with all its other aspects, intensified a hypostatization of the abstract universal already present in neo-Platonism, that conflicts with its dynamic and organic doctrine of intelligible inexistence and involves a certain confusion between the concrete universal, apprehended in aesthetic intuition, the idea as containing and exceeding its particular exemplifications and the abstract universal, the object of speculative intuition or intellection, the minimum common to them all. It is a confusion of which one is sensible even in the doctrine of the neo-Platonic Dionysius, otherwise dynamic and vital, and in its intention and fundamental trend concrete and organic.

But, whatever our opinion on these points, we must admit that Thomism is in the neo-Platonic tradition when it teaches the scale of reality (the presupposition of St. Thomas' fourth proof of Theism), the correlation in that scale of intelligibility, reality, and form, and the exemplarism which everyone allows to be a Thomist doctrine.

As opposed to all partial and inadequate systems, the philosophy which accepts and organizes all data of human knowledge is the *philosophia perennis*. For European thought, at least, this philosophy originated with Plato (including, of course, his master Socrates), was modified for good and evil by Aristotle, was carried forward by the neo-Platonic synthesis, and was Christianized by the Alexandrians, Cappadocians, Augustine, and Dionysius, to culminate in the great Catholic philosophers SS. Bonaventure and Thomas, representing respectively a more Platonic and intuitive presentation and emphasis, and a more Aristotelian presentation, empirical and subordinately rationalist. But in its essentials it is the

[1] *Philosophy of St. Thomas*, p. 219.

same *philosophia perennis*, a concrete ideal realism, a modified Monism which, while accepting only one positive principle of being, admits degree of being—participations of Absolute Being by non-entity—thereby leaving room for creatures wholly distinct from God while owing their entire being to Him. Corporeal matter is subordinately real, but only subordinately, and relatively to mind. For its " matter " is mere potency, and it owes its actual reality to intelligible form. The scales of value and being correspond, as they must, if thought is not to be presented with an irreconcilable dualism. Human knowledge is vindicated as objective in its reference and true, while its insufficiency and fallibility are admitted, even emphasized. This foundation having been securely laid, the data of religion and its culmination, mystical experience, can be accepted in their objective reference without leading to fideism, emotional subjectivism, or that irrationalism which has brought the name of mysticism into such undeserved discredit. In short, it accepts the whole of human experience, and is thus the only Catholic philosophy. In its construction Plotinus was a master builder. The edifice has been modified since he left it, necessarily and rightly modified, and in places demolished. But his work as a whole has never been demolished, not even by St. Thomas, though perhaps in his Aristotelian zeal he destroyed more of his predecessor's work than was justified.

If those who accept the *philosophia perennis*, whether in an Augustinian or a Thomist form, nevertheless regard the philosophy of Plotinus as a system wholly alien, a pantheism or an abstract idealism, they misunderstand either Plotinus or their own metaphysical creed. Let two proofs suffice. No one can deny that Dionysius' theology is essentially neo-Platonic. Neither can it be denied that St. Thomas accepted it wholeheartedly. "By misunderstanding and misinterpretation." That the critic has misunderstood neo-Platonism is a likelier supposition. Nor can Augustine's debt to Plotinus be denied. But,

o

whatever modifications St. Thomas introduced, no one has suggested that he rejected Augustine for Aristotle. On the contrary, he believed himself to be interpreting the more incomplete, less formulated doctrine of Augustine, the Christian neo-Platonist, by the more formulated and systematic philosophy of Aristotle. Did he, contrary to his own intention and belief, reject the former for the latter? On anyone who maintains the proposition lies the burden of proof.

NATIONALISM ENERGETICISM AND THE TOTALITARIAN STATE

God alone because He is infinite is all-inclusive Being and Value. All creatures because their being is limited have two aspects, positive and negative, inclusive and exclusive. A by being A and including the constituents of A, Aa, Ab, Ac, Ad, *is not* B and excludes the constituents of B, Ba, Bb, Bc, Bd, etc. It is the same with the group which we call a nation. It has a positive aspect and value—the positive values of the factors which constitute it and unite its members. Such are race, though races are so mixed that this is a subordinate factor, landscape, climate, geographical contiguity, and more important than these, language, common traditions and customs, a common culture. These distinctive national factors and characters enrich by their diversity the total store of mankind. A cosmopolitanism which should obliterate in a featureless " humanity," common to all nations, the distinctive national characteristics and functions would spell impoverishment and emptiness. On the other hand the nation with its values and qualities inevitably possesses its negative aspect. It excludes other nations and lacks their distinctive values and qualities. In itself this inevitable exclusion is not an evil. For it may and should be transcended in a wider inclusiveness. Though each nation and its culture must exclude other nations and their cultures by being other than they, they can and should supplement each other in a humanity which comprehends them all. French literature, for example, should not abandon its distinctive traditions to adopt those of English or German literature. For not only do the literatures of the three nations contribute, precisely in virtue of their distinctively national characters, to the literature of Western Europe and ultimately of the world, but their mutual influences and borrowings have assisted the development and enrichment of each as a distinctive national literature. It is the same with the scientific and philosophic thought of nations and even, if they are not too far apart, with their languages. As the infinitely rich Totality of the Divine Being is reflected in the multiplicity of diverse creatures, so the vast potential wealth of humanity is realised and can only be realised by a manifold of subordinate groups.

Actually, however, these national groups are not subordinate to a higher and more comprehensive unity. The nation tends to be and in the majority of cases is a sovereign state. This means that the negative aspect of difference from other nations and their cultures becomes a conscious opposition, an actual or latent hostility. Competition replaces co-operation. Mr. Wells is right when he says that the mere existence of a sovereign state is a latent war, and peace between such states, if their interests in any way conflict, a truce rather than peace. It is at this point that the virtue of patriotism, the love and service of the nation in its positive aspect and value tends to pass over into nationalism the love and service of the nation in its negative aspect, its opposition to other nations and their values. Patriotism prizes and promotes the contribution made by the nation to the intellectual and spiritual treasure of mankind. Nationalism prizes the wealth or the power which the nation has seized from the rest of mankind, and it promotes further usurpations or, if the point of satiety has been reached, their retention in face of just claims for their surrender. Nationalism it is true, also values cultural achievements, not in themselves detrimental to other nations but actually beneficial to them—artistic creations for example or scientific improvements. But it esteems them less than the aggressive achievement of the soldier or statesman. And it abuses them as pretexts to belittle and neglect the culture of other nations. In extreme cases it even refuses to enjoy or utilise the products of a foreign culture and attempts to keep its citizens from contact with it. Nazi Germany, for example, is trying to ban Jewish music because the Jew is an alien. Nationalism subordinates the higher and more comprehensive values to national egoism. Mussolini frankly declares that the moral and cultural accomplishment of the nation must be in the last resort subservient to "military and even militarist" aims. The moral law itself must give way to the material interests of the nation. "My country right or wrong" is the motto, avowed or unavowed, of nationalism. Any war the national government may choose to declare is to be considered just and therefore justifying the wholesale slaughter of innocent soldiers even, if aerial and gas warfare requires it, of non-combatants, women and children. Yet the criteria of a just war laid down by theologians condemn the overwhelming majority of wars. "A State," wrote Victoria, "is part of the whole world: so if a war benefits one State but injures the whole world or Christendom I consider such a war unjust." As the late war proved to the hilt, under modern conditions a war must injure the world more than it can possibly benefit the victor even if it benefits him at all, which there is little reason to believe. Therefore a modern war must be unjust and, if unjust, to kill in battle is murder. Nevertheless in every country, more or less, the nationalist state is training its citizens to regard this wholesale murder as their duty and glory. But the Fascist states do it more frankly and more thoroughly. Nationalism in fact teaches that most of the moral laws binding between individuals are to be reversed in the mutual dealings of nations. Thou shalt kill, if the national interest or prestige demands it or fear suggests the safeguard of the first blow. Thou shalt covet the territory, wealth and power of thy national neighbour. Thou shalt steal and hold up successful thefts to the admiration of the citizens. Pride is glorified as national honour, envy as the claim of national justice. And lying is extolled in Foreign Offices as diplomacy, in the schools as patriotic history. When from childhood men are taught at least by implication this double morality, are educated in the belief that conduct which in the individual is immoral becomes moral and laudable when practised by the nation, it is not surprising that the morality of nations is enormously lower than the morality of the average individual.

Nationalism with its evil fruits can be repressed only when the national state is no longer sovereign. Only when the nations are subordinated to a world federation of states armed with power to restrain or punish the disobedience of any member can they be co-ordinated to the common good of mankind, can assist each other in construction instead of destroying each other. Only then can each produce its full quota to the common store of humanity and develop its distinctive qualities to supplement those of other nations, not to compete with them or cancel them. Only then can patriotism replace nationalism. Already in the Middle Ages Dante in his *De Monarchia* pointed out that man could achieve his end, the development of the entire possibilities of his spirit, in Scholastic terminology " the actualisation of his potential intellect " only if mankind were subject to a common government. To-day when applied science has made the nations interdependent as never before the need is incalculably greater. But this goal seems as remote as ever. Indeed nationalism has never been more powerful. Not only is a world federation at present a Utopia, the more urgent federation of the European States for which the late M. Briand pleaded, is impossible. Every nation, however small, must be a sovereign state. It must set up its tariff barrier though the trade of the world be stifled. It must develop its own industries though the goods could be manufactured better and more cheaply elsewhere. Economic self-sufficiency must be achieved whatever the cost to the citizens. For the device

of nationalism is not " We are members one of another "
but " We keep ourselves to ourselves," a policy as impoverish-
ing in one direction as cosmopolitanism in another. And,
after all, self-sufficiency is possible only for sufficiently large
territories. These territories must therefore be secured even
if, as is often the case, they can be obtained only by annexing
openly or virtually the territory or colonies of another nation.
True, there is a League of Nations. But it was conceived in
the original sin of Versailles, and bears the taint till this day.
Far from achieving disarmament it is impotent to prevent
a rearmament race which, as Pope Leo XIII pointed out long
ago, must inevitably lead to Armageddon. And a body which
has no authority over the nations which compose it tends
to become the sphere in which they intrigue for power and
position. This is not to say that we can dispense with the
League. At least it embodies the idea of international peace
and co-operation and, if the conflict of interests is not too
great, can stop and has stopped war. And if it had prevented
only one war its existence would have been amply justified.
But it must be strengthened and purified or it will perish in
the conflagration of the second world war. And this can be
done only if the citizens of the nations which compose it
fight without compromise the nationalism which threatens
to destroy it.

Catholics who are members of an international Church
and accept a moral code which binds the conduct of nations
equally with the conduct of individuals and lays down the
conditions of just warfare should determine to make that
code a reality. If the governments of Europe knew that not
a single Catholic would fight in a war which was unjust
because it injured the whole world—to apply Victoria's
criterion—they would be more ready to accept the mediation
prescribed by the Covenant of the League. For in almost all
the more powerful states Catholics are either a majority or a
powerful minority. And in our education we could combat

nationalism by insisting upon these fundamental principles.
(1) The moral obligation of nations under the same code as
that which binds individuals. (2) The mutual membership of
nations in the more comprehensive society of mankind even
though the latter has not yet received a juridical expression.
(3) The consequent duty of a patriotism to mankind which
takes precedence over the more restricted patriotism whose
object is the individual nation. These are principles of natural
reason which could and should be held and taught by all.
But, as M. Bergson shews, these principles however valid
theoretically are in practice too weak to resist the instinct which
has actually determined the formation of human groups, the
instinct of mutual defence against some hostile group. As
Aldous Huxley has remarked, only the threat of an invasion
by the inhabitants of Mars could unite all the nations of
mankind to oppose a common enemy. But, as M. Bergson
also perceives, there is a higher principle of unity which
alone has the strength to resist the instinctive exclusiveness
and hostility of nationalism. It is not a humanitarian, but a
religious principle. It is the supernatural union of men in
God through the Holy Ghost and the charity which He
inspires. Catholic theology knows this union as the mystical
body of Christ, the Communion of Saints or Kingdom of God
embodied visibly in the Catholic Church. If Catholic education imbued Catholics with a " real " instead of a merely
" notional " conviction of this fundamental doctrine, it would
become impossible for them to kill their fellow members of
that One Body in the selfish quarrels of the nationalist state.
For it is impossible to subordinate this doctrine of Christian
solidarity to " the military and militarist " objective which
for a Mussolini or a Hitler is the supreme purpose of the
nation and as such must dominate and largely determine its
education, culture and work. Nationalism in as much as it
invests the nation with an absolute and sovereign independence
not only in fact, but in right, so that it need acknowledge no

superior rule nor yield to any more comprehensive society is an idolatry with which Catholics should make no terms.

I have said " Idolatry " and I mean it in the strictest sense. For in so far as nationalism invests the national state with an absolute and unqualified supremacy it invests it with the absolute value proper to God. And idolatry is precisely the ascription of absolute value to the relative and limited creature. As we have seen, Absolute Being is necessarily a Whole embracing in Itself all forms and categories of being so that no being lies outside it. Created being therefore adds nothing to the sum of being. For it is but a half-being which reflects in one aspect or another the fulness of the Divine Being. The national state which implicitly or explicitly claims an absolute value by that very fact claims to be a totality including all other human values and subordinating them to itself. Art, science, philosophy, religion are valuable only in so far as they subserve the nation-state and represent aspects of its life. It admits no law or right above itself, no society, not even mankind which can limit its claims or demand its service. Neither will it admit any right or autonomy of its individual citizens or of voluntary or natural societies within its jurisdiction. Nationalism, that is to say, has made the nation-state the totalitarian state, an idolatrous mimic of the essential totalitarianism of the Godhead. Neither the individual nor the family has or can have any rights against the totalitarian state. For their sole function and *raison d'être*, therefore their sole right is to be members agents and tools of the totalitarian state, cells of its living body with no independent life or function beyond. Still less will the totalitarian state tolerate among its subjects societies of international membership, for example, the Catholic Church.[1]

Strictly speaking, the totalitarian state need not be national. A world state or federation might make this totalitarian claim.

[1] That is in so far as it is true to its totalitarian logic. Expediency may, as in Fascist Italy, dictate a practical compromise. This however is purely external and aims at the enslavement of the Church.

Indeed it probably would make it, and therefore, if there were any likelihood of its formation, it would be necessary to restrict its competence to the organisation of law and order between the nations and to take most careful precautions against its encroachment upon the rights and internal self-government of other societies. In practice, however, the totalitarian states of the contemporary world are national. The most strictly totalitarian of them all, Soviet Russia, claims, it is true, to represent, not a nation, but the international proletariate. But in fact it is a national state and proudly conscious of its nationality. By identifying the cause of the international proletariate with its own and claiming to be the instrument for the establishment of world communism it has secured a moral power over the Communists in every nation. Russia is the despot of the Third International. World Communism must take its marching orders from Moscow. This is the aggrandisment of nationalism, not its surrender. In the sixteenth century the Spanish monarchy claimed a similar championship of Catholicism and leadership of Catholics. But the Pope was not a subject of Spain whereas the Communist papacy is identical with the government of Russia. The signal of *Pravda* " For the fatherland, for its honour and glory, might and prosperity " is a far cry from the original slogan of Marx : " Workers of the world unite." Thus the professedly international totalitarianism of Russia proves to be in fact a national totalitarianism like the rest. Moreover, the Fascist totalitarian states are not averse to surrounding their nationalism with an aura of international Fascism. Sir Oswald Mosley looks to Rome and Berlin as his Mecca and Jerusalem as his Communist opponent to Moscow.

In the last resort Fascism and Communism are forms of the same thing, the totalitarian state. For this reason totalitarianism as a concrete political reality of the contemporary world may be called Fascisto-Communism. No state indeed is perfectly totalitarian. For no ideology can be completely realised in the concrete. Imperfections of material prevent the perfect expression of any form. Nor is every totalitarian state equally totalitarian. Bolshevik Russia is more totalitarian than Nazi Germany, Nazi Germany than Fascist Italy. But in all alike the logic of the totalitarian principle is continuously operative and tends to realise itself more perfectly. However hostile Fascism and Communism may be at present the totalitarianism of which both are varieties must tend to bring them together. Communism will never attain the goal its name denotes, and already admits a considerable measure of private property. And the economic planning of the Fascist state will increasingly encroach upon the economic freedom and financial control of the individual. The doctrine of class war which at present arrays the Communist against the Fascist totalitarian will lose its point when all classes except the proletariate have been liquidated in Russia, and all classes gradually assimilated by the Fascist states. Meanwhile the resemblances exceed the differences.[1] And they are all essential features of the totalitarian state. The government is in the hands of one party which tolerates no other. Its power rests on the triple basis of propaganda, that is to say a continuous and exclusive mass suggestion, state controlled education and terrorism. A system of intensive training, military, nationalistic and ideological, moulds the citizens from childhood. The Pioneers and Komsomol educate a population of Communists; the Children of the She Wolf and the Balilea, a population of Fascists. And the Nazis have organised the Hitler Youth for the same purpose. Loudspeaker and newspaper pour forth an incessant stream of political advertisement on the

[1] Under Stalin's dictatorship Soviet Russia having restored a larger measure of private property, strict discipline in the schools and a greater respect for the family, and even more by fostering patriotic sentiment and admitting the army to political power has been approaching her Nazi foe. In this connection the judicial slaughter of the Old Guard Bolsheviks is extremely significant. We can only wonder why Hitler fails to see this internal rapprochement. By a policy of collaboration with Russia and by mediating between Russia and Italy—as ideologically and in his system of government he is intermediate between them he could build up an impregnable block of the totalitarian powers against the Western democracies.

principle which has made the fortune of many a patent medicine : what is repeated a sufficient number of times must be true. Historic or scientific truth is frankly to be sacrificed to the official ideology. A Congress of German Philologists and Teachers was held at Trier. Its avowed object was to adjust scientific study and teaching to racial and political ideology. Nazi speakers declared that National Socialism must prefer political subjectivity to scientific objectivity, was indeed opposed to pure objectivity. In plain terms National Socialism does not value truth for its own sake but prefers falsehood when it is better propaganda. The majority of the Congress it is true, refused to accept this denial of scientific truth. But the totalitarian state has not had time to mould all its subjects. Its view of the matter is clear and it will educate the next generation accordingly.

A fatal mistake, which the Liberal democracies and the League of Nations have made, to despise the sensible and emotional appeal to eye and ear, has not been repeated. There are flags, parades, uniforms and anniversaries. Nazi labour day, the anniversary of the March on Rome or the anniversary of the October Revolution are celebrated by emotionally intoxicated crowds. In the dictator, a blend of the demagogue and the tyrant, the totalitarian state is individualised and exercises the appeal of personality, evoking the loyalty which an impersonal group could never secure. Freedom of opinion does not exist. No man who does not subscribe the official creed can speak his mind frankly. The administration of justice is avowedly made a weapon with which the government combats its opponents. Such weapons are the Russian courts, which administer the class justice of the ruling party, or the Peoples Courts of Nazi Germany. Campaigns are conducted against " wreckers " or " grumblers " that is against those who are regarded as hostile or insufficiently friendly to the omnipotent state. Secret terrorist tribunals—whether they are called Ogpu or Gestapo matters nothing—served by spies,

agents provocateurs and political police condemn the innocent
for the sole crime of hostility to the regime. And political
opponents are often punished without a trial of any kind—
a revival of the *Lettres de Cachet* for which the *Ancien Regime*
is so justly blamed. Evidently in such a state there is little
room for the freedom of individuals or societies. Russian
Bolshevism attempted to destroy the family as a check upon its
omnipotence, the Fascist and Nazi governments abuse it to
provide subjects for its training. And since the latter method
is less unnatural and equally efficacious, it is in fact replacing
the former in Russia. An Italian, German or Russian parent
who wished to educate his children in a doctrine hostile to the
official creed would find it an extremely difficult task. They
would be trained against his will in an ideology he detests.
There is not much left of parents' rights. In the totalitarian
state all the professions, even those to which liberty is most essential, journalism, education, literature, the fine arts, drama and
music are organised by the state and utilised as instruments of
propaganda. And the economic weapon is ruthlessly
employed. For the man whose conscience rejects the orthodoxy of the Communist or Fascist Caesar the totalitarian
state has neither employment nor food. In Russia the victim
is the bourgeois and the priest, in Germany the Jew, the
Socialist and the Pacifist. This economic persecution is not
indeed employed in all cases in its extremest rigour. But it
is employed, and its potential victims must live in terror
of a more rigorous enforcement.

The totalitarian state is a reaction against nineteenth century
Liberalism. The latter however united a valuable truth with
a disastrous blindness. The truth which Liberalism perceived
was the right of individual conscience. Because the state
rests and must rest on force, and force has no place in the
sphere of spirit the state has no place there. Its competence
is confined to the sphere in which alone the use of force is
legitimate the protection of its citizens from force or fraud.

(This, however, includes, though Liberalism refused to perceive it, the economic sphere.) The higher levels of human life, science, philosophy, art and, above all, religion of their nature demand a free activity. The use of force here is the violation of spirit, a practical materialism. Therefore the force bearing society, the state, has no right to interfere. At this point, however, blindness overtook Liberalism. Having secured this freedom it was content to stop. Rejecting an ideology forcibly imposed by the state, it ignored the necessity of a social tradition based on a free vision of truth shared by the members of a community. Aware of no social bonds other than those of state authority it could not establish an organic society. The societies of the *ancien regime* were organic. For they embodied a system of belief and tradition accepted by the society as such. But they were not free. For they attempted to maintain that system by the force of the state. The Liberal society on the other hand is free. For it rejects state compulsion of opinion. But it is inorganic. For it accepts no social forms, expressing social views of truth, which could bind the community into an organic whole. The direct line of advance should have been from the organic but unfree society to the society both organic and free : organic, because the embodiment of a vital social form a vision of truth ; free, because that form was not enforced upon the members of the society by the state, but was the product of their genuine insight or voluntary acceptance of the insight of others. That is to say the state should have become the organ of a wider organic society functioning only within the sphere in which the use of force is legitimate. The failure of Liberalism to make this advance has led directly to the servile state of totalitarianism. For it left a void in which the individuals it had freed could find no social organism to combine their efforts to a common end, no philosophy or creed on which such an organism could be founded. Having no ideal and supervital community of intellectual and spiritual vision they necessarily fell back upon the biological community of the nation, and nationalism grew up with its national militarism, or upon the economic community of class and Socialism flourished with its class war. But the sole community beyond the family left for a secularist Liberalism—the religious Liberalism of England compromised with the old social tradition—was the state conceived as a compromise or contract of selfish individuals. Such a state was thus left in undisputed occupation of the social field and the way was open for its totalitarian claim. It had only to identify itself with the absolute claim of nationality or the absolute claim of class to produce respectively Fascist and Communist totalitarianism. For man's innate capacity and need for religion must find satisfaction in some absolute to which he can give an unqualified surrender and allegiance. Having lost vital faith in the true Absolute, God, our contemporaries are finding a sham absolute in a deified human group, the absolute nation or the absolute class as embodied in the pseudo-church of a totalitarian state. The national state, the sole community which the solvent " rationalism " of the Enlightenment had left standing is only too ready to accept the rôle. And this pseudo-church has its pseudo-pope, the dictator. In the nineteenth century, happily for human freedom, the popular leader who based his power on mass suggestion, *e.g.*, Mr. Gladstone in his Midlothian Campaign ; and the militarist statesman who relied on force, *e.g.*, Bismarck the Iron Chancellor : were distinct and mutually hostile. To-day they are combined in one man—the dictator of the Totalitarian State, Stalin, Mussolini, Hitler.

But the pseudo-church must have a creed as well as a hierarchy. What is the creed of the totalitarian state ? I will define it in brief : it is a pantheist energeticism which deifies a human society as the expression and flower of a cosmic force. Materialism is the philosophy which teaches that corporeal matter is the ultimate reality, the mental but an epiphenomenon which it wholly determines. Idealism, at least as understood since Berkeley, is the philosophy which teaches that reality is solely mental, matter a state of consciousness. Analogously energeticism should mean the doctrine that reality is energy. In this sense, however, I should have to admit myself an energeticist. For I hold that all objects are energies, whether the energy be of the lower order which constitutes a corporeal object, physical energy, or of the higher order which constitutes a spirit, the spiritual energy we call will. Intermediate is the vital energy of the plant and on a higher plane of the animal. This view, however, is not what I mean by energeticism. For it does not hold that an energy pure and simple is the ultimate and Absolute Reality. Besides energy there is another factor of being, the character of an object, its form. God the Absolute Reality is the perfect identity of energy and form. And in creatures form has everywhere the primacy over energy. For it is the form which by its union with a merely potential energy, its matter, constitutes the actual energy, the energy-object in question.[1]

Moreover, the mind apprehends not energy but form, whether through the senses, the external form of bodies or mental forms, ideas. And these perceptions of form by reason must in turn determine our action, if it is to be truly intelligent.

Energeticism, on the other hand, gives the primacy to energy to force. For energeticism, Absolute Reality is an unintelligible force. And everywhere form is the product of a force which determines it, which moreover, is conceived as a blind force, not as itself determined by a form. Corporeal form is determined by physical energy, spiritual form, idea, by the higher energy we term volition. Everywhere energy is prior to and more important than the form, corporeal or ideal, which is, so to speak, its deposit. Indeed this energy

[1] For a detailed explanation of this I must refer to my *Philosophy of Form*, Chapter I.

continuous in its lower and higher manifestations, is primarily conceived as biological—a vital force between the physical and the spiritual orders though somehow manifesting itself on both these levels. It is moreover a cosmic energy which of itself without any transcendant Creator has developed the world. This cosmic force whose immanent law is a dialectical process of evolution and history flowers in man and in the perfect human society he is destined to establish. Man is the priest, this society the church of this cosmic deity. But in as much as man is the most perfect expression of this divine energy he or rather the human society of which the individual is a cell, is also the god of his own worship.

In accordance with its exaltation of cosmic energy, in man energeticism exalts vital energy, instinct, desire, will, or practical activity above intellect, the function which apprehends form and above contemplation its concentrated exercise. Energeticism as I have defined it, is, in one form or another, and whether explicit or merely implied, the predominant philosophy of the present and, in all probability, of at least the immediate future; and it is the ideology of the totalitarian state in all its forms, Fascist or Communist, and as such the theology or rather the " anthropology " of a pseudo-religion which is already opposing and persecuting, and will continue to oppose and persecute, genuine religion because it affirms a God Whose wisdom has created and ordered all things.

As Christopher Dawson has pointed out, in an address to the Rationalist Association, confidence in human reason is justified only if the universe is regarded as ultimately rational, the work of a Divine Reason. The rationalism which affirms reason on the basis of materialism is self-stultifying. To which I would add that genuine rationalism is possible only if we admit the power of the human intellect to apprehend form in its various categories and levels directly, not by an impossible conclusion from purely sensible data. It was, in fact, this misconception of the nature of rational proof

P

which left human knowledge naked before the scepticism of a Hume and dissolved it finally into a mere association of phenomena, ideas or sensations without any other justification than inveterate and invincible habit. (J. S. Mill and Mach.) In practice the process of disintegration was delayed by many factors. Such were Christian beliefs held on faith, moral perceptions accepted rightly or wrongly as self-evident or bolstered up by a grossly inadequate utilitarianism. There was also the strength of a social code : " It isn't cricket." And the amazing triumphs, theoretical and practical, achieved by the mathematical reasoning of the physical sciences, justified in practice the claim of reason, which could no longer be justified in theory, and made the universe appear intelligible even though it were in the last resort the expression and product of an irrational force.

But the end came. Christian beliefs, divorced from an adequate intellectual foundation and reduced to sentiments, vanished as the mists they had become. Traditional morality was questioned in every sphere. The theoretical triumphs of the natural sciences left unanswered all the questions to which an answer is most urgently necessary and their practical triumphs made possible the unprecedented horror of modern warfare. And sooner or later logic will out. If reality is unintelligent, human reason can no longer be sure of itself. It may be nothing more than a tool forged by blind forces, making for biological survival and its seeming apprehension of truth an illusion of biological origin and utility. Men should, it is true, have argued conversely : reason self-evidently apprehends truth, therefore the universe in which it arises and in which it functions must be itself intelligible, the expression and product of reason. But they did not. Even Lord Balfour was content to argue for a Christian fideism on the basis of an intellectual scepticism. In fact the researches of sociology, economics and above all of psychology were showing how many and how powerful were the irrational factors at work in determining our perceptions and judgements. And, as is the way with novel theories, the influence of these factors, great as it undoubtedly is, was exaggerated into omnipotence. The factor in question might vary—might, for instance, be a method of economic production, the herd instinct or a repressed complex. But for its devotee it explained everything. Thus " the flight from reason," to employ Mr. Lunn's striking phrase, became general. Men were certain of nothing beyond their sensations and desires. They drifted hither and thither, trusting no chart—some listlessly, others despairingly.

Some sought refuge in feeling—for example, in the artistic emotion of that æstheticism fashionable in the " naughty nineties," whose motto was " Art for art's sake," or in the emotion, half æsthetic, half religious, of a Celtic twilight, or, more nobly, in the religious sentiment into which many modernists within or without the Church sought to dissolve religious truth. And more recently Mr. Aldous Huxley, sceptical almost of mathematical truths, will base a practical philosophy on moods recognised as nothing more, on a skilful balance of emotional excesses. Others turned to action—a few advocating the theoretical pragmatism which reduced truth to that which works, multitudes living by the practical pragmatism which gets on with its job without asking what its ultimate value and purpose may be. And emotionalism and pragmatism united in an undoctrinal religion of practical charity.

The emotionalists were superficial, mistaking a mere concomitant of reason and volition for man's deepest function. But the pragmatists were implicitly exalting energy, the force which action expresses, above reason—were therefore energeticists. And this energeticism appeared even more clearly in such a philosophy as Nietzsche's, for which the ruthless will of the superman is the supreme value. For M. Bergson also the intellect is simply a crystallisation due to the arrest by matter of a vital force—the celebrated élan vital. This life force is the reality of which the entire process of evolution is the product and expression. Years later M. Bergson has improved on this conception by distinguishing from the infra-rational élan a higher super-rational energy, man's spiritual will united in mystical religion to a transcendent God. But even here, where it is presented in the noblest and the least objectionable form, energeticism has not been overcome. Intelligence and the fixed forms it apprehends are still arrests of the cosmic process, obstacles to life. And the Deity Himself is, it would seem, energy, will, rather than intelligence, intelligible Form self-understood, the pattern of all form and the Truth in whose light we see truth. In short, though M. Bergson has reached a belief in the Holy Ghost, the Lord and Giver of life, he has not reached the knowledge of the Divine Word, the light of light. Moreover in the long interval between the publication of *L'Evolution Créatrice* and *Les Deux Sources de Religion et de Morale* his biological and *apparently* pantheistic energeticism had ample time to foster the movement towards irrationalism.

Another manifestation of this energeticism was the exaltation of the sexual instinct by D. H. Lawrence as the supreme manifestation of an instinctive life which alone grasps concrete reality and flouts the empty shadows of reason. It was his dark religion of the blood.

The two leading schools of psycho-analysis are two most influential forms of energeticism. For Freud and his followers man's entire mental life is determined and moulded by sexual desire (in the widest sense)—a biological and irrational energy. For Adler and his school this psychological sovereignty belongs to the desire for power—an energy equally instinctive and unintelligent.

But all these forms of energeticism are individualist. It is the desire, the instinct, the will of the individual which is exalted as autonomous and sovereign.[1]

---

[1] The statement needs qualification in the case of M. Bergson—but is, roughly speaking, true.

But of all philosophies (I am using the term in the widest sense as an outlook on the world and life, a Weltanschauung) energeticism least of all could remain individualist. The individual must necessarily be too keenly conscious of his own weakness in face of an environment, natural and human, so largely hostile. I am not simply stating the truism which the most stalwart individualist must admit—that the individual cannot accomplish *his own* will, attain his *private* ends without the co-operation of others, without society. For this is equally true of the theoretical aspect of human life. Without learning from others a man can know nothing, can think nothing : without their assistance he cannot make his thought known. The dependence I have in mind is far deeper and more intimate. The man for whom energy in some form or other, vital, volitional or both, is the supreme reality is normally too conscious of his individual weakness and too strongly bound by the social instinct to make his personal energy-instinct, his individual will, the centre of his thought and practice. He must merge it in a social or collective energy by which it is supported and in whose strength it partakes. His social instinct is thus satisfied by his incorporation into a society inspired by the same purpose and the same loyalties, moved by the same emotions, sharing in a common life—that is in a common energy which is the sovereign reality. And he is conscious of being taken out of himself and raised above himself by this greater and more comprehensive power. He is no longer confined by his individual limitations, condemned to his private impotence. He shares in the vaster and mightier energy with which he has identified himself.

The strong man, the man of powerful personality and tenacious purpose, the natural leader, is also attracted to a social energeticism. For in proportion to his gift of leadership he may hope to wield and direct this social energy, to make it fulfil his aims. The latter are by no means necessarily his private and purely selfish interests. Indeed, this base form of egoism is hardly compatible with the qualities which evoke the loyalty inspired by the great leader. The leader's typical characteristics are love of power, the determination to impose on others what he believes to be good for them, the ruthlessness which refuses to tolerate opposition and the firm belief in his capacity and vocation to rule. And the man who successfully claims the sovereign command of a society, inspired by and embodying a social energy, regards himself as the supreme instrument, indeed the supreme embodiment, of that energy—that social life or will.

Thus both types of energeticist, the follower and the leader, tend to pass from a purely individual to a social energeticism. And this is the process which is being accomplished under our eyes. It is the rise of the totalitarian state. For the totalitarian state is a society which is constructed by and embodies a social energy. And this social energy incarnate in the state is held to be the supreme value which must dominate and comprehend all others. Its intellectual deposit is a philosophy which affirms the supremacy of this energy and its social embodiment. The Liberal society, nowhere, of course, existing in its pure state, but the political ideal and partial accomplishment of the nineteenth century, was inorganic. For it regarded society as a compromise and contract between its individual members for their common interests and mutual protection. The totalitarian society on the contrary is united by a common vital principle, is a social organism. In this respect it is more organic and more perfect than the Liberal society. But it is vitiated by a fundamental deordination—the energeticism which it embodies. The ideal society embodies a social energy determined by a spiritual form or order, a structure of truth perceived or *freely* accepted by its members. It cannot, therefore, embody an irrational force of which the social form is merely the deposit and product. It cannot, express and be constructed by a biological energy; for example, race or the herd instinct embodied in a national state, nor by an economic force such as the interest, real or alleged, of an economic class. Still less can it depend upon, or even be upheld, by mere physical force, with its extension the mechanical instruments of war. For this is the lowest and most irrational kind of energy. But in a world of sin and ignorance a society which uses force is indispensable. Therefore, the force-bearing society, be it a state or superstate, cannot be the supreme human society even in the natural order. It must be no more than its instrument for police purposes, with its competence strictly confined to the sphere within which the use of force is justifiable because inevitable, namely, the protection of individuals and groups against force or fraud, the latter including unjust economic pressure and exploitation.

In all these respects the totalitarian state as realised to-day —though like the Liberal state more or less incompletely— perverts the true order. On the surface the energies expressed by the totalitarian state differ. In Russia it is the class interest of the proletariat, in Italy Italian nationality with a revival of the Roman empire in the background. In Germany it is the Nordic race. But all these alike are irrational forces which determine not only the structure of these states but to a large extent, the ideas, the ideologies they respectively embody. And so far are these societies from restricting force to its proper sphere that they impose their ideologies, their official creeds, with a relentless intolerance, penal and economic—above all by their forcible monopoly of propaganda and education—the Press, the wireless and the school. Thus the state becomes co-extensive with the entire society, sovereign in every sphere. If the Nazis by the mouth of Herr Rosenberg declare that the state is but the organ of the racial community; since its competence is universal, for all practical purposes it is identified with the latter. And if the ultimate disappearance of the state is a Marxian dogma, it is postponed to a shadowy millennium while in practice the state is omnipotent. There is no place for the supernatural claim of religion. The state has its own religion, the deification of the force it professes to embody, and thus of itself as the social incarnation of that force and of its chief as its individual-social incarnation. Any compromise with any other creed, as in Italy and still partially in Nazi Germany, is a matter of pure opportunism. Ultimately the totalitarian state must mould religion to its service or destroy it.

Nor can subordinate groups enjoy a free existence within the state. They can be no more than its organs, wholly dominated by its purpose. They can pursue no aim inharmonious with the will it incorporates, uphold no doctrine which does not conform to the ideology officially prescribed. Even science must teach no truth unwelcome to the state—in history least of all. For the social energy which the state represents must determine truth—which of course is a naked assertion of the energeticist fallacy. At a congress of German historians Nazi speakers openly declared that only Nazi truth must be taught. Rosenberg and his followers propagate and are seeking to impose a Nordic religion avowedly dependent upon and peculiar to a particular race. Thus the ultimate truth about Reality with which religion is professedly concerned is made dependent upon and relative to an irrational force, biological race. It is a " religion of the blood." This is energeticism in excelsis—and moreover the social counterpart of Lawrence's individualist energeticism—his " dark religion of the blood." For in both the deified energy is biological—race and sex. The inherent absurdity of energeticism could not be more clearly displayed than in this frank declaration that the truth about the universe depends on race, is different for Nordic and Mediterranean humanity. The metaphysical falsehood is supported by the anthropological myth contradicted by Rosenberg himself—for what is consistency to a thorough-going energeticist?—of a pure Nordic race and the unscientific assumption of an Aryan race corresponding to and presumably co-extensive with the linguistic group of that name.   This racial energeticism—not to speak of its affiliations with Gobineau and that wild Anglo-German Houston Stuart Chamberlain—has much in common with the energeticist philosophy of history invented and popularized by Spengler.[1] For Spengler the historic cultures are expressions of an irrational force and their intellectual systems, their creeds and philosophies, even their sciences and mathematics, are therefore not insights real or supposed into the nature of reality and thus true or false, but purely subjective creations of these cultural forces without reference to any objective truth or error and without a common standard of comparison or mutual intelligibility.

If the orthodoxy of Communist Russia does not deny objective truth so blatantly, it measures the truth of philosophies and even of scientific hypotheses by their conformity with its official ideology.   Any metaphysical doctrine or scientific conclusion which cannot be reconciled with orthodox Marx-Leninism, as expounded by the infallible anti-church—the Communist party—is denounced as bourgeois, and an instrument of the exploiting capitalist to delude and enslave the masses, and as such to be refuted not by argument but by the police. Law has been regarded hitherto as the impartial assertion of an objective justice, reflecting the natural law of right reason with its objective standards of right and wrong and maintaining the intrinsic rights and liberties of man as an intelligent being. For law, so understood, the social energeticism of the totalitarian state has no more room than it has for objective truth.   Law is avowedly but an instrument of that state—a weapon forged and employed by the organism embodying

[1] *Untergang des Abendlandes*

a social force. Justice must be a weapon of the class struggle, declared Lenin. And Bolshevik Russia has been faithful to his command. Nazi justice is equally cynical. Nor was it by a scrupulous observance of law that Italian Fascism climbed to power. Imprisonment—preventive detention is the Nazi euphemism—even execution without trial, as in the Nazi murders of June 1934, or more extensively in the Red Terror : political trials in which there is no justice for the accused—the class enemy or the traitor—savage penalties for the mere expression of opinion—torture secretly inflicted—not to speak of castor oil or rubber truncheons for political opponents—all these illegalities and barbarities are manifestations of a practical energeticism which translates the energeticist ideology into an actual violation of justice, the form of a rational community, by an irrational force. And this practical energeticism is also displayed by the Fascist exaltation of war as man's noblest social and moral activity. When Mussolini glorifies militarism as the crown of the Fascist national culture and praises the soldier at the expense of the musician—implicitly of all who in every branch of art and letters raised an Italy, politically divided and impotent, to the cultural sovereignty of Europe, he is frankly proclaiming the supremacy of physical force over the intellect which apprehends and produces form and is itself the form of intelligent life and action. Catholic Fascism is therefore self-contradictory—an attempt to combine obedience to the Divine Reason, the Word of God with obedience to an irrational social force, self-deified, and expressed by the arbitrary acts of the Duce. And the Bolshevik exaltation of the inferior activities of mechanical construction and economic organization (though unlike war these are constructive, good and necessary) above activities determined by higher insights and purposes—is but another manifestation of energeticism in practice.

On closer inspection the energeticist ideologies of the

several totalitarian states will be discovered not simply to represent different forms of energeticism but actually to be reducible in the last analysis to one fundamental energeticist philosophy, humanist and pantheistic. And that philosophy when it has been finally worked out and clarified is, I believe, destined to unite the ideologies, at present in subordinate points so hostile, of Fascism and Communism. And as the orthodoxy of the Fascisto-Communist state of the future it will prove the archenemy and persecutor of theism in general and Christianity in particular. For the social energeticism professed more or less explicitly by the various totalitarian states and movements is fundamentally identical. The ultimate power is the force of a human society which, since humanity obviously did not originate itself, must be regarded as the flower of a cosmic energy which is the true and sole absolute. That is why the logic of these totalitarian ideologies leaves no room for religion, even if they may compromise with it for opportunist reasons. Fascism has not yet worked out a complete philosophy. Its metaphysic is still largely implicit. And this would seem to be particularly true of Italian Fascism. The state as incarnate in the Duce, its collective will as represented by his, are indeed declared the sovereign authority and value—religion therefore being relegated to a subordinate position. But this social will is not, officially at least, declared the self-expression of the absolute cosmic force. This, however, is the logical implication of the absolute supremacy demanded for the will of the nation as embodied in its leader.

The official philosopher of British Fascism, Raven Thomson (Alexander Raven), in a book bearing the significant title, *Civilization as DIVINE SUPERMAN*, proclaims his faith in the social " super-organism " which is the true superman whose power is shown in its mighty technical achievements, " the towering skyscrapers . . . great tunnels . . . huge liners . . . vast airships and radio " which are " investing mankind with the collective attributes of supermen."[1] And for James Drennan Fascism embodies " The passion for infinity of western man " : the Faustian Man of Spengler. " There is a *blood-urge*, a spiritual passion, a mighty mystical import . . . which seeks—with an infinitude of proud ambition—to master the material bases which have hitherto brought the men of all time to the doom of an inevitable end." Here once more we meet with the religion of the blood, animal instinct, individual in Lawrence, social in Herr Rosenberg, also Nietzsche's superman with his will to power collectivized as a superhumanity. This combination of blood and power as an ideal unites in a social form the physiological energeticism of Freud, and the power energeticism of Adler. And this social energy is a cosmic force which thrusts forward its supreme human embodiment and bears it irresistibly to the victory its omnipotence guarantees. The belief is no doubt as consoling and as inspiring to the individual or group which believes itself the instrument of this cosmic energy as was the Calvinist's conviction that he was the chosen and predestined instrument of God's will. If the language of Sir Oswald Mosley himself is more restrained he sees in Fascism the final wave of a collective Cæsarism which will sweep man to his final triumph—in other words, the social Cæsar embodied presumably in the individual leader enthroned and worshipped as god, a god whose every word and deed is an utterance of the divine cosmic energy which inspires its human mouthpiece.

The official philosopher of National Socialism, Herr Rosenberg, makes it clear that he has no belief in the Transcendent God of the theist and the Christian. His deity is the human spirit and the racial society which is its noblest

---

[1] Since writing this book Mr. Thomson has modified this collective humanism. But though it no longer represents the personal belief of its author, the book may be taken as expressing the tendency of that collective humanist energeticism of which Fascism is a manifestation. And its quotation by Mr. Drennan in his Fascist manifesto proves that it is acceptable to British Fascists.

expression and embodiment. And this human spirit is conceived biologically rather than spiritually. It is the development of a dark irrational cosmic force which he appears to identify unwarrantably with the Godhead above God preached by Eckhart. For Eckhart although an energeticist in so far as he envisaged It primarily as energy rather than form, understood by the Godhead the spiritual reality which leaves little room for the reality of creatures and thus tended to an acosmic pantheism or theopanism akin to that of the Vedanta. Herr Rosenberg's deity is wholly immanent, the underlying energy of the cosmos which is its self-evolution. In short, though he rejects Hegel Rosenberg is an Hegelian who has transposed Hegel's self-unfolding cosmic intellect into a corresponding energy. And as for Hegel the Prussian state was the ultimate and the noblest self-expression of the cosmic intelligence, the Teutonic or Nordic race is for Rosenberg the supreme self-expression of this cosmic energy.

At first sight the official ideology of Communism may seem remote from this social energeticism of the Fascists. For it is professedly the orthodox doctrine of Karl Marx. And the philosophy of Marx was not energeticism but materialism. Taking over through Feuerbach the Hegelian philosophy of an immanent reality unfolding itself by its inherent dialectic Marx replaced Hegel's intellect, not like Rosenberg, by energy, but by matter. But from the outset this matter was regarded not as an inert stuff mechanically moved from without but as invested with an intrinsic motion. For dialectical materialism the world is a cosmos of energies passing into one another by the inherent dialectic whereby each motion involves and produces its opposite. It is a Heraclitean world of constant flux in which opposites are born of each other and flow finally together in a higher unity. But this self-moving matter is energy and such a materialism an energeticism. And although in contradistinction to mechanical materialism dialectical materialism admits the objective existence of forms of motion higher than the mere local motion of material particles, quality as objectively distinct from quantity, sensation, thought, these are the automatic products of the former when it has attained a given complexity. They are not products of superior forms pre-eminently contained in the Divine Mind and derived from it upon a given complex of lower energies. They arise spontaneously out of the latter into which they are once more transformed in the endless interchange of cosmic forces, their inherent dialectic. Moreover since philosophy is held to depend upon and express the interests of a particular economic class the knowledge of truth is determined in the last analysis by an irrational social force, as thought itself is determined by an irrational cosmic force. Berdaiev is thus justified when in his Essay on the General Line in Soviet Philosophy he maintains that it is not strictly materialism but what he terms a " lightless spiritualism." For matter is invested with what is called autodynamism, self-movement, an inherent energy whereby it evolves itself. And this autodynamism manifests itself as the collective activity of the Communist proletariat and its leaders. The consciousness of this proletarian anti-church is, therefore, the measure of truth, its work the highest achievement of the cosmic force which gave it birth, namely, autodynamic matter. Indeed, since natural laws are but its self-posited expressions they are in principle as subject to the collective will of Communist humanity as are the laws of morality and justice. All who resist the collective will of the Communist society are therefore resisting the absolute cosmic reality, sinners against it, as for the Christian the man is a sinner who resists the will of God. Evidently the Soviet philosophers are working out to its logical conclusions the social energeticism implicit and partly explicit in the various forms of Fascism. The logic of Fascist philosophy is Communist philosophy. For if the sole ultimate and absolute reality is a purely immanent self-developing energy which finally produces and is embodied in a human society whose power is as absolute as its source and substance, there can be no room for any other Deity. Any practical Fascist compromises are illogical and transitory. It is true that, as Berdaiev points out, the official terminology of Soviet philosophers is still inconsistent. A self-determining energy whose highest expression is human will should not be termed matter, even autodynamic, but frankly the energy which it is. And moreover, since its most perfect expression is human volition, it is primarily spiritual, material forces being but its inferior manifestations. Here the Fascist energeticisms may seem more logical. But it is simply a question of terminology. And after all is Rosenberg's divine blood flowering in the Nordic race so much more spiritual than the autodynamic matter flowering in the proletarian class?

And there is a sense in which all these social energeticisms are materialist. In as much as human thought and therefore human purpose depend upon and are the product of the lower quantitative motion which is irrational and unconscious, dialectical materialism still retains, no doubt as its inheritance from the nineteenth century, a genuine materialism. This materialism however is incidental and may disappear as the energeticism latent in the systems develops its inherent logic. All forms of energeticism and therefore its social expressions are, however, materialist in a more fundamental and permanent sense. For they are in Berdaiev's phrase, lightless. They exalt energy, even though it be the spiritual energy of will, above intellect, life, therefore, above light. But it is precisely form which is everywhere the intelligible factor of being and on the higher levels the principle of subjective intelligence, that is to say of mind. Form constitutes the potential energy which is its metaphysical matter, the actual energy which is an object, corporeal or mental, in accordance with the character of the form in question. Energeticism, therefore, since it exalts energy above intelligibility and intelligence, force above form, and regards the latter as the product and deposit of the former reverses the metaphysical order of being. For it makes its formal dependent upon its material factor. It is therefore a materialism of a subtler description, a materialism of metaphysical though not of corporeal matter. And, moreover, it tends to a practical materialism in the grosser sense. For since a formless energy is a metaphysical impossibility, by exalting energy above mind it exalts energies informed by lower forms, mechanical, economic or biological, at the expense of the higher energies whose forms are spiritual principles of a higher order. Such inferior energies are racial purity, bodily health and fitness, economic organization, technical achievement as in the machine worship of Bolshevism and its idolatry of mass production—even for Mussolini the destructive energy of war. The Duce differs from the Bolshevik in as much as for him the cult image in which the divine energy resides and finds expression is not the machine but the machine gun. But as we have already seen, all these lower activities, though with the exception of war in themselves good and necessary, should subserve the higher activities of the human spirit—for example, art, theoretical science, philosophy, and, above all, religion. Instead the latter are subordinated to the former; and the highest, religion, wherever energeticism is logically carried through, is denied and proscribed. And it is but the logic of this energeticist deordination when physical force in its crudest form is freely employed to suppress unwelcome ideas.

The feuds dividing the totalitarian states which at present embody this social energeticism will no doubt prove long and bitter. They may well involve the world in the conflagration of another war. For they concern the nature and determination of the society which is to embody and fulfil the cosmic force, and to be the anti-church of divine superhumanity. Since, however, these differences cover a fundamental identity, the energeticist creed of a world force flowering in social humanity, that identity will in the end prevail over the more superficial divergencies. It will produce the totalitarian society of the future, the society of man self-deified as the purpose and fulfilment of the absolute energy immanent in the world it has evolved and in the totalitarian community which is its final achievement. It will fashion the " religion " of pantheist energeticism as the orthodoxy of the totalitarian state. For believers in the transcendent God, in His Divine Reason and in the Holy Spirit of Love, one with that Reason in the identity of the Godhead, truce or compromise with such a creed is impossible. It is as impossible as was a compromise with its predecessor and counterpart, the Cæsar worship of Imperial Rome. The sole possibility is relentless war, the sole alternative death or victory.

The energeticist ideology which is taking shape in the totalitarian societies of Fascisto-Communism will be the pseudo-religion of the coming age. It is undeniably seductive. To a generation which rationalism has bereft of faith in reason it offers a faith in life as expressed by the collective social energy, to those who have lost faith in God the worship of a self-deified human group. The tendency to appeal from reason to life was already evident in pragmatism and in the cult of individual self-expression in art, success financial and social, or sex. But this individual energeticism was too feeble, too isolated, too disintegrating. Social energeticism is constructive and comprehensive. It flatters man's pride and stimulates his energy. For it presents himself and his achievement as the climax of a cosmic energy which is bearing him irresistibly to victory. It satisfies his social and combative instincts in the tasks and struggles of a militarised society. It covers the inner emptiness created by loss of a transcendental religion and hides its theoretical deficiencies with the exhilarating enthusiasm of practical work and comradeship. For action is exalted above thought, production above knowledge. There are visible achievements to strike the imagination and soothe the soul into oblivion of her supernatural destiny. It is above all a creed of youth with its eagerness to be up and doing, its impatience of a speculation without immediate tangible results. In place of the lost communion with God it bestows a keen sense of communion with the life of nature. Man feels her life blood in his veins, her force in his activity. For he and she are one, expressions and creations of one vital cosmic energy, in whose self-creation both partake, and man in the supreme degree. For in him the life of nature is self-conscious and her instinctive operation has become the accomplishment of a deliberate purpose. Nor can any limit be set to this cosmic power immanent and conscious in man. It has already transformed the face of the globe. Why should it not create an earthly paradise free from poverty and pain and postpone death till man has had his fill of living and is ready to cease ? For the same human will which has harnessed the forces of external nature may harness the obscure psycho-physical forces which determine the nature of man. Nor should we feel surprise that energeticism and the totalitarian society which embodies it should offer such attractions. The number of the Beast is not ooo but 666, the perfect number minus one.

The inevitable conflict between the sham religion of the totalitarian state, the worship of deified man, and the true religion which adores the transcendent Creator of man has already begun. In Russia it is a war without compromise or quarter. In Fascist Germany hostilities have opened without a formal declaration of war. In Fascist Italy there is for the moment a truce. But the latent hostility between Fascism and Catholicism came to the surface in the conflict of 1931 when the Pope's encyclical displayed the intrinsic incompatibility which makes a final and genuine reconciliation impossible. Moreover, in face of a determined religious opposition the Fascist state can afford to compromise and wait.

For by its monopoly of education it possesses the children and therefore the future. In this war between the totalitarian state and religion the prospects of the latter are dark. A state which wields every weapon of propaganda and penalty, and has a complete control of economics and education, can and will persecute with a scientific thoroughness approached in the past only by the successful persecution conducted by the Japanese Shoguns. Of the attractions held out by energeticist humanism to contemporary mankind I have already spoken. Transcendental and other-worldly religion, already sapped by the rationalism of the eighteenth and nineteenth centuries, will seem pale and unreal beside the tangible fruits of the humanist tree of knowledge. Nor can we hope that the totalitarian state will break down. Individual states may, but not the totalitarian type of social organisation. Liberalism cannot defeat the totalitarian state. For the totalitarian state is the offspring of its defects and will devour its parent with those good qualities by which it excelled its supplanter.

What then is our hope? Truth and the God of truth and the human soul in its capacity and destiny for both. Not for ever will the efforts and victories of social achievement conceal intellectual inconsistency or stifle spiritual need. The central depths of the soul will throw off the weight of humanist work and enjoyment superimposed by the totalitarian state, in a gigantic effort to satisfy its innate craving for the God who made it for His dwelling. Man's hunger for God will not finally be satisfied with the substitute religion of a deified humanity. The struggle will be long and bitter. But the victory of truth is secure. The society at once organic and free of souls united supernaturally with God and in Him with one another will vanquish the servile society whose bonds are falsehood and force.

The kingdom of a social humanity deified by the self-donation of God will overcome the kingdom of a social humanity self-deified. The totalitarian state of antiquity, the

Roman Empire which worshipped Caesar as divine, was conquered after three centuries of martyrdom by the Christian Church. And the organisation it had built up served its conqueror. In like manner the true totalitarian national states, even perhaps in a remoter future, their federation, erected by Fascisto-Communism will be defeated by the Church of God. And the organisation which they are building up will become the framework of a world order inspired by religious faith and the charity infused into our hearts by the Holy Ghost. The work of a social energy exalted above form, a community of wills which acknowledges no order of objective truth above itself will surrender itself and its products to the Absolute Will, the Love which proceeds from the Absolute Reason, the Logos, conjointly with Absolute Power, the Father. The totalitarian state which proudly thought to usurp the place and prerogative of God will have prepared the way and constructed a social instrument for the sovereignty of Divine Wisdom.

NATION AND STATE

It is too often taken for granted that the terms nation and state stand or at least ought to stand for the same thing— the national sovereign state. The doctrine of national self-determination understood as the right of every nation to constitute a completely sovereign state which has split Europe into twenty-four states barred and bolted and largely arming against each other is founded on this principle. Indeed all the excesses of modern nationalism—above all the rise of the totalitarian state have been made possible by it. Yet the simple fact that the nationalities of Europe are in many regions so intermingled that unless populations were forcibly trans-planted on a gigantic scale its complete application is a geo-graphical impossibility should give its advocates pause. And there are few I think, who would maintain that the nationhood of Scotland and Wales makes it right or expedient that they should become independent sovereign states ; or that French Canada should become a sovereign state, not only outside the British Commonwealth of Nations but separate from British Canada. And who can think that South Africa would be more prosperous or freer if an attempt were made to divide the Dutch and English speaking populations into two inde-pendent states with customs, barriers and military defences against mutual aggression ?

Evidently it is neither desirable nor even feasible to make nation and state co-terminous. The utmost that can be said is that wherever a nation occupies a reasonably large conti-nuous area it tends to form a state. And even this tendency is far from universally operative. Not until the nineteenth century did the Italian and German nations form unified states. And even now the process is incomplete. The Ticino is no part of Italy; Austria and the German cantons of Switzerland are outside the Reich.

It may be replied that the Italian and German Swiss though of the same race are not of the same nation as the Italians and Germans of Italy and Germany. How then does their situation differ from that of the Italians of the Trentino before the war, or of the Bavarians before 1870? The sole difference assignable is their sense of membership in a nation which, originally artificial, has been welded into a genuine nation by centuries of political community.

For in the last resort a nation though a very real thing is indefinable. Many factors go to its making, race, language, territory, a common history. But a nation exists only when these are informed by a distinctive group feeling. In so far as a human group feels itself a nation, a nation it is. Even when the Cornish spoke their own language they did not feel themselves a nation. The Welsh do. And even had there been no Gaelic speaking highlands the Scotch would no doubt still have been conscious of a distinctive nationality.

The state on the other hand is essentially a group wielding force. As usually understood it is a sovereign state—a society which enforces its will upon its members but itself admits no higher authority to whose will it is in any respect subject. Protectorates and the states which compose a federation prove that a state is not necessarily sovereign. Indeed, I am convinced that H. G. Wells is right in holding that in the reduced and interdependent world of to-day the sovereign state is a mischievous survival, a principle of anarchy which involves at best a latent condition of universal war. Only a supreme super-state with power to impose on the states a legal settlement of their disputes can save human civilisation from perishing in the flames of a war unprecedented in its devastations. This, however, must remain a dream so long as nation and state are identified to the present degree. For every nation

will believe that by surrendering the absolute sovereignty
of its state it will derogate from the fulness and freedom of its
nationhood.

Moreover, as I have already pointed out, the totalitarian
state—the state which claims omnicompetence and absolute
control over its citizens—is based upon this identification
between nation and state. For it demands an unqualified
loyalty. And loyalty is not inspired by the state as such.
The policeman, judge and tax-collector, however indispensable,
do not evoke it. It is the nation which by the instinctive
attraction of its various factors—in the first place a common
soil and a common speech—inspires that variety of group
instinct which we term loyalty to our native land or patriotism. Indeed, as we have seen, it is this patriotic loyalty which
in the last resort constitutes nationality. It is by identifying
itself with the nation that a state is able to claim the loyalty
the nation inspires and can therefore go further and make
an absolute claim upon its citizens. Only when the wielder
of social force (individual or group) is identical with the
representative of the nation is a totalitarian dictatorship
possible. Not even the nation indeed has an absolute claim
upon its individual members. For it neither embodies an
absolute nor even a supreme value. Neither truth nor beauty
are determined by it. And the notion of a national God is a
blasphemous absurdity. Nevertheless nationality plays a part
in every sphere even the highest. Though it is absurd to
suppose that religious truth can differ for an Englishman and
a German, the Englishman and the German will probably
regard the same truth from a different angle, determined in
either case by a difference of national temperament. And
their respective emotional reactions to it will often differ.
So long as the state does not intervene these national
influences are less likely to prove harmful. Education, rational
reflection and criticism, and international intercourse can do
much to supplement the exclusiveness and correct the

deficiencies which the operation of national feeling produces. When however the state identifying itself with the nation employs its control of force to uphold and impose these nationalist limitations they are rendered so powerful that for the majority of citizens it becomes a moral impossibility to overcome them.

The ideal is not indeed a featureless cosmopolitanism which flattens out national differences. It is the inclusive and positive patriotism which seeks to make the best of distinctive national endowments for the wider service of mankind and displays a generous appreciation of the endowments and achievements of other nations. And this ideal is most likely to be reached, if the nation is not identified with a state which asserts itself against other nations and measures the national welfare not by the nation's contribution to humanity but by the extent of its power, as against, and at the expense of other nations.

Thus from every point of view the nation should be kept distinct from the state. Normally indeed to the nation a state will correspond. Without some state organ a nationality is likely to prove too weak or indefinite for its full development. And a full development of the distinctive cultures of all nations is required for the full development of human culture as a whole. Some measure of local home rule would therefore seem desirable for such nations as Wales and Scotland —as it is in fact possessed by the far smaller communities in the Isle of Man and the Channel Islands. But the state, be its competence wide or restricted, must be regarded as no more than the organ of the nation within the legitimate sphere of government. It is not sufficient merely to distinguish between the state and the nation. The Nazi ideology as voiced by Herr Alfred Rosenberg makes this distinction. But after Soviet Russia, if indeed after it, Nazi Germany is the most totalitarian state in existence. For if the state is to be the organ of the nation *in every sphere*, its competence is co-extensive with the nation. For practical purposes state and nation are identical. The sole way in which a distinction between the state and the nation can be maintained is by limiting the former strictly to its rightful sphere of jurisdiction. This is the sphere within which the use of force is justifiable because inevitable. And the use of force and therefore the competence of the state should be confined to the protection of the citizens from oppression by force or fraud. The state must guarantee their security and freedom. Under modern economic conditions however these cannot be effectively guaranteed without such a degree of state control as must constitute at least a serious menace of totalitarianism. The problem of combining the necessary economic control with respect for the liberty of individuals and voluntary societies, though not insoluble with good will, is extremely difficult. Next to the maintenance of international peace it is the most urgent political problem of the present day. If however the economic control of the state is strictly confined to the production and distribution of necessaries, and in other spheres does not go beyond the enforcement of satisfactory conditions of pay and work it should be possible to prevent any state control of art or opinion. And if the state's educational jurisdiction were limited to the provision of sufficient opportunities for its citizens without compulsory education, and, if conscription with its tyrannical and unjustifiable claim that the state has a right to take by force the lives of its innocent subjects, were also abolished, these restrictions would go far to neutralise the inevitable increase in the economic interference of the state.

That the power of the modern state will in fact be thus reduced in the near future I have little hope. At present the tide is everywhere running more or less strongly in the direction of the totalitarian state. Already in many countries the most sacred of all individual rights, freedom of conscience in matters of religion, has been restricted, if not altogether refused. But it is not the business of the political philosopher to acquiesce in what is or in all human likelihood will be. He must attempt to discover and proclaim what should be, hoping that in the long run, at least, reality will correspond more closely with the ideal.

In place of the totalitarian state which in practice, if not always in theory identifies nation and state, our ideal must be the nation of which the state is but a departmental organ inspiring no deeper loyalty than the police force. The bond which would unite such a nation would be an organic bond, not the force of physical compulsion, but an integral complex of vital forces partly biological and partly spiritual. And this complex and its component forces would be determined by the citizens' intuition of social forms. Such forms are biological forms of racial kinship, the external features of the national landscape, historical forms that have moulded the national past, the intellectual forms of common ideas, aesthetic forms of national art and craftsmanship. And the intuition of these social forms must be free, not imposed on the individual by force or by a propaganda and educational system which do their utmost to blind him to anything beyond. Of a common vision will be born a free co-operation in a common task. Those who cannot share the vision or contribute to the task must be at liberty to take their own way so long as they do not positively hinder their fellows. For their solitary vision and work may finally enrich the common store. To secure this freedom it is well worth our while to make every citizen a minimum payment sufficient for a frugal subsistence irrespective of work—the vagabond's wage advocated by Lord Russell or the national dividend of the Social Creditors. The modern community can produce sufficient wealth to give it. Thus freed from the stigma of slavery and moved solely from within the life and therefore the work of the nation will be an organic process analogous to the life of an individual organism determined from within by its organic form. But since it is a free co-operation of individual vision and labour not enforced by violence or a mass hypnotism organised by an all-powerful government, this life process and the work it inspires will be the nation's not the state's. The Liberal nineteenth century continuing the work of the eighteenth produced the thesis of individual liberty. The twentieth is producing the antithesis of the organic society. The former forgot that the national society is an organism, not a mere aggregate of individuals. The latter forgets that an organism whose members are rational human beings must be free, if it is to be genuinely organic. The synthesis which we must expect, if the dialectical process of history is not frustrated by some intrusive factor from without, must combine the freedom of the liberal thesis with the organisation of the totalitarian antithesis. But the freedom will be greater than it was in the old liberal strife because the economically stronger will not be permitted to exploit the economically weaker. And the organisation will be more perfect than in the totalitarian state because it will be the genuine organisation effected by an intrinsic vital principle, not a largely artificial organisation imposed by the force and craft of a dictatorship.

This free social organism whose life principle is determined by a social form accepted voluntarily by the reason and heart of its members is, as we have seen, possible only where state and nation are clearly distinguished. Moreover, it is only by this distinction that we can solve satisfactorily the problem of the relations between religion and the temporal society, between God and Caesar. Ideally a society should be religious, not merely the individuals who compose it. Religious truth should be the highest of those forms which I have called social, the forms which render a society organic when freely accepted by its members. That is to say a nation should have a religion. On the other hand experience has abundantly proved that an established Church is an enslaved Church. When Caesar patronises religion it is to exploit it for his own ends. The exceptions have been extremely rare and confined to individual rulers. Moreover, a state must rest upon force and use force. But force lies wholly outside and below the order of religion in which everything from first to last must be the free conviction and choice of the soul. Therefore the state can no more be religious than the post office or the system of sanitation. If, however, the state and the nation are distinct, the nation can have a religion, although the state which it employs as its organ of government has none. If a nation can be Catholic, though there is and can be nothing distinctively Catholic about its post office or system of transport, a nation could be Catholic though its state, as befits its compulsory character, were purely secular. Under present conditions, it is true, even the nation must be secular. For its members do not in fact share a common religious conviction. But in this respect the contemporary nation is not and cannot be organic. And any attempt to achieve this religious unity by any state action direct or indirect would, as we have seen, violate the nature of religion. But the ideal, however remote its realisation must be, is the religious nation employing the secular state.

Is there anywhere in the modern world even the rudiments of that distinction between nation and state which alone can secure our freedom from the tyranny of a totalitarian state? It would seem as though everywhere the state were extending its control over every department of the national life. In Marxian theory it is true the state is nothing more than a temporary expedient, a weapon defeating the class enemy and an instrument for setting up the ideal economic society, destined therefore to disappear entirely when its task has been accomplished. But this is pure theory. In practice the Russian state is totalitarian imposing its official Marxian creed by a tyrannous proscription of recalcitrants. Nor does its tyranny shew the least sign of diminishing. And, as we have seen, Rosenberg's distinction between state and nation is equally unreal. There is, however, one nation and group of nations in which nation and state are partially though very partially distinct. And it is no accident that of all the major powers that nation and group of nations are still the freest, though their freedom is lamentably imperfect. I refer to Great Britain and the Commonwealth of self-governing British dominions.

The fact of this distinction, however incomplete, between state and nation in Britain and her Commonwealth was most forcibly displayed by the Jubilee of the late King George V.

Who then was the centre of an empire's loyalty, the point on which its patriotic devotion was focused? The head of the state? In theory, yes, in fact, as certainly, no. Only in theory is the King the head of the state, the "supreme governor" as the Anglican Prayer Book terms him. In fact he is not head of the state, not a ruler. He is the head of a nation, of a group of nations. He can command no force to compel our loyalty, can make no law nor prevent any law from being made. Whereas the continental dictator can slay men untried, he cannot condemn even in the course of law. Nor does he even pardon an offender. He cannot declare war nor, if war is declared, wield the armed forces of the country. Nor can he conclude peace. No officials are of his appointment though they hold his formal commission. Therefore that natural group sentiment which is patriotic loyalty can be directed to the King where it could not without the gravest danger to liberty be directed to a genuine ruler. The instinctive need to focus loyalty to the nation upon an individual whose humanity appeals to the imagination and touches the heart can be gratified without risk of slavery, if that individual does not govern. Because our King can no longer compel our homage, he is a fit object for the homage of freemen. Because he is head of the nation, not of the state, loyalty to him does not tend to an idolatry of the state. Political power there must be, if we are to escape anarchy, the prestige of a national head, if the nation is to be united and vigorous. But only when the power of the head of the state is divorced from the prestige of the head of the nation is liberty secure. The unity of an allegiance to a national head who does not rule is not achieved by force. The power of the sword is not perilously redoubled by the power to stir the hearts of a people. The crowds who lined the streets to see King George pass or gathered night after night to await his appearance on the balcony of Buckingham Palace were paying their affectionate homage not to their commander, but to the father of a vast family of free adults.[1]

When we turn to the commonwealth the King is no longer head of the state even by a legal fiction. As the Statute of Westminster makes plain, he has not even authority to retain their allegiance. But as their super-national head he holds the Dominions in a voluntary union which has saved the world from the curse of several new sovereign states. If the British Commonwealth of Nations is in some respects a model of what a free union of all nations might be, this is largely due to the existence of a super-national head without real jurisdiction. If we are wise we shall not forfeit our unique advantage by centring our patriotism on some actual ruler, be he a dictator or merely the leader of a party. Nor shall we forfeit it by reinvesting the monarch with the least tittle of real sovereignty. For we should be throwing away the invaluable distinction between the head of the state and the head of the nation which we at present possess. Too easily does patriotism destroy freedom. Against that danger our loyalty to a monarch who does not govern is a safeguard not lightly to be surrendered. We should rather realise consciously the nature and value of the institution to which our constitutional development has unwittingly given birth—a genuine national head who is not the head of the state. The French President indeed, like several others, is not the head of the state. But he owes his position to the operation of the

[1] It is however deplorable that the Sovereign should wear a military or naval uniform and hold military and naval rank. As head of the nation, not the state he should be entirely divorced from any connection with force.

governmental system and is not in any profound sense head of the nation. He is merely its figurehead. Elsewhere patriotic sentiment is focused on a tyrant who exacts by terrorism the adulation of those who are not hypnotised by propaganda. If we would continue members of a free nation, not slaves in a servile state—and even here the jurisdiction of the state has unduly encroached upon our liberties—let us watchfully maintain and logically develop the distinction between nation and state represented in germ by the position of the British crown. Never has it been more valuable or more necessary than now. Precisely because, to adapt a resolution moved in an eighteenth century Parliament, "the power of the state has increased, is increasing and ought to be diminished," we should cherish the throne of a King whose monarchy is and must continue to be confined to his peoples' hearts.

There is indeed a danger, and unfortunately by no means remote, that in the event of war the government will prostitute loyalty to the national head to the service of militarism. Middle-aged men like myself can remember how loyalty to the Crown was employed to encourage recruiting for the Boer war, a war every whit as unjust as the Italian conquest of Abyssinia. But this danger, real as it is, would be greater not less, if already the nation's loyalty were directed to the head of the executive. And if we make it clear to ourselves and others that we are loyal to the King only because and in as much as he does not wield force, we shall be able to resist this perversion, if and when it is attempted. It is the combination of patriotism, loyalty towards the nation and a national head, without control or use of force, with devotion to the state, the organisation of social force, which is fatal to peace and freedom. And against that combination, the distinction between the nation, the object of true patriotism, and the state, the indispensable organ of force, but with no more claim upon our emotional loyalty than the post office, is an effective safeguard.

THE PHILOSOPHY OF MARXISM

To speak of a Marxian philosophy may seem a misnomer. For Marx and his disciples disclaim philosophy and profess only a universal conspectus or synthesis of the sciences, a comprehensive view of their interconnections. Since, however, this synthesis is a doctrine of reality as a whole it is a philosophy. Indeed it must be a philosophy. For it can synthesise the special sciences only with the aid of a principle more universal and more ultimate than the departmental principles which the sciences employ. And the preoccupation of Marxists with certain philosophic systems whether to modify or oppose them, notably the philosophies of Hegel and Feuerbach and the sensationism of Mach and Avenarius is another proof that Marxism possesses a philosophy. It is in truth among its merits that it is not content with an empiricism or positivism, not content to accept the detailed results or even the general laws established by the special sciences without co-ordinating and sub-ordinating them in and to a picture of the universe as a whole. Engels criticised the older materialism for its failure to take this step and thus, as he aptly put it, failing to see the wood, the general pattern of reality, for the trees, the detailed facts and sequences of facts. This general view is, in fact if not in name, a philosophy. And this official philosophy of Marxian Communism is dialectical materialism.

Dialectical materialism is a compound of Hegelianism and materialism. For Hegel the universe is the unfolding of an immanent reason by a dialectical process. This dialectical process in which the logic of the cosmic reason unfolds itself is threefold. There is first an affirmation, a thesis. This is followed by the contrasted truth, the negation of the former, the anti-thesis. Finally this antithesis is in turn replaced by its contrast, the negation of its negation of the original affirmation. Since this final stage denies the denial, the antithesis, of the first stage, the thesis, it restores the positive truth of the latter, but in combination with the positive truth of the former, and is thus the synthesis, which includes the thesis and antithesis while transcending the limitations in virtue of which they contradicted each other. But whereas for the idealist Hegel this dialectic was the development of a cosmic idea, for Marx and Engels it is the movement of a material reality of which ideas are subjective reflections.

As against mechanical materialism which conceived reality as a series of mechanical interactions between material objects, this dialectical materialism conceives motion, and motion in accordance with the dialectic discovered by Hegel, as the essential mode of material, that is, of all being. Matter is self-moving, autodynamic. Consciousness and thought, and above all will, are thus higher forms of this cosmic motion, not mere epiphenomena of a mechanical process.

This materialisation of Hegel had indeed, as Marx recog-nised, been already effected by Feuerbach. But whereas Feuerbach was content with a theoretical philosophy, for Marx speculation, ideology as it is now termed, is subordinate to action. The object of philosophy is not to know the nature of the world but to change it. Indeed it is through action, because we are able to act upon and change objects, that we know that the latter are objectively real, not mere projections of human sensation and thought. This practical criterion, however, as Lenin pointed out in his critique of Mach and Avenarius, does not mean that, as pragmatism holds, truth is merely what works in practice, a working hypothesis. On the contrary what is found to work in practice must be objectively true. Because we can change external objects, these objects must exist independently of our knowledge of

R

them. Nor is the dialectic process insignificant or barren. On the contrary it is teleological. For it results in a progress, an ascent from lower to higher forms of being and motion.

The supreme achievement of this progress is the rational and purposive life of man. By his knowledge and manipulation of material laws, above all of the universal law of dialectical motion and in particular its exemplification in the economic-social development of human society, man is able to build up the perfect human society. On the other hand, since he can do this only in accordance with the inevitable process of economic-social development he cannot, as certain Utopian Socialists imagined, produce this society at any time or place and at a single stroke. He can do so only by understanding and utilising the course of economic-social development, as it unfolds in accordance with its dialectic. Capitalism must therefore precede Socialism and Socialism " a system of planned production for use in which the products (of labour) are distributed in accordance with the quantity and quality of the work done," roughly the system actually established in Soviet Russia, must precede Communism " in which the products are distributed according to needs and work is done according to ability," " from each according to his ability, to each according to his needs." Moreover, as material objects determine our sensations and thoughts of them, not vice versa, the economic conditions of production determine the type of society and its institutions and beliefs. " All ideas and tendencies without exception have their roots in the condition of the material forces of production." This is the materialist conception of history. It does not, however, mean, as is often supposed by its critics, that economic facts are the sole causal agents in human history. It affirms merely that all the factors of an historic situation, ideal and material, are interconnected and that in this causal complex economic causes are ultimate, or more strictly penultimate, since they are themselves determined by geographical factors. " According to the materialist conception of history," wrote Engels, " the determining element in history is *ULTIMATELY* production and reproduction in real life. . . . If somebody twists this into the statement that the economic element is the *ONLY* determining one, he transforms it into a meaningless, abstract and absurd phrase. The economic situation is the basis, but the various elements of the superstructure—political forms of the class struggle and its consequences—constitutions established by the victorious class after a successful battle, forms of law—and even the reflexes of all these actual struggles in the brains of the combatants: political, legal, philosophic theories, religious ideas and their further development into systems of dogma—also exercise their influence upon the course of the historical struggles and in many cases preponderate in determining their *FORM*."

Criticism of this Marxist philosophy must conclude (1) that it is conditioned by the particular historic situation in which it arose, (2) that *within certain limits*, it states or attempts to state the truth, (3) that outside those limits it is totally blind to the truth and (4) that this rejection of more ultimate truth, while not invalidating the truth it affirms, leaves that truth incomplete, unstable and vitiated by fundamental error. Marxism attempts to erect into a solid self-contained philosophy the rationalist materialism for which the material world made known by sense perception and the sciences based upon it is the sole reality. And it was essentially a reaction against the pure idealism of German philosophy, in particular its most massive expression, the philosophy of Hegel.

Marx and Engels oppose their materialism to this idealism, as Lenin later, to the subjective sensationism of Mach and Avenarius. They are concerned to refute the notion that the material world reflects consciousness and thought as they manifest themselves in human sensation and thought. To hold that material objects exist independently of our knowledge of them and determine that knowledge is in their view materialism. To be a materialist is to regard knowledge as wholly determined by the external universe. " A return to the materialist standpoint means . . . to comprehend the real world-nature and history just as it presents itself to everyone who approaches it free from pre-conceived idealist fancies . . . to sacrifice every idealist fancy which could not be brought into harmony with the facts conceived in their own and not in a fantastic connection. Materialism means nothing more than this."[1] That this realism has always been held by the Aristotelian philosophy accepted in the Catholic schools and is not necessarily materialism, but realism, of which materialism is but one variety, seems not to have entered the minds of the Marxists. For when Marxism arose this scholastic philosophy was almost universally discredited. Even within the Church, though its fundamental realism was of course maintained, for this alone was compatible with Christian dogma, it had largely been abandoned in favour of various makeshift systems. It is not therefore surprising that Marx and Engels had eyes only for two extreme positions, pure idealism and materialism, and never seriously considered the ideal realism of scholastic philosophy. And as against all forms of pure idealism, as later against the sensationism which resolves objects into complexes of sensations and the pragmatism which rejects objective truth, their realism, miscalled materialism is fully justified.

Certain systems of philosophy are radically perverse. For

---

[1] Engels, *Ludwig Feuerbach*, Ch. IV. " The materialistic outlook on nature means no more than simply conceiving nature just as it exists without any foreign admixture." (*Ibid*. From a fragment hitherto omitted.) This of course is simply objectivism, realism and as such a true and sound principle. The denial that even the facts of corporeal nature imply a spiritual principle as their ultimate ground and explanation is indeed suggested by Engels' language. But on their face value as they stand these definitions do not express their genuine materialism. They affirm nothing more than realism.

For Plekhanov that " being determines thought," not vice versa, is the " fundamental thesis of modern materialism " (*Fundamental Problems of Marxism*, Eng. Trs., p. 42). It is, in fact, the fundamental thesis of realism, and therefore, as Pater Lippert has pointed out, a fundamental principle of Catholic philosophy.

they start from a false premise. Such, for example, is the idealism which regards the material universe as a form of sensation or thought, whether this be conceived more object-ively as an immanent cosmic thought or consciousness or more subjectively as human consciousness and thought. And as Lenin rightly argued, the latter and indeed even the former type of idealism leads logically to solipsism. For since our knowledge of other minds is given through and in the action of bodies, if we deny the objective existence of bodies, we can be certain only of our individual consciousness. Moreover, if we extend practice to include the primary apprehension of resistance we can agree with Lenin that the objective existence of external objects is apprehended by our practical dealings with them. What we are up against must exist.

In starting with this immediate apprehension of objective reality, as it has always been taken for granted by unso-phisticated common sense, Marxism set out from a funda-mental truth. And for this reason it is rather partial truth falsely claiming to be the whole truth than a positive error like the idealisms, sensationisms and scepticisms against which it was primarily directed. However little it may rise above the ground it is at least solidly built upon it.

Idealism hangs in the clouds, an unsubstantial if beautiful construction.

> "I would build that dome in air
>   That sunny dome, those caves of ice."

Of such a castle in the air Hegelianism was the most ambitious example. And it was followed throughout the nineteenth century by many similar castles in the air, for example the absolutisms of Bradley and Bosanquet. And because they were built in the air, they had no influence upon the living thought of the century, which was a crude, scientific positivism, and finally collapsed altogether, yielding place to scepticism and various forms of irrational energeticism. In contrast with them Marxism may be compared to a bungalow, low and narrow but firmly planted on the soil.

Marx was justified in taking over from Hegelianism its doctrine of the historical dialectic. It is possible to discover in human history and indeed in the course of evolution, before man appeared on the planet, a movement from thesis through antithesis to synthesis. Advance in one direction yields to advance in an opposite direction and this in turn to an advance which combines what is positive in both. Physical size, for example, is developed to its utmost in the giant reptiles of the Mesozoic age. This is followed in the mammals by the development of brain until its climax is reached in man whose brain is the instrument of reason. And human reason in turn makes use of physical magnitudes as its instrument on a scale incalculably exceeding the physical magnitude of the hugest body. In human history freedom pushed to the verge of anarchy tends to give birth to despotic rule and this in turn to a system of government in which freedom and authority are combined.

Both Hegel and Marx, it is true, pushed the dialectic to unwarrantable extremes. The factors at work in the history of the universe and of man are so numerous and so complex that their mutual interactions forbid any attempt to explain human history in detail by the dialectic process. What in one aspect is a synthesis may be a thesis or an antithesis in another. Nor is it always clear what movement we are to take as our thesis. The determination must be often an arbitrary choice determined by our particular interest. Nor can any dialectic movement develop simply and purely. For in the intricate web of cause and effect no factor can operate in isolation and develop unhindered and unmodified by other factors. Nevertheless we can detect a dialectic process in the development of the world and mankind. And it results in a spiral movement of evolution and history in which the lowest point of the upper spiral is above the point reached by the corresponding point of the spiral below it. Moreover this dialectic and the spiral movement in which it tends to result are in truth due to matter, though not matter as the materialist understands it. As I have argued elsewhere,[1] all finite and contingent being is composed of matter, that is potential energy and form, their union constituting an actual energy-object. In itself form is of infinite implication and involves the entire order of being. Therefore the realisation, the thesis of any form, would in itself involve the realisation of all forms of the entire ideal order. Matter, however, in its inherent deficiency permits only a limited reception and realisation of form. Form can therefore be realised only to a limited degree and to the exclusion of complementary form which it implies of itself. Therefore this realisation must be one-sided, along a particular line and involve an absence of this complementary form. When, however, this realisation has proceeded so far that this particular form cannot, at least under the actual conditions, be further realised or has reached the utmost limit of its isolated realisation it yields to the realisation of its complementary and contrasted form, the antithesis. And when this antithetical realisation of form has reached its limit it in turn must yield to the realisation of the original form on the basis of its own realisation, and in co-ordination with it. Thus the new form realised is not a simple restoration of the original but a synthesis of both forms by the realisation of a form comprehending both. That is to say an ideal realist philosophy of matter and form must accept the dialectic taken over from Hegel by Marxian materialism, though, as we have seen, we cannot ascribe to it the exaggerated scientific value accorded to it by Marx and Hegel alike. It is an underlying principle of evolutionary and historic development operative throughout their infinitely complex course, and dimly visible in it, but not a scheme precisely determinable and applicable

[1] *The Philosophy of Form,*

with scientific accuracy. Moreover the deficiency of matter which produces the dialectic prevents its inherent logic working itself out with rigid accuracy. As its embodiment of form is defective, its embodiment of the logical development of form must also be defective.

On the other hand we must reject the Marxian contention that the dialectic contradicts even partially the fundamental laws of logical thought, identity, contradiction and excluded middle. Because in a process of change, A is not completely realised but coexists with a partial realisation of B which, moreover, has always been potentially implied by A, for example, to use Plekhanov's illustration, when a head is turning bald, there is simultaneously a measure of hair and a measure of baldness, it does not follow that A is also B. The hair as such excludes baldness, and the baldness as such excludes hair. And if we can say with some truth that the head is and is not bald, two contradictory predicates are not thereby applied to the same subject. We do not affirm that A is and is not B. Both statements are partly untrue. Strictly speaking we should say not that the head is or is not bald but that it is partly bald and partly covered with hair. This may seem rather elementary. But the fact that the Marxian and indeed the Hegelian statement of the dialectical principle should be deformed by this error shows how much accuracy of metaphysical thought had declined since the Scholastic epoch.[1]

Moreover, even where the dialectic can be detected in a particular sphere it is not susceptible of indefinite repetition. A final synthesis may be reached which concludes that particular dialectic process because the form developed by it has

---

[1] The corresponding Marxian error that motion involves the contradiction that an object is and is not in the same place at the same time is less obvious. Its solution, I am convinced, is to be found in the ultimate discontinuity of motion, a view which should indeed have appealed to Marxism which rightly emphasises the sudden character of decisive changes. (See Plekhanov, *Sudden Changes in Nature and History*. Plekhanov, however, unwarrantably identifies sudden historical changes with outbreaks of violence. They by no means always coincide. The advent of Christianity though a sudden was not a " violent " revolution.)

been fully realised. No doubt this achieved synthesis and closed dialectic is itself part of a wider dialectic which can never be closed while the world and humanity continue. But the particular process is complete and its dialectic closed. If, for example, materialism is the antithesis of idealism its synthesis must be ideal realism. Therefore the thesis of Hegelian idealism and the antithesis of Marxian materialism must be succeeded by the synthesis of ideal realism. But in fact this synthesis had been already achieved by scholasticism and the Hegelian thesis itself arose not from any intrinsic disintegration of that synthesis but from its unwarranted abandonment, due to external causes. Here then the synthesis must be a restoration of a synthesis long ago achieved, the re-established synthesis of a metaphysical dialectic achieved and closed in the past. Moreover, since the Marxian ascribes a final truth, if not to the details, at least to the fundamental principles of dialectical materialism he is compelled to regard it as the closed and finally achieved synthesis of philosophic truth, however he may attempt to escape this consequence by appealing to its unlimited capacities of detailed application in the future. For however extensive these may be supposed, they cannot, if Marxiam is true, alter the fundamental truth and finality of dialectical materialism as opposed to conflicting philosophies, idealism for example, or pragmatism.

It has been argued that a professed materialist has no right to affirm an historical and cosmic dialectic. The dialectic of an idea is, it is said, conceivable but not the dialectic of matter. The objection does not seem to me valid. Granted the Marxism view of matter as mass in constant motion it might well be that the necessary limitations of this movement compelled it to assume the dialectic pattern. Advance in one direction might well be exclusive or at least excessive until the excess in this direction was balanced automatically by movement in the contrary direction. And this second movement equally exclusive or excessive would in turn be balanced by a reverse movement which, however, would not be a simple return but, having, so to speak, assumed momentum from the second movement, would reach a point beyond that reached by the first of the three movements. This would not indeed happen in a purely mechanical system, where motion would be but the swing and return of a pendulum to the same point. But dialectical materialism is not mechanical, since it ascribes to matter a power of spontaneous, that is, self-generating motion.

The term dialectic is however a misnomer when used by a materialist. For it essentially implies the unfolding of an idea.

But although, the name apart, a dialectic is not inconsistent with materialism, a qualitative progress is incompatible with it. If the ultimate nature of reality is corporeal mass in motion its development cannot achieve a higher order of being. Quantity and complexity might increase. But this is not genuine progress. The dialectic, that is to say, would express itself only by such processes as the movement of one barley corn to the many produced by the grown plant, which Engels adduces, not very happily, as an example of it. In a materialist universe there might be many spirals but they would be isolated fragments jumbled together confusedly. There could not be the spiral staircase which we actually find. Without mind the dialectic could not be teleological.

When therefore Engels dogmatically affirms " that in spite of all seeming accidents and of all temporary retrogression, a progressive development asserts itself in the end [1] this optimism has no warrant in his materialist philosophy but is a pure act of faith which the founders of Marxism shared with the vast majority of their contemporaries, for whom progress was an unquestioned axiom. But it is a faith which can have no foundation apart from belief in Divine Providence.[2] Engels is fond of charging and justly charging his opponent Duering with propositions which imply theism.

---

[1] *Ludwig Feuerbach*, Ch. IV.   [2] See Christopher Dawson *Progress and Religion*.

But his own belief in an inevitable progress belongs to the same category. In a universe which is the product and development, even the dialectic development, of irrational matter there can be no reason why this development should be an inevitable advance in a rational and moral direction.

The conception of autodynamism does not really overcome this objection. For if the self-movement is intelligent and purposive, materialism is abandoned. In fact, since all matter, even inorganic, is autodynamic, materialism has yielded to a pure idealism. If, however, the self-movement which determines the course of cosmic development, the motion of inorganic matter, which preceded all other motion, on which the higher forms of motion depend for their existence and which must ultimately destroy them—we are speaking of course only of this empirical universe which is the sole reality the Marxian admits—is irrational, a blind spontaneity, it could not have given rise to a teleological evolution culminating in human reason and will.

Nor is this progress explained by Marxism when it states as a law which conditions the dialectical process, the transformation of quantity into quality, for example of water into steam when boiling point is reached. For this law simply states an empirical fact, a phenomenon, what happens. It does not explain why it happens. Such a change of quantity into quality is indeed unintelligible on the materialist assumption. For the sum of a particular factor A cannot of itself produce a new factor B. If empirically this seems to be the case, reason compels us to go below the phenomenal surface and perceive that a given quantitative intensity having prepared the material substratum a new form, the novel quality, has supervened. And since this form cannot supervene from no-where, it must come from the ideal order, from the Divine Source of Form, the Word of God.

It, is however, precisely the fundamental error of Marxist materialism that it confines itself to the phenomenal surface, or rather, since this is impossible, if any view is put forward of the nature of reality as a whole, that it starts from the phenomenal surface and admits no data taken from a deeper level of being. Metaphysics is not only concerned with being as an extensive whole but with being as an intensive whole, not only with being in every department but with its profound essence. Though Marxism claims to teach the nature of reality in every department, namely that it is mass in motion, it avowedly sets out from the phenomena of nature and human history, the data of the departmental sciences, not from the properties of being as such. Any attempt to scrutinise the properties of being and argue from them to the fundamental nature of being is rejected as abstract metaphysics, philosophy in the sense in which Marx condemned it. It is, however, impossible to answer the ultimate problems of being without this scrutiny. Only an intellectual gaze steadily fixed on the properties, the forms of being as such, will reveal the metaphysical composition of form and matter in all limited and contingent being, the impossibility of higher being arising of itself from lower being, and the implication in the nature of contingent being of an Absolute Being transcendent of the contingent universe, and its creative source. Without this metaphysical apprehension of metaphysical form the utmost that can be achieved by a survey and co-ordination of empirical phenomena is a system such as Marxism, a system containing indeed general truths apprehended by this co-ordinated survey, a frank and sound acceptance of the witness borne by the senses and by common sense to the corporeal universe, but unfinished, without an ultimate and satisfying explanation of the truths it affirms or a consistent statement of them. For the part cannot be understood apart from the whole, the phenomenal surface of reality in isolation from its depths. Nor can its various aspects be reconciled; for example the appearance of reason in an irrational universe. If the Marxian bungalow, unlike the idealist dome, is built on the solid earth and much sound material has been used in its construction, the human mind cannot live under its low roof and in its confined space without being intolerably cramped. For it needs a metaphysical home which, however firmly founded on the earth, soars upwards to the heights of spirit, therefore not Marxism, but the ideal realism of the philosophia perennis.

The Marxist may reply that his system does culminate in a dome, the spacious and lofty dome of the perfect Communist society, stateless and classless; and moreover since this society will be the product, not of unreal supernatural forces, but of the inherent law of the economic process, it alone is built not in air, but on solid foundations. But even if this classless society were the inevitable product of economic social forces, it could not be the dome to which the human spirit aspires. It is not high enough. No merely human social order, however perfect, can satisfy a spirit made for an eternal life and an Absolute and Infinite Good.

But in fact this earthly paradise does not and cannot follow from the premisses of dialectical materialism. Why should irrational forces result infallibly in an order of reason and social righteousness? That they should produce any reason and any righteousness whatever, even the modicum which has been actually realised in human history, is indeed, as we have seen, inexplicable and impossible. That they must produce a perfect order of reason and righteousness is more inexplicable than the inexplicable, more impossible than the impossible.

Moreover, for Marxism the dialectical process never ceases to operate. It is not even admitted that a particular dialectic, e.g. the metaphysical dialectic which has produced a satisfactory view of the nature of reality, for Marxism, materialism, in our view ideal realism, ceases when its synthesis has been achieved. Marxism emphasises the factor of motion in the universe of flux and change, not indeed to the exclusion of the complementary factor of rest and endurance, but so excessively that no synthesis can be final. Why then should

the social dialectic cease when the Communist millennium
has been achieved? Actually Marxism regards this ideal
society as a perfect social equilibrium bringing to an end the
pendulum sweep of the dialectic which produced it. It
attempts to reconcile this finality with the continuance of the
dialectic by holding that the latter will continue indefinitely,
but as an indefinite progress within and beyond but not
against the Communist society. But if this further progress
does not change the fundamental principle of the Communist
society, society will remain Communist until the end of
human history, though it did not and could not have remained
permanently patriarchal or permanently capitalist. That is
to say the Communist society in its fundamental constitution
will be exempt from the process of universal change which
destroyed all its predecessors. But this exemption is
arbitrary. Moreover, permanence leaves no room for
the negation of the previous movement which is an
essential part of the dialectic. In fact the dialectic will be
replaced by a rectilinear progress within a permanent social
synthesis, and therefore cease to operate, which on Marxian
principles is impossible.

The Marxian millennium, incompatible, as it is, with
Marxian materialism, with the excessive emphasis on the
factor of motion and the unendingness of the dialectical process
which is to produce it, did not originate in the logical development of dialectical materialism. It was imported into it by
Marx from another source. This was a disguisedly religious
faith in an ideal social order, a kingdom of truth and justice
in which the poor would be exalted, the wealthy and powerful
abased. This kingdom is in fact the Kingdom of God on
earth which the Jewish prophets had proclaimed, whose
advent was the burden of Our Lady's revolutionary hymn,
" He hath filled the hungry and sent away the rich empty,"
and which has never ceased to haunt the Jewish mind. Here
indeed was the distinctively Jewish contribution to Marxism

of its Jewish founder. No longer believing in God, he clung to the kingdom of God, reinterpreted as a kingdom of self-redeemed man. This social ideal is the noblest feature of Marxism, though the most remote from the actuality of Soviet Russia where the coercive state, doomed to disappear in the Communist "kingdom," holds millions in the grip of a relentless slavery. For although the belief in the advent of a social order of justice and universal peace cannot be justified on the premisses of dialectical materialism, it is justifiable in the religious context from which it was taken. If for all the resistance of human sin and folly there is a Divine plan for mankind, if our prayer for the coming of God's kingdom, in which His will shall be done on earth as it is in heaven, is no empty dream we may or rather must believe that this kingdom will indeed come on earth. What dialectical materialism has no right to believe, Christian faith may and should believe. It is not enough that the community of supernatural and deified men should be expressed outwardly in the directly religious sphere by a Church. It must also be expressed outwardly by a society—not a state, for the state is bound up with force—in which social justice reflects the justice of God; peace, His tranquillity; and mutual charity, His love. And for such a society we could not find I think any better economic principle than the Communist slogan, " from each according to his capacity, to each according to his needs," though its application will involve a measure of personal private property which the Communist would not admit.

If, therefore, the anti-Semitic prejudice of the Nazis and their English disciples charges the Jews with Bolshevism because Marx was a Jew, it must be replied, that, in fact, the only Jewish constituent of Marxism, the specific contribution of Marx *the Jew* is its noblest feature, the ideal of an earthly order of social justice and peace. The materialism, the evolutionism and the dialectic on the other hand in their blend of truth and error can boast an unimpeachable " Aryan " pedigree. But, as we have seen, the millennarianism, however secularised, is incompatible with the materialism.

Dialectical materialism hangs dubiously between mechanical materialism and energeticism, indeed ultimately idealism. Autodynamism cannot be reconciled with the Marxian conception of matter as moving mass. For moving mass, a conception taken over from mechanical materialism, is substance fixed in its permanent self-identity, yet in motion. And for autodynamism this substance is not only moved but is itself a source of motion. Why and how the constant mass should generate this self-motion is nowhere explained. Moreover, in so far as it moves, it changes, is in process of flux. What then is the relation between the factor of motion and the factor of rest? Does the entire mass participate in the motion and indeed in so far as it is self-motion generate it? If so, how can it be at rest, a fixed self-identical mass? If, however, it moves only in part there must be a fixed and a changing part of the substance, somehow an unchanging core and a changing surface. But in this case we have, in fact, two substances respectively at rest and in motion. What precisely is their relationship? If masses in themselves fixed move, motion must be a changing relationship between motionless substances, very much as mechanical materialism conceived it. And if the fixed mass remaining unchanged throughout its motion generates motion as autodynamism affirms, it must change in doing so. We cannot conceive of a material particle as an unmoved mover. And for Marxism motion is an essential mode of matter, therefore of the moving but persistent and self-identical mass. Autodynamism leaves no place for any fixed substance or mass, its unchanged source. Matter must be wholly in flux, in motion throughout, and fixed objects and knowledge must therefore be impossible. Moreover, thought cannot acquiesce in an ultimate dualism of fixed mass and the motion it generates and undergoes.

Dialectical materialism refusing to scrutinise the depths of being ignores these problems. But to ignore them is not to answer them. The ultimate enigmas and contradictions remain and demand a solution. And in accordance with the law of dialectic these contradictions must negate the antithesis of dialectical materialism which involves them and thrust thought forward to the synthesis in which they are resolved, namely ideal realism.

For ideal realism, resolving finite being not into two physically distinct factors but into the metaphysical factors of matter, which is potential energy and form, is able to do justice to rest and movement alike and reconcile them in a higher unity. For every object is an actual energy, dynamic through and through and capable of the subordinate autodynamism which alone is consistent with contingent being. On the other hand, in as much as it is constituted by a form and in so far as its matter, its potential energy is and remains in metaphysical union with that form, it is at rest, self-identical. And the union between matter and form, therefore the energy objects and their activities which that union produces, is explained by the creative will of an Absolute Being that is the perfect identity of form and energy, and thus without any admixture of matter, potential being ; and that produces finite beings, actual energy objects by actualising their possibility through their forms, of which this possibility, potential energy, is the matter. Thus ideal realism answers the fundamental metaphysical problem which dialectical material-ism cannot answer and refuses to see. And where the latter fluctuates between mechanical materialism and energeticism, ideal realism moves with a sure step, recognising fully the two factors of rest and change, accounting for their co-existence and referring them to the ultimate unity which effects it.[1]

[1] The system here outlined differs in certain respects from the traditional scholastic system. I would, however, claim that it is true to the fundamental principles common to all varieties of ideal realism, but applies them more comprehensively and brings out more explicitly the dynamic character of reality.

As conceived by dialectical materialism matter is somehow endowed with a nisus pushing upwards, like a plant to the light, from the dark soil of inorganic matter to the rational organisation of the perfect human society. That is to say it is conceived as somehow alive and even intelligent in its unintelligence. Plekhanov indeed, in his *Fundamental Problems of Marxism*, is sympathetic with the view that " matter in general " is " animated," that is endowed with a measure of life and " a certain degree of sensibility," though this is pre-eminently the prerogative of organic matter.[1] This animism[2], for despite Plekhanov's disclaimer it is a form of animism, is incompatible with materialism. For, if it is true, reality is nowhere just moving mass but living, even conscious energy. The conception of matter as essentially autodynamic has thus substituted for the matter of the older and genuine materialism a vital energy, subconscious when not fully conscious and endowed with an active urge. This vitalism, however, does not account for the rational purpose which is found, and which the Marxian claims to find, in human history. Mere life, even sentient, cannot of itself produce reason. " Dialectical materialism," Plekhanov maintains, supplies " a method competent to solve the problem of *the rational character of all that exists*."[3] If however existence manifests an intelligible character, that intelligibility cannot be explained by any irrational cause, whether the purely corporeal mass of mechanical materialism or the self-moving matter, even if living and in some sense conscious, of dialectical materialism.

To affirm the rational character of all that exists is indeed to restate in less accurate terms the scholastic equation between being and truth. The restatement is inaccurate inasmuch as it equates intelligibility, objective truth, not with being but with

---

[1] English trs., p. 29.
[2] I should agree that even inorganic matter possesses an active nisus akin to though less than life. This nisus which is not strictly living nor conscious, is what Professor R. Lossky has termed psychoid.
[3] *Fundamental Problems of Marxism*, p. 31.

concrete existence; and the latter, when finite, is not pure being but partial being, between pure being and non-entity. As such its intelligibility is incomplete. For this finite existence is not completely identified with its form nor its perfect embodiment. Its material factor involves an irrational element, so that all that exists is not purely rational but partly irrational. That is to say Plekhanov is here actually too idealistic and insufficiently materialist and were the implications of his position worked out would be forced back upon the pure immanental idealism of Hegel.

The intelligibility of being here affirmed by Plekhanov is, however, incompatible in any formulation with materialism of any kind or indeed with vitalism. The product and self-development of matter or even of irrational life cannot be an objective intelligibility. Intelligibility is the product and expression of intellect.

This idealism is, however, but a passing concession, though a concession that exposes the fundamental weakness of dialectical materialism. In the main, as we have just seen, dialectical materialism tends to the position intermediate between materialism and idealism, a vitalist energeticism; and, though this vitalism breaks with materialism without accounting for rationality, it is employed to cover the unbridgeable gulf between materialism and the Marxian teleology. If matter is a self-moving energy, man's rational volition which must dominate nature and establish the just society need not be regarded as a mere epiphenomenon of physical processes but can be regarded as the highest form of auto-dynamic matter, in which it is both fully self-conscious and rational. For of all existing energies on our planet man's rational will is the highest. Moreover, since like the other energies this volition is self-moving, autodynamic, it must be free. This, however, is not genuine materialism but, as Berdaiev terms it, a dark spiritualism, for which the supreme manifestation of reality is the spiritual force of human will.

This energeticism is the practical philosophy of contemporary Russia, though the profession of materialism is as vehement as ever and the older conception inherited from mechanical materialism, that motion is the movement and mutual shock of corporeal masses, has not been discarded. But in practice, as Berdaiev points out, the power of human will over material forces is emphasised. This emphasis finds embodiment in the ambitious Five Year Plans to revolutionise the production of the Soviet Union. Nowhere is there a stronger conviction of the power of human will to control and harness natural and social forces than in Soviet Russia.

Freedom according to Engels is nothing but the recognition of necessity, the knowledge of 'natural laws,' and freedom of the will therefore means nothing but the capacity to make decisions with real knowledge of the subject. Recognised necessity, however, is not freedom. Were it so the prisoner who recognises the inevitability of his sentence to penal servitude would be free. And if the decisions I make with knowledge are inevitable so that I could not have decided otherwise, they are not free. Engels is indeed groping in the right direction. For freedom is founded on reason, and full knowledge of every relevant consideration if held actually before the mind would secure the higher freedom which cannot make the wrong choice. But this knowledge is impossible on earth. The problem of freedom therefore is whether our wrong choices are always inevitable, whether we could have chosen otherwise.

Engels shirks the issue. He does not, and, as a materialist, he cannot, believe that the will is free in this the only sense which admits a genuine moral responsibility. But he will not say so explicitly. He prefers to fall back on a definition of freedom which makes it no more than the power to manipulate natural forces and make rational choices whenever our temperament and environment permit us to act rationally. In short, freedom is merely emancipation from bondage to subhuman forces, by their scientific manipulation, not free will. And even this freedom is in the last resort produced by the irresistible operation of these natural forces. If material well-being were man's sufficient good this necessary freedom[1] might perhaps suffice, though even then it would be destroyed by the successful revolt of nature against man in the death of individuals and the extinction of the human race. But man's true good is spiritual and requires a genuine freedom of choice with its consequent responsibility.

Theoretically of course the Marxists follow Engels in this indirect denial of free will. In practice however the will is regarded as truly free. If the Bolsheviks really viewed human acts as the necessary results of forces beyond the agent's control the outbursts of moral indignation against political opponents which fill the Soviet press and make Russian political trials resemble the courts in which Scroggs and Jefferies presided would be impossible. For everyone would realise that they are as ridiculous as a child's anger against a toy which will not work.[2]

By this practical exaltation of the human will as the supreme and quasiomnipotent manifestation of autodynamic matter Marxism, though its ideology is impregnated with the rationalism of the eighteenth and nineteenth centuries, has in fact exalted will over intelligence, energy over form and thus become a form of immanental social energeticism which approaches the social energeticism of National Socialism and Fascism. And this energeticism is likely to become even more marked in future, thus bringing the ideology of Communist totalitarianism closer to that of Fascist totalitarianism and its more thoroughgoing variety, National Socialism.

[1] Marxism boasts that it has reconciled necessity with freedom. Not with genuine freedom.

[2] If even adults are often angry with animals their anger is partly the emotional reflex of the angry gestures they must assume to train the animal and partly due to the fact that they half-consciously ascribe to it a freedom analogous to our own. Even so, no sane man would write and publish a moral invective against an animal or introduce it into a public speech.

For all energeticist ideologies, inasmuch as they ascribe a primacy to force as against form in man, therefore to will as against intellect are, as we have seen, materialist according to the metaphysical acceptation of matter, even if Marxism alone professes materialism according to the scientific and popular acceptation of matter. And all alike are therefore unable to account for the formal or ideal factor in reality. This exclusive preoccupation with the material factor finds expression in the materialist interpretation of history by Marxism. The mode of production in material life determines the social, political and intellectual life-process in general. "All the social and political relations, all religious and legal systems, all the theoretical outlooks which emerge in the course of history are to be comprehended only when the material conditions of life of the corresponding epochs are understood and the former are derived from these material conditions."[1] It was all very well for Engels to deny later that the economic factor, the system of production is regarded by Marxians as the sole cause of historical phenomena, the sole determinant of cultures. For if it is the sole ultimate cause, it is at least the indirect cause of every historical phenomenon, every aspect of culture. For in the last resort it has caused their immediate causes.

"Men," wrote Engels,[2] "make their own history, but in a given environment in which they live, upon the foundation of extant relations." This does not take us very far. What, we must enquire, makes men make their own history? The Marxist must reply that in the last resort whatever ideological factors may be interposed, it is the material factor, the economic system of production which makes them act as they do.

When, indeed, Lenin affirms that "all ideas and tendencies have their *roots* in the condition of the material conditions

---

[1] Engels *Ludwig Feuerbach*, Appendix: from a review published in 1859.
[2] Letter written in 1894, quoted by Plekhanov, *Fundamental Problems of Marxism*, E.T., p. 56.

of production " the statement may be understood in a true sense. A scientific worker in the field of comparative religion, so little suspect of Marxism as Pater Schmidt, has in fact argued that the principal types of early religion owed their distinctive features to a social system, itself determined by the mode of production.[1] Thus even the religion of a culture has its roots in the conditions of production, and to this extent Marxism is justified. And in fact since the conditions of production are themselves determined by geographical conditions[2] the roots of a culture and therefore of the religion embodied by the culture are literally in the soil. But only the roots. No plant is explained by its roots, though it cannot dispense with them. Nor are the roots, though indispensable, the most important portion of the plant. When Marxism regards the economic and geographical roots of a culture and its ideology, including its religion, as the sufficient final though not immediate explanation of the latter, it is maintaining that the root is a sufficient explanation of the plant and all its distinctive qualities. This, however, is as untenable as the corresponding attempt to explain quality by quantity, mind by matter.

Just as a particular material complex is required as its necessary basis, before a given form can supervene upon it, so a particular system of production is required as its necessary material basis, before a given ideology can supervene upon it, as the distinctive form of a culture. And the core of this ideology is a religion, be it only the pseudo-religion of Communism. But this economic basis no more produces of itself this ideological and religious form than the material basis of a particular plant or animal form produces that form. In the latter case the material basis merely determines which form shall supervene, in the former case the economic basis merely determines which ideological and religious form shall

---

[1] *Studies in Comparative Religion*, No. 3 : The Religions of Primitive Peoples.
[2] See Plekhanov, *Foundations of Marxism*, Eng. Trs., p. 31 *sqq.*

supervene. Moreover a particular economic structure may admit, that is may be capable of receiving, more than one ideological form. The economic structure of the Roman Empire, for example, was not appreciably different before and after Constantine's conversion. In such cases other factors determine which ideology shall prevail.

A given complex of material factors must be brought into existence before the form of an individual, organic or even inorganic (*i.e.* the form of a mineral or chemical compound), can supervene upon this matter. Similarly a given complex of socio-economic factors must be brought into existence before a new cultural form, ideological and religious, can supervene upon it as the form of the social group, constituted by the union of social matter and social form. But in both cases, and here we break with materialism, this new form, whether individual or social, cannot be itself the product of the matter prepared for its reception but must be derived from the ideal order of forms in the Divine Wisdom. And it thus supervenes upon a given material complex in virtue of the Divine Creative Will ordaining the process of evolution and human history and expressing itself as the immanent law of that process.[1] And as it is the form, not its material basis, which makes a plant or animal an organism, a living organic whole, so it is the ideological-religious form not the economic basis which makes a culture an organic whole, a religion culture as Christopher Dawson terms it. Engels indeed, in the passage quoted above, admits that ideal factors, among them religious beliefs, may even preponderate in determining the form of a culture. These factors, however, he regards as themselves determined by the material economic factor which thus indirectly determines and explains the form

---

[1] The deficiency of matter and later the failures of human free-will prevent the perfect embodiment of the ideal order and limit the intrinsic possibilities of fulfilling the Divine law, though God's eternal purpose takes account of these intrinsic defects and limitations and overrules them for the Divine glory and the happiness of those who freely serve it.

of the culture. And Engels plainly regards the form as subordinate and comparatively unimportant, nothing but an external manifestation of the material reality below it, which determines, not as in fact it does its embodiment in a given historic situation, but its actual nature. And this is precisely that inversion of the respective rôle of matter and form which, as opposed to the physical materialism nowhere consistently maintained, is the consistent metaphysical materialism of Marxian philosophy.

Granted, for example, that a particular family system, itself dependent on the mode of production, has determined as Pater Schmidt holds, whether the Godhead is conceived primarily as masculine, a heavenly Father, or feminine, an earth Mother. The conception of Deity is not therefore itself produced by the family system and its economic basis. Nor do they explain the belief that the ultimate Reality must be more not less than human personality and has therefore more not less than whichever sex, masculine or feminine, is regarded by a particular society as the higher, though this is in fact decided largely on economic grounds. The idea, therefore the religious belief, is different in kind from the economic facts which enable it to find expression but which depend upon it for their cultural significance. It cannot, therefore, be produced and explained by them though its historical appearance may be explicable in this way.

In his *Fundamental Problems of Marxism*[1] Plekhanov quotes Tylor's words, " It is obvious that, among all nations, man was the type of divinity. This explains why the structure of human society and its government have become the models for celestial society and the government of the heavens." " Here," comments Plekhanov, " we already have a materialist conception." It is indeed obvious that if man is to form any image of Deity he must employ the highest form of being he knows, namely himself.

[1] Eng. Trs., p. 46.

In this sense he must make God after his own image. Moreover, if God is to reveal Himself to man through human images and concepts these must be anthropomorphic. So long as this human image is not regarded as representative of God as He is in Himself there is no idolatry in this nor anthropomorphism in the objectionable sense. For God is known to transcend this anthropomorphic image, and to be infinitely more than anything we can imagine or conceive. It is therefore absurd to speak of a materialist conception of religion in this connection. For the material factors do not determine the apprehension of Deity as transcendent but merely to some extent the images and concepts employed to express this transcendent religious apprehension. Hence the diverse religious images which fill the anti-religious museums of Soviet Russia illustrate only man's various endeavours to translate into the terms of his finite thought and imagination his experience of a Godhead which infinitely transcends them all, containing what is positive in each while rejecting its limitations. We might as well call the recognition that the language of religion is and must be ultimately derived from language expressing physical objects, e.g. Father, and Spirit, literally breath, a materialist conception of religion.

It is therefore not the religious form of a culture but only the possibility and conditions of its social acceptance and embodiment that depend upon the material conditions which are its social matter. If the plant cannot strike root except in the fitting soil, the soil cannot by itself produce the root. Here, as always, Marxism is content to study the material factor of finite reality and neglect the formal, as on the other hand religious believers have been too disposed to concentrate upon the formal and neglect the material factor. The Incarnation of the Word, the Absolute Idea in the flesh of His Mother is the culmination of a cosmic process which is throughout an Incarnation of the form, the idea in matter. A philosophy of Incarnation completed by a theology of the Incarnation is thus alone in a position to do full justice to both factors of human history, the material basis exclusively studied by Marxism, and the spiritual form too exclusively put forward by excessively idealistic philosophies and excessively spiritualist theologies.

It is perhaps more than coincidence that Russian religious thought has of late been much preoccupied with the Divine Wisdom, Sophia. For it is precisely the Divine Wisdom with its order of forms which is the complement of the material factor of finite being to which dialectical materialism attributes an unwarranted primacy over form, and which everywhere determines and actualises this material factor. A sound doctrine of the Divine Wisdom, involved indeed by ideal realism, thus overcomes dialectical materialism by including and subordinating its positive truth: its insight into the material factor in evolution and human history, while reversing its radical inversion of the rôle played by the two factors, matter and form.[1]

Thus the metaphysical materialism of Marxism for all the energeticist insistence upon autodynamism and will is constantly pulling dialectical materialism back to the mechanical materialism from which as materialism it originated. When Lenin approves Plekhanov's dictum that mind is the inner function (the inside) of matter he reduces mind to an epiphenomenon of matter. Even if this matter at its highest includes human will, if this will is a blind though self-moving energy and thought no more than its by-product, human purpose must be automatic, therefore mechanical. Men are after all puppets, manifestations of blind force. It is indeed possible to understand the doctrine that mind is the inner function of matter to mean that it is the inmost reality of which matter is but the surface, the outward expression. And it may be that in their exaltation of human

---

[1] This is not to say that we can approve every detail of Russian sophiology. I have in mind its general principle and orientation.

purpose Soviet philosophers are moving in this direction away from materialism. But neither Plekhanov nor Lenin understood it thus and any idealistic reinterpretation is liable to be checked by the official exponents of Marxist orthodoxy.

This uncertainty and fluctuation between materialism and a crude idealism or rather energeticism is inevitable so long as the only alternative is immanentist materialism or immanentist idealism or vitalism.

Obviously human knowledge, thought and sense perception alike, depend upon a physical universe external to the mind. "Being determines thought." The universe cannot therefore be the creation or reflection of human mind or some cosmic mind of which the human mind is a portion. But this, however, does not justify the materialist in asserting that mind is the creation or reflection of matter. On the contrary, since human mind arises in the universe of corporeal objects, and knowledge of them can within limits change them, there must be an Absolute supermind of which both the human mind and the material universe are the creations, and the reflection. Though the material world far from being the creation of human thought determines our thought of it, it is less real than the transcendent Mind which brought it into existence and which is not thought as contrasted with being but the concrete identity of both. It is indeed less real even than the human mind. For the human spirit is not identical with its knowledge of the material universe nor indeed with its entire knowledge. It is a substance which is the subject of that knowledge. It is thinking being, as God is the identity of thinking and being. Nor is it passive in its relation to the outside world. Even in perception and knowledge it selects and attends. And in the employment of this knowledge it is predominantly active. A philosophy which, like Marxism, stresses action and boasts that in contrast with the speculative philosophies of the past it knows reality in order to change it should not have subordinated mind to matter, because knowledge of material objects is necessarily determined by them and abstracted from them. The Bolshevik defence of materialism on this ground is simply the defence of epistemological realism, not of materialism. Yet when Plekhanov seeks to shew that the dialectic is compatible with materialism he is content to defend, naturally with success, realism against Hegelian idealism on this epistemological ground. This radical confusion between realism and materialism is revealed when Engels in his statement of the difference between materialism and idealism[1] tells us that the issue in dispute is " The relation of thinking to being, the relation of spirit to nature." Evidently the two questions whether spirit has a primacy over nature or vice versa, and whether " our thoughts about the world" are capable of knowing it, are " a correct reflection of reality " or reality is the reflection of thought, are for Engels two aspects of the same question. That is to say he equates thought with spirit, being, *i.e.*, objective existence with nature, though elsewhere he inconsistently distinguishes nature from human society. But, as we have just seen, thought whether it be understood as thought about reality or the function of thinking is not spirit, the subject of thought. Because human thought about the world is determined by its nature it does not follow that the thinking subject, human spirit, is not a being *at least* equally real as nature, or that there is not a Superspirit infinitely more real than either and the source of both. Engels, however, by assuming identity between thought and the thinking spirit, objective reality and material nature, though the latter identification is implicitly contradicted by his distinction between nature and human society, takes it for granted that the latter proposition that only nature is objectively real follows from the former that our thought about nature is determined by it. In short he believes that

[1] *Ludwig Feuerbach*, Ch. ii.

he has proved materialism by proving realism, " We comprehended the concepts in our heads—*materialistically*—as images of real things instead of regarding the real things as images of this or that stage of development of the absolute concept." Apart from the slovenly use of terms which can speak of concepts as images we must agree that human concepts and images are derived from and determined by real things. But why call this realist epistemology materialist? Engels failed to see that though our human concepts are founded upon real things these objects in turn, real though they are in their own order, may nevertheless be expressions of Divine Spirit, of the Divine Wisdom and its ideal order. For this Wisdom is not exclusively Superthought, the Logos, but at the same time Supersubstance, Superbeing and Superenergy, Superwill and their Identity as one God. Clearly he was not entitled to deny this, as he does, merely as the self-evident implication of epistemological realism. This is the great ignoratio elenchi of Marxian apologetic explained, as we have seen, by the philosophic environment in which Marx constructed his system.

As against the relativists and sceptics Lenin, following and explaining Engels, affirms the existence of absolute truth. And like Engels he regards certain propositions, for example that Napoleon died on May 5, 1821, as examples of absolute unqualified truth. But he also holds that most truths, all the more general truths, are partial and involve their contradictory truths which will succeed them in the dialectical process. And he regards absolute truth as a whole as being the sum of relative truths.[1] There is a confusion between contradictory and complementary. The contrasted truth which rectifies and completes a half-truth does not contradict it. Moreover, a sum of relative truths cannot produce an absolute truth, but at most truth complete within a particular field of reference however enormous. Engels and

---

[1] *Materialism and Empirio-Criticism.*

Lenin were indeed right in finding absolute and relative truth in human knowledge. But they drew the frontier between them incorrectly.

All human truths without exception are partial and relative. The more detailed a truth is and the more narrowly defined the terms of its statement the closer does it approximate to an absolute truth, for example, the proposition that Napoleon died on May 5, 1821. But even this statement could have been denied by a follower of the Julian calendar. And a believer and a disbeliever in personal immortality would not attach the same sense to " died ". Thus even when by narrow definition which makes the content of a proposition correspondingly more relative, for example when May 5 is defined as relative to the Gregorian, not the Julian calendar, and the margin of error in a proposition has thus been reduced to a minimum, it still falls short of absolute truth and as we have just seen, approximates to it only by the increasing relativity of its content. The truth about half being—created being as intermediate between Absolute Being and nothingness—is always half truth, the concrete truth of any proposition is never absolute. On the other hand the abstract truth, the quality of being true which attaches to every proposition, in so far as it is true, however partial and relative its truth may be, is as such absolute, valid for every time and place and for all beings.

That in spite of these confusions and misconceptions Marxism has held tenaciously to absolute truth as against the philosophic scepticism of late so fashionable in various forms, is in fact one of its healthiest features and a feature that offers a valuable starting point for any one who seeks to convert Marxians to a more adequate philosophy. For absolute truth implies absolute Mind, its source and guarantee, absolute abstract truth an Absolute Concrete Truth. St. Augustine's defence of certain truths against the Academics was bound up closely with his religious apprehension of

God as the source and warrant of its truthfulness, of what I have termed its abstract absolute truth. A philosopher of Marxist tendencies quoted by Lenin in his critique of Mach, Joseph Dietzgen, professes a belief in absolute truth so passionate and powerful that it brings him for the moment close to Augustine. "When I say that the consciousness of the endless, absolute truth is innate in us, is the one and only knowledge a priori, I am confirmed in my statement also by the experience of this innate consciousness." When I came across this flash of Augustinianism breaking through the mist of materialism it gave me a sense of exaltation, as of a witness from the heart of a professed materialist to man's native capacity for pure Truth and therefore for God. In fact its writer actually approaches along this line a statement of unrecognised theism. "How then, do we know that behind the relative truths, there is a universal, unlimited, absolute nature which does not reveal itself completely to man? . . . Whence that knowledge: it is given us with consciousness." Though the conception of the relationship between the phenomenal universe and this absolute nature behind it is no doubt conceived too immanently, the theistic implication of this passage is evident. Dietzgen has been led by his apprehension of absolute truth in the abstract to the Absolute Concrete Truth. Because its anti-materialist implications were perceived Lenin repudiates this last statement of Dietzgen's as "Incorrect and unessential." But he endorses the former, the affirmation of an innate knowledge of absolute truth, which logically leads up to it. Dietzgen had taken a further step on the road to Truth and we must hope that hereafter the Marxians will take it with him and moreover the final step Dietzgen failed to take.

This aspiration after absolute truth is, however, doomed to sterility in a system of materialism dialectical or otherwise. For truth is form, objective intelligibility and it is known by mind. And as we have seen, in dialectical materialism form is secondary to matter, the product rather than the determinant of energy. This fundamental defect finds expression in the practical materialism of Soviet Russia. Much, very much, is done to provide the material foundations of the good life. But there on the whole it remains. The higher life, the spiritual life is starved and atrophies. The Communist convert Gide has remarked on the " depersonalisation " of the Soviet citizens, the reduction of their intellectual life to a common pattern turned out by official propaganda like the mass production of the modern factory. That is to say, minds are being materialised, human personalities mechanised. Self-sacrifice indeed there is for the common welfare. But it is squandered on the production of material values, lower, therefore, than itself. It is not surprising that there are indications that it is giving out and yielding to a self-seeking petty ambition and the worship of success. And there is an emptiness and a drabness, evident even in the radio-propaganda from Moscow, eager as it is to present Russian conditions in the most favourable light.

As we have already seen, a particular dialectic comes to rest when its synthesis has been achieved and metaphysics cannot therefore progress in its essential principles beyond the ideal realism fully achieved in medieval scholasticism. Nevertheless, when this synthesis owing to a combination of circumstances was disfigured and then abandoned, so far as the main current of European thought was concerned, the dialectic was renewed and must continue till the equilibrium is once more attained. In this new dialectic the thesis was pure immanental idealism, of which Hegel was the greatest and most thoroughgoing exponent. It represented an excessive emphasis upon form, the idea at the expense of matter, and therefore of the concrete energy-object, constituted when matter, potential energy, receives a form. Since the universe is regarded as the necessary development, the unfolding of a cosmic thought purely immanent and culminating in human

T

thought, this Hegelian thesis was academic. It made no attempt to change the actual order of society but rather canonised it as being the perfect expression of the idea at the human climax of its development. It was followed by the antithesis dialectical materialism in which matter, understood, moreover, not metaphysically but as corporeal stuff, is exalted at the expense of form, of the idea whether objective or subjective. Even when it tends towards an energeticism or vitalism it maintains this subordination of the ideal and the mental. Since it holds firmly to the concrete world of corporeal objects it has been able to achieve a concrete social embodiment; as Marx put it, to change the world and thus to realise part of its ideal. Hegelianism remained the speculation of "remote and ineffectual dons"; Marxism has created Soviet Russia and maintains a world-wide organisation and propaganda. But the antithesis must yield to the synthesis, which must be the restoration of the thesis in a higher and more comprehensive expression which shall include the truth contained in the antithesis. Materialism therefore must yield to a system which will reaffirm the ultimate primacy of form, of the idea, therefore, of mind, which idealism affirmed. But it must reaffirm it so as to include the truth of the materialist antithesis. It must affirm the primacy of existence, the object of knowledge as against knowledge of it, its subjective apprehension. It must therefore agree with Marxism that our preception and understanding of the universe are determined by its nature as it exists independently of and prior to our knowledge, and that corporeal objects are, as such, real. This synthesis, however, must be an ideal realism. Mind is supreme because all things have been created by an infinite Supermind. And all things reflect it. On the other hand corporeal objects are real in their order and our knowledge is dependent upon them. Moreover the ultimate Supermind is not pure thought. It is the absolute unity of thought and existence, of energy Superwill, and form

Superunderstanding. As ideal realism this synthesis must indeed re-establish the synthesis achieved in the classical and medieval past. But it will not be a mere restoration. For the scholastic ideal realism though containing the basis of a dynamic view of the world and history was actually static. In view of the social conditions of the age and men's pre-occupation with metaphysical and religious truth, of its nature predominantly unchanging and eternal, it could not have been otherwise. The restored ideal realism of the future must, however, do full justice to the dynamism of finite being, must in short be a dialectical ideal realism. And in this respect scholasticism will stand to it in the relation in which, according to Marx, the static mechanical materialism stood to his dialectical materialism.[1]

THUS THE METAPHYSICAL DIALECTIC MUST PASS FROM THE THESIS, DIALECTICAL IDEALISM (HEGELIANISM), THROUGH THE ANTITHESIS, DIALECTICAL MATERIALISM (MARXISM) TO THE SYNTHESIS, DIALECTICAL IDEAL REALISM. For dialectical idealism is the one-sided affirmation of the formal factor of being, dialectical materialism of the material, and dialectical ideal realism does full justice to both factors, thus correcting the excesses of dialectical idealism and dialectical materialism and embracing and reconciling their partial truth in its comprehensive synthesis. That is to say dialectical materialism has mistaken the antithesis for the synthesis.

Dialectical ideal realism will accomplish the huge task of integrating and co-ordinating the masses of detailed fact discovered by the natural sciences since the Renaissance. Since it is a realism it will be able, unlike idealism, to embody itself in an actual society which it will inspire and inform.

---

[1] Marxism however, as we have seen, exaggerates and universalises the dynamic factor and therefore the dialectic process. This was inevitable. For it ascribes a false primacy to the ground of that process, the material factor of finite being, and moreover regards this finite being as co-extensive with reality. The dialectic process has no place either in the Absolute Reality in which form and energy are one or in the order of finite spirits wholly united to this Absolute Divine Reality by a super-natural union and thereby emancipated from the dialectic process.

Since it is an idealism that society will be a genuine culture, not like contemporary Russia, merely the material framework of a culture. And since it is a dialectical ideal realism it will encourage the active attempt to control and to a large extent remodel man's material and social environment by applied science, which is the distinctive feature of the modern world.

And since it is theistic this culture, as indeed all genuine culture must be, will be a religion culture whose " form " is a religious faith, though its roots are planted in the material order of economic production, which is its material basis, in short its " matter." The labour and devotion which have gone to the social embodiment of dialectical materialism are building up a powerful material framework, have produced a muscular and strongly knit body which lacks a soul. May we not conjecture that as in the course of the ideological dialectic the materialist antithesis must by its own development produce the ideal-realist synthesis, this ideological synthesis will find its social embodiment by assuming the body constructed by its predecessor and infusing into it the missing soul? The Roman Empire, as materialist and as secular as any society could be at that epoch of human history, though far less materialist and secular than Marxian Communism, after centuries of struggle provided a social framework for the Church which defeated it. The Pope succeeded to the inheritance of Cæsar. May not a " Communist " society, whether Soviet Russia or a world-wide extension of its social system, likewise provide a social framework for the Kingdom of God which it seeks to destroy? Pure Communism or indeed pure Socialism is no doubt impracticable. But Russian Communists are not in fact building up an order of pure Communism or approaching it more closely. Nor are they even constructing a pure Socialism in which all private property is abolished. Jesuit Paraguay, probably the best society hitherto known, was as " Communist [1]" as Soviet Russia.

[1] The family shaken at first is being restored in the U.S.S.R.

We cannot deny that a genuine and profound desire for social justice has inspired and does inspire whatever is noblest in Communism. This desire is projected in the ideal of the society of justice, peace and freedom which is to succeed and be produced by the actual proletarian dictatorship with its state tyranny. But if one thing is certain from human history, it is that holders of power do not, apart from individual exceptions, willingly relinquish it. It is inconceivable that the Russian dictator and his supporters will ever voluntarily abandon the power they hold, that the totalitarian state will abdicate. And dialectical materialism, with its exaltation of corporeal matter at the expense of mind, of force at the expense of form, cannot inspire the abandonment either of the practical materialism which worships the machine and sacrifices quality to quantity, contemplation to utilitarian production, or of the tyranny of the state and its rulers who represent and control the social organisation of force. But the ideal synthesis which must follow and overcome this materialism, namely dialectical ideal realism, can inspire this new social revolution, a revolution, however, in which the only blood shed will be that of the revolutionaries. It can set up an order of social justice, freedom and peace which dialectical materialism is unable to produce. For such a society must be the expression of charity and inspired therefore by the Divine Charity, the Holy Ghost. Since man can never be sinless even this society cannot be perfect. Some measure of compulsion will be indispensable and therefore a state. But this compulsion, and accordingly the sphere of state action, can be reduced to less than they were even under Victorian *laissez faire* when economic and social compulsion supplemented a weak and restricted executive.

Marxism postulates two social movements in opposite directions, one to the totalitarian state, the other to the stateless society which, however, both embody the same ideological movement. But the former social movement alone expresses and embodies the ideology of dialectical materialism and the latter is reserved for the dialectical ideal-realist ideology which will succeed Marxism and with which alone it is in harmony. For inasmuch as the material foundation of this relatively ideal society will be an efficient and just system of production and consumption it will embody the realism of the ideal-realist synthesis which continues the positive truth of dialectical materialism in its conflict with pure idealism. And inasmuch as it is an order of charity in which force is reduced to a minimum, it will embody the idealism which in this synthesis restores and re-affirms the positive truth contained in dialectical idealism. This, I believe, is the course indicated by the dialectic of human history whereby in spiral progress it fulfils not the blind urge of material energy but the Will of Divine Wisdom as It embodies Its ideal content in this created universe of informed matter.[1] And in this dialectical process Marxism, the antithesis, like its Hegelian precursor the thesis, can be no more than a stage on the road to the final ideology, the ideal realist synthesis and its social embodiment, no more than a passing phase of material preparation on the way to a richer and more comprehensive religion culture than the world has yet known, God's Kingdom on earth foretold by Prophet and Apostle, at last achieved as historical reality.[2]

[1] Since the human will is free, matter in its deficiency recalcitrant to form and any isolated dialectical process liable to interference from a host of external factors, we cannot emulate the confident predictions of Marx. We can but argue that the dialectical process in question developes in a particular direction and is likely to work itself out in the concrete. We can however be certain that the grossly onesided and inadequate ideology of Marxian materialism and its social embodiment cannot be permanent.

[2] From the belief that Marxism and its society are a stage on the road to the general acceptance of an adequate ideology and to its social embodiment and therefore that Communism is unwittingly preparing the material basis for the Kingdom of God it does not follow that we should acquiesce in its present advance. Before its positive achievement can be utilised Marxism must be defeated. The primitive Christians far from acquiescing in the irreligious claims of the Roman Empire resisted them to death. But they did not attempt or even desire to replace the Empire by the obsolete forms of government it had superseded, as the Jews attempted the hopeless task of restoring the temporal independence of the Jewish state. Similarly we should not attempt to resist Communism by supporting movements of forcible

Besides the metaphysical dialectic from dialectic idealism through dialectic materialism to dialectic ideal realism there is a social dialectic which in Marxism met the metaphysical and has partially co-operated with it. It is a dialectic process from Liberal individualism, the thesis, through the totalitarian state the antithesis, represented not only by Communist Russia but by Fascism in its several varieties, to its future synthesis, a society at once organic and free since the principle of its organic unity is not the compulsion of the state but a common faith freely accepted and a common purpose achieved by free co-operation. And this precisely is the society which Marxism promises but cannot produce, but which can be produced by an adequate philosophy fulfilled by religious faith, and by the charity which translates that philosophy and faith into individual and social practice. And this society will in turn be, as we have seen, the social embodiment of the metaphysical synthesis which must close the metaphysical dialectic. It will thus, unless external factors prevent their effects, be the joint conclusion of both these powerful dialectic movements of modern history, the metaphysical and the economic-social.

Beyond these dialectic movements of modern history, the ideological movement from dialectical idealism through dialectical materialism to a dialectical ideal realism and the social economic movement from Liberal individualism through the totalitarian state to a society free and organic, individualist and " socialist " there is another dialectic process, more comprehensive in its scope and older in its origin but working towards the same conclusion through the lesser dialectics subordinated to its operation. It is the dialectic from the vertical or transcendental through the horizontal or

---

reaction whose primary inspiration is not religious truth but the secular interests of a nation or class. We should combat it solely by the spiritual and intellectual methods of prayer and argument and by a refusal, where possible organised, to obey any claims of the Communist state incompatible with the dictates of conscience.

immanental movement of human thought and practice to a synthesis of both.

The great nature religion cultures of antiquity had achieved a synthesis of the patriarchal religion culture of masculine dominance and its sky-god and the patriarchal religion culture with its feminine dominance and its earth-mother goddess. And the supreme social and political embodiment of this natural religion culture synthesis was the synthetic totalitarian Empire of Imperial Rome. The synthesis was followed by a vertical movement away from the plane of nature and natural forces to the depths or height or interior, whichever metaphor you prefer, of spirit and the transcendent and supernatural God there revealed. This movement, the thesis of a new dialectic process, tended to turn away from and disparage the natural and merely vital level of reality, as indeed was inevitable if the human spirit were to be emancipated from nature and raised to the supernatural. It was crowned by the Christian revelation. For although as a religion of the Incarnation Christianity was not exclusively vertical and transcendental; in practice, the vertical aspect was onesidedly and excessively emphasised, an excess illustrated by the Augustinian concentration upon God and the soul and by the desert ascetics. Later, it is true, the horizontal movement towards nature and the world implicit in the Incarnation and the ideal realism it presupposes began to assert itself. And it found expression ideologically in the scholastic synthesis, socially in the medieval attempt to realise the ideal of a universal empire working in subordination to a universal Church. But the vertical movement remained predominant. As M. Maritain has shown, the social order was conceived as " sacral," a direct domination of civil society by the Church. And Catholic spirituality continued to be suspicious of the natural and vital order, in particular of its flower, sexual love. Moreover, theoretical and applied science were so rudimentary that the horizontal-immanental

movement was unable to develop while the vertical-trans-
cendental was still sufficiently powerful to control it. The
material for a synthesis of nature and supernature, the religious
and the secular, was lacking. Hence the theoretical synthesis
was but an unfulfilled and unfulfillable programme, Thomism
but the forecast of a development to come, as the vision of
the Jewish prophets had been a forecast of a reality not to
be achieved until the hour of Christianity should strike in a
remote future. The horizontal movement, therefore, along
the natural and secular plane inevitably broke away from the
vertical and asserted itself in opposition to the latter. The
horizontal and immanental antithesis negated the vertical and
transcendental thesis.[1] Scientific knowledge accumulated,
and the practical inventions based upon it. Metaphysics and
religion, activities and insights of the spiritual depth were
progressively abandoned in the absorption with work and
knowledge on the empirical surface. Outlook replaced
"inlook." The logical end and perfection of this horizontal
antithesis is dialectical materialism and its social embodiment
the Communist totalitarian state. Here the horizontal movement has been developed to its logical conclusion, to the
complete and deliberate exclusion of the vertical movement,
both as metaphysical insight into the ultimate properties and
implications of being as opposed to its empirical surface, and
as religious insight.[2] Inlook is abandoned as visionary
dreaming, outlook is the sole direction of mental vision.
The material basis of human life with which the horizontal
movement is conversant is the sole field of human thought
and practice, and the superficial and inferior forms which
determine that material basis, which should be the matter

[1] This horizontal movement can be subdivided into subordinate movements
vertically superimposed on the inorganic, vital sentient and positive rational planes.
But for the present purpose they can be ignored.

[2] Such a complete exclusion of the horizontal movement by the vertical movement
was impossible. Man cannot altogether ignore his animal nature or his corporeal
environment, as he can ignore the depths of his soul and of being and God there
apprehended.

of forms, deeper, superior and more comprehensive, are alone perceived. The sister species of totalitarian society, the various forms of Fascism are but less logical and more imperfect embodiments of the same movement in which the materialism is more or less thinly disguised by an idealistic veneer or an external compromise with organised religion. They must therefore either amalgamate with the Marxian society or be destroyed by it.[1]

But the full embodiment of the horizontal or immanental antithesis must reveal its essential inadequacy, the falsehood it conceals. To use Engels words its " latent false side " must " manifest " itself.[2]

Marxian materialism, as we have seen, in spite of itself is pointing through an intermediate energeticism to the spiritualism which negates it. For a matter whose development has produced an intelligible world and human intelligence must be derived from and dependent upon spirit. Thus the negation of the vertical transcendental movement and its spiritualist thesis, by the horizontal immanental movement, the antithesis must be in turn negated by a synthesis in which the vertical and transcendental movement dominates the horizontal and immanental, utilises its material and scientific achievements and informs the social body it has constructed. And this society which embodies the synthesis is that spiritual-material kingdom of God on earth which fulfils socially the individual Incarnation of Divine Wisdom, the Form of Forms. It is the kingdom of " justice and peace " to which Marxism aspires but which it cannot achieve. For it must be from above and from within, from the Divine Spirit, revealed to and in human spirit, not from the lower order which is but its material substratum. Thus the conclusion reached by our view of this wider and more ultimate dialectic reinforces the conclusion reached by our study of the two minor

---

[1] We may, however, hope that some Liberal societies may survive as a refuge and base of operations for those who cannot accept the false totalitarian ideologies.

[2] Engels is speaking of the dialectical antithesis. And Marxism is an antithesis.

dialectics, namely the supersession of dialectical materialism and its social embodiment, the totalitarian socialist state, by a dialectic ideal realism completed by the religion of Divine Incarnation, and its social embodiment, the kingdom of God on earth. For this ideology overcomes by including the positive truth in Marxian ideology, and its society overcomes the Marxian state by including its positive achievement.

Surely these considerations should encourage us not to fear the temporary triumphs of Marxism, or, for that matter, of its rival totalitarian ideologies, but while refusing our surrender, to see in them, so far as God permits their success, the unwilling preparation for His earthly Kingdom and to pray more confidently for its advent. " Thy Kingdom come. Thy will be done ON EARTH as it is in heaven." And God's will is " the perfect law of liberty," the law of love, His Kingdom, therefore, a kingdom of liberty and a kingdom of love.

PEACE AND WAR

At the present juncture no issue of public morality is so urgent as the justice, that is the justifiableness or otherwise of war. For the horizon is dark with threatening war clouds. For the time at least the collective system of organised international peace has broken down. The pledge not to employ war as an instrument of national policy has proved but a scrap of paper to be torn up by any great Power that may find it convenient. Yesterday Japan and Italy, to-morrow perhaps France, Germany, Britain, or Soviet Russia. It serves no purpose for pots to wax eloquent upon the blackness of kettles. The brutal fact remains : in a world in which modern communications have made the nations willy nilly members one of another as never before in human history, in which a war between the " civilised " or more truly the technically equipped powers must be suicidal, and in all countries the people fear and hate war, the sovereign states are preparing for a war which for slaughter and suffering is likely to dwarf even the late war into a comparative insignificance. For the powers that have will fight rather than yield even a little of their possessions and prestige, and the powers that have not or think they have not will fight as soon as they believe they have a reasonable prospect of taking by force what they regard as their just due.

Faced with this dire prospect what should be the attitude of the Catholic? He believes in reason as light from the Divine Word. And war replaces reason by the arbitrament of brute force. He believes in spiritual force, in the power of the Holy Spirit; and in war material force, above all the machine, is supreme. He believes in love: and war is organised hate. He believes in truth: and war involves organised lying. He believes in the victory of the Cross, the victory of suffering love : and war seeks a victory won by inflicting suffering and death. His heroes are the martyrs, the victims ; war's heroes are the conquerors, the slayers. He believes in a mystical body of Christ whose members belong to all nations, one Christ Head and members. And he therefore believes that any wrong done to any of Christ's members is done to Christ Himself—" Saul, why persecutest thou ME ? " War rends this body asunder—one limb fighting against the other and all slaying Christ anew in his members. He believes in the Kingdom of Christ on earth with the peace of Christ in Christ's Kingdom—" A kingdom of truth and life, a kingdom of justice, love and peace." Shall he at the bidding of an earthly sovereign, for ends of worldly policy, national prestige, empire, markets and the like, acquiesce in, if not actively assist, war which produces and is itself a disorder, the very reverse of this Divine order ?

And yet. The Baptist did not forbid war and the military profession. Nor Christ, who recognised that if His Kingdom had been of this world His servants would as a matter of course have fought for Him. Nor St. Peter whose first Gentile Convert was a Centurion who did not " send in his papers." And although the Primitive Church, in those blessed days before the fatal wedlock between Church and State had been concluded under Constantine, discouraged for various reasons the military profession, she never condemned it out and out, as she condemned the gladiator, actor and professional musician. On the contrary there were Christians, large numbers of Christians, in the army, and among them many martyrs. Obviously we were too hasty in drawing an unqualified contrast between military service and martyrdom.

Was then the opposition between Christianity and war

depicted above mistaken ? Is there after all a companionship between Mars and Christ ? Ought Catholics in future, as in the past, to support any war a government may see fit to declare ? Ought they to acquiesce in the suicide of civilisation ? In the appalling slaughter and torture, first and foremost, of the civilian population, the women and children ? Is poison gas, the weapon with which Mussolini has achieved his noble Roman triumph over half naked tribesmen, the lawful weapon of a soldier of Christ ?

So long as we proceed on these lines there is no way out of the impasse. Sentiment has its place. Positive or negative as the occasion demands, it should normally accompany the apprehension of truth vitally important for human life. But it must be concomitant. Feeling is not itself knowledge. In fact even the highly emotional considerations urged above were not, could not have been, pure sentiment. They embodied glimpses of truth. But these glimpses were incoherent and obscure—like fragments of a landscape discerned dimly through a mist. We must therefore adopt another approach to our problem, the approach of pure reason. It may indeed seem at first sight an unchristian approach. An enlightened atheist could take it. Certainly he could, and many do. But the objection implies an opposition between natural reason and its moral judgements and the doctrine of supernatural religion, therefore between the orders of nature and grace which is fundamentally uncatholic and fundamentally irrational. If there is only one God, He must be the author both of nature and grace and the source and therefore directly or indirectly the revealer of all truth, secular as well as religious. Whatever moral truth, therefore, is attainable by the natural use of reason is the revealed will of God binding the conscience as such. That Protestant pacifists tend to neglect, if not to reject altogether, arguments of natural reason and appeal exclusively to religious principles and motives is not perhaps unconnected with the anti-rationalist tradition endemic among the Protestant Churches since Luther denounced the " whore reason."

Nor can we expect religious teaching on matters within the competence of the moral reason. As well might we expect miracles to supply the place of human research and effort. Where the light of the Divine Word, as through natural reason He enlightens every man that cometh into the world, is sufficient, we cannot expect a supernatural illumination. And in fact we do not find in the Gospel any clear, complete and final teaching on war and peace. Nor has the Church ever issued a body of magisterial pronouncements on the subject. In the early Church the divergence of opinion among Catholics on this issue extended so far that the calendar of Saints includes not only soldiers like the Theban Legion and the forty martyrs of Sebaste but conscientious objectors such as St. Martin of Tours with his reply to the Caesar Julian, " I am a soldier of Christ, I may not fight," and St. Maximilian, who owed his martyrdom, not to his profession of Christianity but his refusal to serve in the army.

But if there is no official teaching there has gradually come into being, constructed by fathers, schoolmen, and canonists, a moral code on this question of war and peace. It does not indeed contain anything which could not have been known without religious revelation. On the contrary it rests upon principles and embodies conclusions of natural reason. This, however, should not detract from its weight with Christians, while giving it a claim upon the consideration of all thinking men, even those who have no religious faith.

It is agreed that war is not intrinsically and as such immoral. If it were, all use of physical force which might involve the infliction of death would be immoral. This, however, would spell an anarchy, an orgy of lawless violence incalculably more terrible than the force which the police must employ against criminals, which in fact is under normal circumstances more potential than actual. Here indeed the absolute non-resister will reply that, if the police were disbanded and citizens trusted solely to the spiritual power of love this manifestation of love would destroy once for all the reign of force and put an end to aggression. This may be true. But in this world of sinners there is no likelihood of a society of any size adopting this heroic course. And its adoption by a minority would be ineffective and if that minority were of any considerable extent would positively assist the forces of anarchy. But what is true within the State is *in principle true* in the international sphere. And in fact when Catholic theology first began with SS. Augustine and Ambrose to elaborate a doctrine of the just war, armed resistance to the barbarians pressing in upon the Roman Empire was an imperative necessity. Submission would not, did not, save the inhabitants of the Empire from massacre, pillage, rape, arson, and slavery, or the organisation of civilised life from destruction. Only in the Eastern Empire, where the government was able to organise an efficient military defence, did the Empire and its civilisation survive for a further millennium to become the Byzantine Empire and culture. And to resist Attila the sword of Aetius was needed as well as the words of St. Leo.

And in later times—though the Crusades cannot be justified in so far as they were attempts to conquer Palestine—the defence of Europe against the invading Turk, as by Hunyadi Janos at Belgrade, and Don Juan at Lepanto was the justifiable self-defence of Christendom. A Turkish Empire comprising the whole or the major part of Europe was not a prospect to be contemplated with equanimity.

But what of wars between Christian nations? What of the mystical body of Christ? Christendom has never been simply identical with the mystical body of Christ. For the visible Catholic Church has never been co-terminous with the invisible. Even for Augustine, as Christopher Dawson has pointed out, the City of God was not another name for the Catholic Church on earth or the Christian Empire. A Christian nation that wantonly attacks another is not, as such, a limb of Christ's mystical body inspired by His Spirit. Whether, therefore, resistance is or is not justifiable, it cannot be declared unjustifiable on the simple ground that since both nations are nominally Christian or Catholic any war between them is war between members of Christ's mystical body. No doubt the war will involve the mutual slaughter of members of the One mystical Christ. But it is also involved by the suppression in a Christian country of a revolt which, if left unchecked, would involve anarchy and the collapse of the entire social fabric.

War may therefore be waged by Christians for a just cause. Such a cause is the defence of one's country, or of an innocent third party against aggression, or to vindicate one's own or his right against injury, that is to say to vindicate justice. As Gratian stated it in his Decretals, " a war is just when it is waged to regain what has been stolen or repel the attack of enemies."

Without disputing this criterion of justice in the stricter sense, I must point out that it is so difficult to apply in practice that it is of little or no use. When it is claimed that often the only effective self-defence is to strike the first blow against the menace of aggression, it is not always so easy as it might seem to determine the question of self-defence. And as for justice—obviously a more or less plausible case can be made out for the claim of any belligerent state. In such obscurity and perplexity neither the soldier nor the private civilian can be absolutely certain where justice lies in a quarrel between his country and another. Not to lay too heavy a burden upon conscience, theologians have therefore laid it down that the individual who is in doubt as to the justice of a war may, in default of a court of higher instance accept the judgement of his rulers. Since, however, a Government will always affirm the justice of its own case

U

this proviso renders the criterion of justice nugatory, no more than a dead letter. Of what use would be laws and a system of jurisprudence if an interested party were allowed to judge in his own cause ? We are therefore faced with the dilemma; either the individual must judge whether his country's claim is just, which, as we have seen, is usually beyond his knowledge. Or all wars are in practice just.

Happily this dilemma is not the last word on the question. There are other criteria of just and unjust war formulated by Canonists which, unlike the criterion of justice in the strict sense, can be applied by the individual. One of these lays it down that a war is unjust, i.e., unjustifiable, if there is a possibility of settling the dispute by recourse to a competent tribunal.[1]

If therefore a State refuses to submit the dispute to arbitration though the other party is willing to do so, the war which it wages is *ipso facto* unjust and all who participate in it commit or assist murder.

Whatever may be the weakness, the lamentable weakness, of the League of Nations in enforcing international justice, it does at least provide machinery for the settlement of disputes. And its members are solemnly pledged to make use of this machinery before resorting to war. Further, even nations who are not members of the League have adhered to a solemn undertaking—the Kellogg-Briand pact—not to make war an instrument of national policy, i.e., to submit all disputes to arbitration. No nation thus pledged to arbitration can refuse arbitration and go to war without breaking its plighted word. And if, like Japan and Italy, it does so, the war in question is an unjust war, sheer mass murder. Nor clearly is the possibility that from political bias the tribunal of arbitration may give an unjust verdict sufficient ground for refusing arbitration. In a sinful world any tribunal may, and too often does, give an unfair decision.

[1] See J. Eppstein, *The Catholic Tradition of the Law of Nations*, p. 122.

And the laws themselves are often unjust. But is this any reason for refusing to accept the jurisdiction of the courts and substituting the anarchy in which every man asserts or defends his claims by force? Obviously not. And if the legal administration were weaker than it should be, and were menaced by powerful forces of disorder, the duty of all law-abiding citizens to rally to its support would be all the graver and the more urgent.

The individual citizen, however, whether soldier or civilian, is able to apply this criterion, unlike that of justice, for himself. If he cannot judge the merits of the dispute, he can discover whether or no arbitration has been accepted or refused and if accepted whether the decision of the arbiter has been obeyed. If his country has refused to submit the dispute to arbitration, or having done so has refused to accept the arbiter's award, the private citizen can be certain that on this ground, at least, the war is unjust and therefore mass murder in which he can take no part without committing or abetting murder.

But there is another criterion of even more universal application which also can be applied without any special knowledge. In the sixteenth century the Spanish canonist Victoria stated it: "A war may be just and lawful in itself and yet owing to some collateral circumstance may be unlawful. . . . For inasmuch as wars ought (only) to be waged for the common good, if some one city cannot be recaptured without greater evils befalling the Commonweal, such as the devastation of many great cities, great slaughter of human beings, provocation of princes" (in modern terms extension of the area of conflict), "occasions for new wars to the destruction of the Church (in that an opportunity is given to pagans to invade and seize the lands of Christians) it is *indubitable* that the prince is bound rather to give up his own right and abstain from war."[1]

[1] Quoted by J. Eppstein, *Op. Cit.*, p. 106.

We may notice that Victoria assumes the existence of a Christendom subject to the Church. To-day when this Christian Commonweal no longer exists, for the direct destruction of the Church we may substitute in the above passage the indirect damage to religion which a world war would most certainly produce, not least by the spread of Communism among its impoverished and disillusioned victims.

And again :

" No war is just if the harm which it seems to bring to the State exceeds the benefit or the advantage, even if in other respects titles and reasons for the justice of the war are not lacking. The proof of this is that the State has no power to wage war except to defend and protect itself and its property. Therefore if its strength is diminished and out-worn rather than increased by war the war will be unjust.

" And so, since any one State is part of the world as a whole . . . if war is made with advantage to one province or republic but with loss to the world . . . I think that that war would be unjust."[1]

Mr. Eppstein sums up the teaching of the neo-scholastics —theologians of the sixteenth and seventeeth centuries, on the conditions of just war in a series of propositions. Among these is the following, " Even if a certainly just cause of war exists, the prince must refrain from going to war if the losses resulting from war to the belligerent States, the whole community of nations or the Church are likely to be so great as to outweigh the advantages of repairing the injury done."[2]

It seems to me impossible to exaggerate the importance of the criterion thus laid down by Victoria and restated in the above terms by Mr. Eppstein. For it involves the conclusion whose importance cannot be exaggerated that under modern conditions all wars between any one civilised State or group of States and another civilised State or group of states is unjust because it must involve incalculably more

[1] Quoted *Op. Cit.*, p. 107.   [2] *Op. Cit.*, p. 122.

evil both to the belligerents and the world as a whole than any possible good it can effect.

Mechanised warfare has revolutioned war, making it a literal hell on earth. Even the appalling slaughter and torture of the last war will be dwarfed by those of the next. Wholesale massacres amid terrors and torments which beggar description or imagination and the maiming of millions among the survivors will be the inevitable result of war from the air. It will not be merely that " grappling of aerial navies in the central blue " which Tennyson foretold in "Lockesley Hall." It will be the indiscriminate destruction of the civilian population of our urban centres. The inferno of Flanders and Gallipoli will be transferred to London, Paris, Rome and Berlin. There will be nothing of that chivalrous knight-errantry *à la Chevalier Bayard* which cast a deceptive glamour upon the wars of the past. It will not be a struggle of human wits or even human strength but of murder machinery. Who outside Broadmoor or the shareholders' meeting of an armament firm can contemplate such a prospect without the conviction that it must be prevented at all costs ? Order, and the civilised life which is based upon order, will be ruined. The amenities and decencies of a cultured and civilised existence will founder in chaos. The whole or almost the whole of Europe will be as Russia was in 1917. There will be revolution and tyranny. Moreover, the war will be waged by means intrinsically unlawful such as the gassing and bombing of civilian populations, even such obvious non-combatants as children and the aged. For even a lawful end cannot justify unlawful means. And the moral atmosphere will be poisoned as foully as the physical. Only by an organised propaganda of lies and hate can the peoples of Europe who want peace and friendly relations with their neighbours be induced to engage in an orgy of mutual massacre. We remember the slogans of 1914– 1918, the war to end war, the war to make the world safe for democracy, the corpse factory, and the "mutilated Belgian babies." The Christmas truce on the Flanders front shewed plainly enough that the British and German privates were men of good will whose natural humanity would have celebrated the birth of the Prince of Peace by receiving the peace He came to bring. But this did not suit the politicians on either side who wanted them to go on with the slaughter as an instrument of national policy.

And when at last the war was over, what of the victory? What fruits were secured by the agony of a world for any of the belligerents or for humanity as a whole in the least commensurate with the suffering, death and ruin? Fear of vengeful victims, terror of reprisals, the bitterness of the defeated nations into whose soul the iron of humiliation had been driven deep, economic depression, insecurity, social revolutions from left or right, these have been direct legacies of the war. And if the late war shook the economic and social fabric so severely, the next must bring it down in ruin. And what did the victors gain? Already in his *Great Illusion* Sir Norman Angell had proved that in consequence of the economic interdependence of modern nations war could not pay—that is to say, war between members of this international economic society. The event proved him right. The indemnities, mendaciously termed reparations, proved a boomerang ruinous to those who imposed as well as to those who vainly attempted to pay them. For they were payable only in goods which the markets of the recipient powers would not receive. The attempt to pay them reduced the recipients' customers to bankruptcy. And bullion proved barren metal indeed in a world without purchasers of the goods which alone give it value. The destruction of the Austrian Empire has not only impoverished Central Europe, it has created permanent foci of future war. And Germany, though shorn of colonies and outlying territory in Europe, has emerged more formidable than ever in the disciplined and organised resolution of her people. The widespread restriction of individual liberty and the rise of totalitarian States claiming to control the entire life, nay the very thought of their citizens, has been directly due to the war. And the sole genuine gain, the establishment of a League of Nations with its hope of collective security, has sadly disappointed our expectations. Why? Because it canonised the peace of Versailles and has been abused to maintain an unjust balance of power. Despite much good work to its credit it has proved too often an instrument in the hands of the victorious powers to secure their victory. It has never been, and is least of all to-day, a League of all the nations to secure peace and enforce international justice. Whatever genuine power for good it has exercised has been mainly due to the adherence of the small States disinterested in the balance of power between the great nations. And they precisely were the neutrals of the late war.

And finally what of the effects of war on religion and the Church which the Catholic must have particularly at heart? The churches desecrated and destroyed, the priests killed, the seminarians who never reached ordination, the religious communities broken up—these were the least of the evil done by war in this sphere. Far more serious and more permanent damage has been done to religion. There is the scandal of religion everywhere employed to encourage instead of repressing war—a commonplace but only too effective theme of secularist propaganda. And there is the triumph of Communism with its frank atheism, and of the pagan nationalisms of the right, equally godless in their practice and results, since they ascribe to a human group and its leader the Absolute value proper to God alone. Though these movements were not actually births of the late war, it was the war which directly or indirectly gave them political power. What the balance may be between war and peace in that profound depth where individual souls by their free choice accept or refuse God, we cannot tell. A man who in good faith gives his life in an unjust war and is therefore in his concrete act, materially, a murderer, may by his self-devotion be in will, formally, a martyr and win the martyr's crown. But precisely because these depths are hidden from man's judgement, we cannot take account of them in striking the balance between the good and evil of war which we are obliged to strike if we would decide upon its justice. Nor can these intimate spiritual decisions be reckoned among those effects for religion and the Church to which the Canonists would have us give particular consideration in making up that account. For we cannot estimate unknowables. And in the only spheres accessible to our scrutiny and of which therefore we can take account, it is evident that a war between two civilised States or alliances does far more harm to religion and the Church than any possible good.

Surely it must be obvious to any fair judgement that war between modern nations or groups of nations does not and cannot fulfil the criterion of just war laid down by the Canonists, that the good to be expected from success must outweigh the evils it will produce. Evidently the contrary is true. Such a war produces incalculable evil and a minimum of good, whether for the belligerents, victors or vanquished or for mankind as a whole.

No doubt this criterion of greater evil condemns the majority even of past wars, for example the Thirty Years War with its wholesale devastation and massacres. But not all. For wars were then fought out between professional armies, not between entire populations. Further the ordinary life and culture of civilians often continued undisturbed. This will be possible no longer. Indeed even in peace time the entire population including women and children is being systematically militarised.

Whatever department therefore of human life, whatever

level of man's being and action accessible to observation you
may choose to examine, it can be established beyond doubt that
under modern conditions any war whatsoever between any
civilised state and another such state or between one group
of such states and another, does and must result " in losses
to the belligerent states, the whole community of nations
and the Church so great as to outweigh the advantage of repairing the injury done" (assuming it to exist). This is a proposition of which I confidently challenge disproof.

But what of self defence ? If we are unjustly attacked ought
we not to defend our country ? Here too I appeal to reason in
the teeth of false sentiment and apply the same criterion. And
the reply is not doubtful. Under modern conditions the
evils of resistance are worse than those entailed by submission. For let us suppose, to make the case as concrete
as possible, that England were at the mercy of Germany.
Would the Germans act like Attila's Huns, massacre, rape
and pillage the population of Great Britain ? Certainly not.
Though the Versailles treaty was a vindictive one the Allies
did not do these things to a conquered Germany. On the
other hand resistance would mean wholesale slaughter,
torment and ruin. Would not the victor, however, impose
crushing indemnities leading to wholesale impoverishment ?
Experience has shewn that under modern financial conditions
this is impossible. On the other hand the devastation caused
by resistance would involve impoverishment. Would he
annex Great Britain ? Certainly not. The annexation of one
great civilised power by another is impossible. In 1918
Germany lay helpless and prostrate before the Allied Armies.
But Germany did not share the fate of Poland in the eighteenth
century. She was not annexed by the victors.[1] Even the

---

[1] In the teeth of this obvious fact the Bishop of London (in an address to his
Diocesan Conference, May 25, 1936) can make a preposterous statement repeated
in Convocation the following year, typical of the attitude which I am attacking.
" If ' pacifism ' had been our policy in 1914 either the German Emperor or Hitler "
(who incidentally would never have been heard of but for the war) " would be
in Whitehall to-day." Is M. Léon Blum in the Wilhelmstrasse ?

Ruhr valley was not permanently annexed. In border regions where the population is mixed and there must in any case be a national minority, the victor as at Versailles will favour, even unfairly, his own or allied nationals. But this has no application to the large homogeneous national areas. Italy, it is true, for strategic reasons annexed a purely Teutonic area in the Tyrol. But can we seriously maintain that the evil constituted by this unjustice to the annexed Tyrolese was so great as to outweigh or balance the evils of world war? But would not Germany annex Austria if she could? She would, but because a very large section of the Austrian people desire union with Germany.[1]

But surely, it will be replied, it is dishonourable to yield so tamely to the aggressor. What of national honour? Is that to be sacrificed to save life and avoid suffering? Is not honour precisely the value which when thrown into the scale turns the balance in favour of resistance at any cost? At this point we must be on our guard against the insidious sentimentality of the militarist. If we believe that Reason, the Word is God we must follow reason to the end. The individual may kill to defend his life? May he do so to defend his honour (I am not talking about sex which is beside the point here)? Certainly not. I must not kill a man who insults or strikes me. When the supporters of duelling taught otherwise the Church condemned them and maintained the condemnation in face of a social code which branded and ostracised the man who refused to fight for his " honour " as a despicable coward. If then it is lawful for the individual to kill in defence of his life but not of his honour, the same principle must apply to the national

[1] Was then the self defence of Abyssinia unjustifiable? Actually it was. For in view of the overwhelming preponderance of Italy in poison gas and other such instruments of " Roman and Christian " warfare that defence was but a useless slaughter. If, however, the League of Nations, instead of luring the Abyssinians to a vain resistance by false hopes of international support, had done its duty in restraint of aggression, the Abyssinian defence would have been justifiable. For it would have supported a successful vindication of international law by an international police force.

group. We may kill to defend the lives of our countrymen but not to defend the national prestige. But as we have just seen the best defence of these lives, if an international police force is unavailable, is non-resistance, and for this reason national self-defence has become unlawful. *A fortiori* it must be unlawful, unjust to fight for national honour. Indeed the passive resistance of a nation to an unjust conqueror best promotes the true honour of that nation, just as the refusal by an individual to vindicate his honour by a duel was its truest vindication. Nor is foreign conquest necessarily the worst dishonour which can befall a nation. The honour of the purified Judaism under Persian and Greek rule was greater than the honour of Israel under the idolatrous rule of the victorious Omri. And the honour of Michael Angelo's Italy was far greater than the honour of Mussolini's. To follow reason, not blind instinct, even herd instinct, is the honour of a rational spirit.

Thus even in the extreme case of self defence war between two states or groups is under modern conditions unjust, i.e., unjustifiable, because it must cause more, incalculably more, evil than good. If, however, such wars are unjust they are mass murder and no Catholic is justified in participating in them. It is his plain duty to be or to support a conscientious objector to service in such wars, that is, in any war between one civilised state or group of states and another.

Nor can he place the responsibility upon his government. For the Canonists allow him to do this only where there is a genuine doubt as to the justice of a war. Where he is certain that it is unjust he must refuse to take part in it. I will quote the words in which Mr. Eppstein sums up for us their teaching on this important issue : " Soldiers (obviously this applies to all citizens who in any way assist the soldiers to fight) are bound to examine the justice of a proposed war. If uncertain of the justice of the cause their duty is to obey their commanders (rulers). If certain of the injustice of the cause they are to refuse to fight " (civilians therefore to refuse their assistance). But war between two modern states or alliances is and in all cases must be unjust —unjust *beyond all reasonable doubt*—because as we have shewn the evils it will certainly produce, even if waged in self defence, enormously exceed any good which it can produce.

Therefore it is the plain duty of soldiers to refuse to serve in any such war and of civilians to refuse to support them. Thus the application of the sane reason embodied in the teachings of the Canonists has led us to the same practical conclusion, as the sentiment of the absolute pacifist with his misapplication of the Gospel. The latter says we must not partake in any war because Christ forbade all war. I maintain that we must not take part in any war between nations or groups of nations because under modern conditions such wars are necessarily unjust, i.e., unjustifiable. While therefore we must disagree with the absolute pacifists, in our theoretical principles, we can and must agree in our practical attitude.

There is, however, a practical issue, or rather an issue that should be, but unfortunately is not, practical, in which we must differ from the absolutist objection to war. It is the lawfulness of international police action. The absolute pacifist, believing that war is intrinsically wrong and forbidden by Christ, denies the lawfulness of such an international or rather supernational use of force to maintain international justice and collective security. Those who on the other hand believe that all war between nations and groups of nations is now unlawful, not because war is intrinsically unlawful always and in any case, but because often arbitration has been refused and because war must produce more evil than good, may well approve and desire such international policing.

From this point of view it is not illogical but strictly logical to stand side by side with the Fellowship of Reconciliation in resisting any war which may be declared against any other nation and on whatever ground and at the same time to support the ideal sponsored by the New Commonwealth. For the same criterion the balance between the good and evil results which condemns all modern wars between nations and groups as unjust, because they produce an excess of evil must make us support a genuinely international police force, because it would produce an excess of good. And if wars are unjust when arbitration is refused, the universal enforcement of arbitration must be just and *ceteris paribus* a just cause of military action.

We must, however, be very cautious in the practical application of this principle. To render a war just it is not enough that it be approved by a group of powers styling itself the League of Nations or waged in the name of collective security. For this League may be no more than a camouflaged alliance of a group of powers to maintain a settlement advantageous to themselves. In that case, even if in the actual dispute their case were just, the war would be in effect another version of the late war, a war between one powerful group of states and another. And such a war, since as we have seen it must produce more evil than good, is unjust.

International military action therefore can be just only if it is a genuine international police action. And it can be such only on two conditions. States with no interest, direct or indirect, in the dispute, must participate. And the League which takes such action must possess an overwhelming preponderance of strength as against the aggressor and his probable allies. If the first condition is wanting, the war is a conflict of national interests, not the disinterested affirmation of international justice and order. If the second condition is wanting, the evils produced by such military action will outweigh the good, thereby rendering it unjust. The only type of international military action, therefore, which we can support with full assurance that our criterion of just war has not been violated, is that taken not by any combination of national forces but by an international police force directly controlled from a supernational centre. If, however, disinterested powers are prepared to participate and the preponderance of strength possessed by the League is such that it is certain that the aggressor will either not resist at all or be reduced to submission at a minimum cost of life and suffering, the clear balance of good over evil will render such action justifiable war. For example, I believe that action by the existing League of Nations against Mussolini's conquest of Abyssinia would have been justified by these criteria, against a hypothetical aggression by Germany would be unjustifiable.

Resolute action by the League of Nations would have saved Abyssinia and vindicated Collective Security without leading to a world-war. Since it was not taken the League is no longer in a position to take any coercive action without involving a world-war. That is to say war under the aegis of the League would now camouflage a war between Russia, France and Britain against a rival group of powers and would as such be unjustifiable. For the disinterested powers, e.g., Holland, Sweden, Norway, ready to co-operate in applying sanctions for Abyssinia would certainly refuse to do so to-day.

And our attitude towards police wars, e.g., the policing of Palestine, will differ from that of the absolute Pacifist. For in this case also the balance of good over evil favours the use of armed force.

Moreover since religious liberty is man's most priceless possession, incomparably more valuable than any secular good, civil war for its defence is not condemned by Victoria's criterion. On the other hand organised non-co-operation is the better method of opposing irreligion. Therefore in so far as Franco's insurrection, to take a particular instance, is inspired by the defence of religion against the persecution of atheism though it is the worse method, since peaceful non-co-operation would have achieved the same result more surely and more successfully, it is not, like international warfare for secular ends, absolutely the worst. It is better than sheer acquiescence. Hence though it is a pis aller in which the individual may well refuse to participate as the more perfect course, it is not like the latter, simply unjustifiable, a war, therefore, in which he *ought* not to participate. And whatever our condemnation of the Fascist and militarist elements in the Nationalist cause we must nevertheless desire the victory of its twilight over the night of its Godless opponents.

Finally we must beware of the reckless and unbalanced anti-Fascism which threatens to drag this country into a war " for democracy " and " collective security " against Fascism and military aggression, in fact for a Russian and French alliance against Germany, Italy and Japan. Even our pacifists are being beguiled by these specious names. War for Communist that is atheistic Russia is unjustifiable, not only for the general reasons which condemn other international wars, but specifically, because it would be a war for open irreligion against powers whose hostility to religion is nowhere so thorough-going and so explicit. Even though, as I have suggested in another essay, it may be God's design to utilize Soviet Russia as the framework of His earthly kingdom, so long as it remains Godless we must not support its attempt to impose atheism on the rest of mankind. Moreover such a war far from being a war for political freedom would be a war for the worst because most totalitarian state against totalitarian states less evil because less completely totalitarian. I therefore conclude my plea for Christian Pacifism with a warning against the pacifist militarism of our anti-Fascist Left, a most serious danger to peace, because it supports a military alliance with Russia through France, an alliance which could only lead where the Franco-Russian alliance led us in 1914, to a world-war. And a world-war to-day would be the ruin of victor and vanquished alike.

The only final solution to the problem of war and peace must be the supersession of the sovereign state, which under modern conditions is a mischievous anachronism. Indeed its very existence has now become an implicit state of war. If therefore civilised humanity is to survive under the conditions created by modern machinery it must constitute a superstate able to enforce order upon all the states of the world. Its decisions might, indeed in view of human sin and error would, in many cases, be unjust. So are the decisions of the Courts. But even this imperfect justice would be infinitely preferable to international anarchy. In the meanwhile since the anarchy continues and even increases and there is little prospect of that efficient and comparatively impartial vindication of international order which alone can render military action justifiable, what are we to do? We must make it clear that we cannot and will not participate in any war not thus justified, therefore in no war, whatever its plea, waged by one nation or group of nations against another. I have sought to shew that this is the sole attitude consistent with a genuine acceptance of the conclusions of moral reason formulated by the theologians and canonists when they are applied under conditions widely different from those which prevailed when they were formulated.

But it is no easy task to stand firm in our obedience to the teaching of reason in opposition to the irrational herd instinct which masquerades under the noble name of patriotism— for true patriotism is to desire that one's country shall best serve the common good of mankind.

If the illumination of natural reason, by which the Word enlightens us as human beings, is sufficient to expose the unjustifiable character of modern war, to be true to its dictates in defiance of Cæsar's command and the mania of a belligerent people we require the supernatural charity infused into our

hearts by the Holy Ghost.[1] Only the service of the one
God and Father of a humanity made in His image and the
One Lord of a Church gathered out of every tongue and
nation and language can enable us to resist the idolatry of
the nationalist war god. And though it did not require the
Cross to teach us that it is wrong to wage a war that must
harm, not benefit, mankind, or which could be settled by
arbitration, at the very worst no more unjust than the administration of law within a state has been in many times
and places, it is through the Cross that we must overcome
the wars which reason condemns. Though in every country
the masses of the people of every class want peace, its
champions against the Government and public opinion will
be very few. And where conscription is established resistance
involves a martyrdom for truth, as painful as and more
prolonged than the martyrdom of the soldier who, in invincible
ignorance, gives his life in an unjustifiable war. The
conscientious objector has little glory from men. But God is
His invincible strength. 'Strive for justice as for thy soul
and even unto death strive for justice. The Lord guarded
him from his foes and kept him safe from his tempters and
granted him to overcome in a mighty struggle.'

[1] A strong counter conviction, e.g., devotion to Communism, may, it is true,
enable individuals and in particular cases even powerful groups, to resist an outbreak
of war mania. But the inspiration here is usually another form of war. And how
sporadic and impermanent its action is, is shown by the slavery and militarism of the
conscript Red Army.

x

INDEX